WIRING
GOVERNMENTS

WIRING GOVERNMENTS

Challenges and Possibilities for Public Managers

JOHN A. O'LOONEY

QUORUM BOOKS
Westport, Connecticut • London

Library of Congress Cataloging-in-Publication Data

O'Looney, John.
    Wiring governments : challenges and possibilities for public managers /
John A. O'Looney.
        p.   cm.
    Includes bibliographical references and index.
    ISBN 1–56720–440–6 (alk. paper)
    1. Public administration—Information resources management.   2. Electronic
government information.   3. Internet in public administration.   I. Title.
JF1525.A8O56   2002
352.3'8'02854678—dc21   2001019867

British Library Cataloguing in Publication Data is available.

Library of Congress Catalog Card Number: 2001019867
ISBN: 1–56720–440–6

First published in 2002

Quorum Books, 88 Post Road West, Westport, CT 06881
An imprint of Greenwood Publishing Group, Inc.
www.quorumbooks.com

Printed in the United States of America

The paper used in this book complies with the
Permanent Paper Standard issued by the National
Information Standards Organization (Z39.48–1984).

10 9 8 7 6 5 4 3 2 1

Contents

Preface

Despite a daily flood of news and commentary about the impact of new technologies on business in America, a recent review of public administration textbooks and journals suggests that the topic of computing in public administration receives scant and inconsistent attention. A. Northrop (1999) suggests that public managers need to have familiarity with generic applications (e.g., spreadsheets, databases, Internet, e-mail and geographic information systems) and with a number of management-specific issues (e.g., quality of data, training, personnel, hardware compatibility and security). These areas are certainly important to the training of new public managers, but with the rapid development of Internet-based information technologies (IT), public managers are facing a deluge of new information technology issues and challenges.

With the expanded possibilities created by the new IT-based economy, public managers will increasingly need to incorporate computer applications into public sector strategies for improving efficiency, effectiveness, responsiveness and accountability. To meet this challenge, public managers will need to increase their involvement both in the details of administration of information and communication technologies and in the orchestration of technology policy development. While the public manager's role in policy development is typically limited by the tradition of nonparticipation by public administrators, the technical nature of IT issues will dictate that professional managers take a more active policy development role than is customarily the case.

Public managers who attempt to stay abreast of the plethora of applications, hardware, resources and skills being created as part of the new economy are likely to be frustrated. Because these resources are generally being developed through private sector rather than public sector efforts, public managers have fewer means of certifying that the specific technologies they are employing are truly those that are needed and that present the best fit between challenge and response. This book addresses this limitation by helping public managers to identify the key characteristics of different information technologies and to understand how these technologies fit within different types of efforts to reform or reinvent government and administration. In addition to distinguishing the impacts of specific technologies, this book offers assistance to public managers faced with finding the proper fit between technologies and current practices and organizational characteristics. Finally, this book will prepare public managers to look into the future with a better understanding of the likely impacts of emerging technologies and systems on the world of public administration and democratic governance.

KEY CONCEPT

The thesis of the book is that "wired governments" will be different, not because of the technology per se, but because they will be organized to adopt and employ technology in a more rapid, integrated and extensive manner than has traditionally been the case. In order for this wired or digital government to evolve in a desirable way, organizational, managerial, and inter-organizational structures, supports, staffing, training, practices, cultures, boundaries and policies will need to change. The challenges of becoming a wired organization are comparable to what business owners faced at the beginning of the industrial revolution. In both cases the challenge is rooted in radical changes in available technologies, but in both cases these technological changes were only a small part of the story. The larger story was (and is) about the potential transformations in management and employment practices, ownership rights, and the distribution and arrangement of political power. As public managers build wired organizations over the next few decades, they will need to keep in mind these larger challenges and assist elected officials to think more deeply about how their policy making can contribute to the development of more effective and efficient public organizations.

ORGANIZATION

The book is organized into five parts. Part I, An Overview of Wired Government, consists of a single chapter, "Introducing the Wired Concept." This chapter is used to define wired government and to help the reader understand how this concept fits within the larger world of core governmental functions and the broader information technology policy challenges facing governments (e.g., issues of access, equity, capacity, enabling law, the architecture of the technology, etc.). Chapter 2, "Electronic Government: Stages and Status," briefly outlines the developmental history of different approaches to using technology in governmental settings. The key characteristics and the effectiveness of these approaches (e.g., data processing, work reengineering, knowledge management) in the context of broad public administration problems are examined. Chapter 3, "Information Technology and Government Business Processes," examines principles and examples of how information technology can be used to streamline the core functions of government.

Part II, The Challenges of Knowledge Management, explores in much more detail the knowledge management approach to developing a wired government. In Chapter 4, "Knowledge Management: The New Frontier of Information-Enhanced Management," I more fully define the appropriate place of knowledge management in a public sector organization and provide a guide to the phases of knowledge management and the types of information technology tools that public managers can use to enhance their capabilities at different phases. This part also presents some emerging knowledge management practices that can be employed or tested by public program managers. Chapter 5 explores four "dark-side" issues of knowledge management. These issues are "dark" in the sense that we do not yet fully understand the social and political consequences of using knowledge management and computer-mediated communications for public administration and democratic decision making. How, for instance, will the use of electronic meeting technologies and associated rules of procedure differ from currently used practices? And how will these change the balance of power between and among citizens, public managers and elected officials? These issues are also "dark" in the sense that there exists a potential downside to the implementation of these technologies and practices. Thus, Chapter 5 is devoted to cautioning public managers about the far-reaching implications for policy development of simple efforts to wire the government.

Part III, Managing the Transformation, which contains four chapters, alerts public managers to the organizational, administrative, cultural and human resources issues that they are likely to face in their attempts to wire their governments, and it identifies points of leverage that public managers can use in managing IT projects. Chapter 6, "Staffing and Design of Wired Organizations," outlines the basic research findings on managing organizations that are introducing or using technology as a key component. Here, issues of organizational design, the role, place and status of information technology within the administrative structure, and the importance of leadership and rewards are addressed. Chapter 7, "Wired Governments and Wired Cultures," looks explicitly at the cultural foundations for transforming government organizations into wired organizations. Ideas for both going with the flow of the existing culture and changing the culture to make it more amenable to adopting new technology are presented. Chapter 8, "Managing the Trade-off between Ease of IT Implementation and Performance Benefits," examines the central question of IT implementation failure. Such failure is often misunderstood because managers are not credited with having to negotiate a difficult risk-reward trade-off. Specifically, public managers who embark on a program to achieve a substantial boost in performance must often simultaneously accept a decreased likelihood of implementation success. In order to increase the probability of success, this chapter presents an IT implementation guide in the form of a matrix of expected IT system benefits under conditions of different degrees of organizational and environmental rationality. In addition, this chapter addresses the issue of managing potentially conflicting technologies. Chapter 9, "Management-Level Policy Development for Wired Governments," identifies sixteen administrative-level IT policy issues that government managers need to understand in order for their departments to become wired. How public managers address issues such as intellectual property, personalization of information and service delivery, open source code, remote work, the sharing of the government's brand, and privacy will determine in part whether government staff, constituents and partners will be able to make digital government work for all concerned.

Part IV, The Network Is the Government, explores the challenge that networked systems pose to the traditional boundaries of governmental organizations. Two chapters examine to what extent wired governments can become boundaryless and how the boundary-spanning possibilities afforded by wired governments can best be managed. Chapter 10, "Wires across Government Boundaries," looks at the efforts and plans of different governments and governmental units to create technology-enhanced alliances or knowledge networks. This chapter draws heavily on the exploratory work being done at the Center for Technology in Government and other digital government efforts being funded by the National Science Foundation. Chapter 11, "Wired Governments in the Context of Wired Communities and Economies," looks beyond public sector organizations to understand how wired governments might act within the context of wired communities and economies.

INTENDED AUDIENCE

This book is written for the generalist or executive-level public manager as well as elected officials and students of government. Unfortunately, because of the nature of the topic, it is not possible to fully avoid technical language and buzzwords. After finishing this book, however, the reader will be familiar with most of the more important concepts in the field as they relate to organizations. While many, many more buzzwords and levels of IT jargon could have been included, my intention was to limit these to the minimum that would still enable generalist managers to communicate effectively on most issues with IT managers and staff. In addition to helping generalist public managers communicate with these specialists, this book will also help alert public managers to important policy issues so that they may educate and prompt public officials to assume their policy-making responsibilities.

EXISTING LITERATURE

The distinct role of public managers as initiators and regulators of information systems has been the subject of only a few studies. This is likely to change in the near future. The history of frontier society provides an appropriate metaphor for understanding the role of public managers in the information revolution. As with the exploration of the frontier, the development of new information technologies has been primarily a private sector endeavor. Freebooting entrepreneurs in both cases have led the charge. However, as the age of exploration gives way to active settlement, the role of the public sector in the regulation and shaping of social relations (through sheriffs, the land offices and the courts in the case of the Western frontier, and through policies, purchases and guidelines for public sector system design in the case of cyberspace) becomes much more important. As the basic capabilities of the Internet evolve through private and commercial action, the call for public sector activity is increasingly heard. At the level of public policy, Lawrence Lessig's excellent book, *Code and Other Laws of Cyberspace*, presents the case for understanding the public's role in regulating cyberspace in order to maintain its more desirable features and prevent undesirable attributes from developing. However, policy, as public administrators understand very well, is often shaped by the thinking and practice of real public managers as they go about influencing elected officials and implementing "policy-in-fact" through their directives and program strategies.

As cyberspace develops, these public managers will exercise influence through their choices of regulations to favor, through their implementation of these regulations, and through the example they will provide by developing wired governments that exemplify public values and meet public expectations about performance. While there are good books that present academic conceptualizations of information technology in the public sector (Garson 1999), and books that present tactical advice on implementing IT projects within the context of reinventing government (Heeks 1999), or that outline the challenges for the emerging digital state (*The Digital State*, 1998; *Some Assembly Required*, 1999), or that address the impacts of new technologies on communities and democracy (Gurstein 2000), or that provide advice on the use of specific technologies such as expert systems, geographic information systems, Internet systems or technology management techniques such as outsourcing (Duffin 1988; O'Looney 1997, 1998, 2000), none of these books is designed to provide an overall strategic orientation to the challenges that public managers face in this age of first settlement of cyberspace. This book, however, addresses this gap.

WHAT'S NEW

While no book can present entirely new ideas, at the heart of this book the reader will discover some novel ways of thinking about incorporating information technology into government operations, service delivery and policy development functions. I explore new ground in four areas in particular:

- The explication of how a fairly innocuous technology in the private sector—knowledge management—presents numerous policy and practice challenges in the public sector.
- The presentation of a cycle of knowledge management that includes a more complete itemization and description of the phases in this process than has been documented to date.
- An examination of how specific IT systems uniquely stress existing organizational cultures. From this examination, practical advice is provided on how public managers can make better IT system choices—ones that match the current realities of the organizational culture as well as realistic expectations for performance gain.
- An outline of the key architectural alternatives public managers will face when they embark on efforts to build new electronic public meeting spaces.

REFERENCES

The Digital State. (1998). Washington, DC: Progress and Freedom Foundation.

Duffin, P. H., ed. (1988). *Knowledge Based Systems: Applications in Administrative Government*. Central Computer and Telecommunications Agency. London: Ellis Horwood Ltd.

Garson, D., ed. (1999). *Information Technology and Computer Applications in Public Administration: Issues and Trends*. Hershey, PA: Idea Group Publishing.

Gurstein, M. (2000). *Community Informatics: Enabling Communities with Information and Communications Technologies*. Hershey, PA: Idea Group Publishing.

Heeks, R. (1999). *Reinventing Government in the Information Age: International Practice in IT-Enabled Public Sector Reform*. London: Routledge.

Lessig, L. (1999). *Code and Other Laws of Cyberspace*. New York: Basic Books.

Northrop, A. (1999). The challenge of teaching information technology in public administration graduate programs. In *Information Technology and Computer Applications in Public Administration: Issues and Trends*, ed. David Garson. Hershey, PA: Idea Group Publishing.

O'Looney, J. (1997). *Beyond Maps: Geographic Information Systems and Local Government Decision Making*. Washington, DC: International City/County Management Association.

O'Looney, J. (1998). *Outsourcing State and Local Government Services*. Westport, CT: Quorum.

O'Looney, J. (2000). *Local Governments On-Line*. Washington, DC: International City/County Management Association.

Some Assembly Required: Building a Digital Government for the 21st Century. (1999). Albany, NY: Center for Technology in Government, March.

PART I
AN OVERVIEW OF WIRED GOVERNMENT

1

Introducing the Wired Concept

WHAT IS A WIRED GOVERNMENT?

In Marion, Ohio, some citizens began to notice what appeared to them to be a very high incidence of leukemia among River Valley High School graduates. Upon examining medical records, it was discovered that the disease rates increased by 122% between 1966 and 1995 among students. Detective work by the parents of some students led to a discovery that the high school was built on a former storage site for military equipment. The site had been abandoned for more than thirty years when these parents began to hypothesize that residues from the earlier facility might cause the high rate of leukemia among students. Ironically, all of the information that might have led people to make the potentially life-saving discovery of an association between disease and environmental factors already existed in government databases. The authors of a report on the interoperability of government information systems tell this anecdote to illustrate an important point about the state of these systems: governments are often unaware of what they know because their systems cannot talk with each other (Landsbergen & Wolken 1998). A wired government is one where connections are made among disparate pieces of information so as to form new insights and new levels of efficiency. Technology, like the wires or transistors in a computer, enables connections but does not ensure that they will be made. Only people and organizations can do that. In this book the term "wired" refers to both the technical linkages that allow connections and to the features of the organization and environment that lead people to use the technology to actually make connections. In this sense, as governments become wired, the people in and around government will begin to know more and communicate what they know more effectively. Public managers, staff and ordinary citizens will be able to use information and communication systems more effectively to know more and to know who to talk to about what. Thomas Friedman, the author of *The Lexus and the Olive Tree*, has argued that one of the results of the world becoming wired is the super-empowerment of individuals. Super-empowerment is no doubt one of the results of the first level of wiring an organization (i.e., for simple technologies such as e-mail). It may not, however, be an impact that will be long-lasting, particularly as governments choose to implement more sophisticated technologies or to use technology to effectively filter and monitor information or communications. As this book will make clear, empowerment is just one of many possible impacts of governments becoming more wired.

In this book, the wiring in "wired governments" includes all those things that enable public managers to use information technology to create new organizational forms and manage these organizations effectively. Becoming wired requires a focus on organizational innovation—not just computer gadgetry. In the process of becoming wired, organizations will change in a number of ways. Connections and paths of communications among employees will change. Boundaries among organizational units will change. The nature and effectiveness of managerial control will change, and the knowledge base, both tacit and explicit, on which workers make decisions will change. In sum, as one changes the physical (e.g., copper and fiber) wiring in a wired organization, the neural and cultural networks that human beings have depended on for ages to organize work will also be transformed or may need to be transformed.

More specifically, wired organizations have a number of characteristics. First, they generally employ a common network that cuts across hierarchies and organizational divisions so as to share, mine, analyze and act on large repositories of information. Second, because they employ high-speed processors within these networks, the sharing, mining and analyzing takes place at unprecedented rates of speed. Third, these wired governments combine sensor, analytic, simulation and networking technology with new operational concepts to enable a dramatically improved sense of reality. That is, such governments do not just count things. Rather, they use technologies to model political, economic, operational and social realities. With more and more accurate models and information, public managers in wired organizations can begin to respond to changing conditions in dramatically improved ways. That is, wired governments apply resources for greatest effect by using real-time information coupled with flexible and highly skilled personnel, research-tested approaches, customized communications and command-and-control connectivity to spin decision loops so rapidly that mistakes are short-lived, successes are rapidly reproduced, and service satisfaction continually increases. Finally, wired governments use these new technologies to build new relationships to citizens, other governments, constituents and stake-holders.

WHERE DOES THE IDEA OF A WIRED GOVERNMENT FIT WITHIN THE RANGE OF DIGITAL GOVERNMENT ISSUES?

Digital government involves the full range of policy and program chal-lenges that governments face in moving toward electronic delivery of their own services and in facilitating and regulating the development of wired communities and economies. The latter role is much broader than is the focus of this book. It involves establishing legal, programmatic and regula-tory frameworks that apply to the full range of social, political and economic transactions. As a consequence, government's responsibility for managing the movement into a new age is much broader and more complex than is the case in the private sector. Whereas private firms can often move a large portion of their transactions onto electronic networks by overcoming only technical hurdles, governments will often struggle with issues of privacy, intellectual property, fairness and openness of access, the legal standing of electronic documents, and the impact of policies on economic development, democracy and jurisdictional rights and resources.

More particularly, digital government presents challenges in seven often interrelated areas: (1) service capacity; (2) electronic transaction enabling law and infrastructure; (3) network infrastructure; (4) citizen and public em-ployee access; (5) network architecture; (6) intellectual property and privacy; and (7) connectivity and information/knowledge management. These areas are discussed below.

Assessing the vast body of theory and resources that is quickly developing around each of these areas is beyond the scope of this book. However, I do wish to address the policy areas of digital government in light of the man-agement challenges they may pose. These challenges generate questions such as "What role should public managers take in framing policy debates vis-à-vis the role of elected policy makers?" or "When should public managers be proactive implementers of new technology?" Because of the technical nature of information systems policy, public managers are likely to have a large amount of discretion to create "policy in practice." As such, public managers need to be aware of the broader ethical and practical implications of their making policy and of the potential alternatives to employing their discre-tionary power. Specifically, public managers are advised in many cases to engage a broader group of stakeholders in the making of these decisions (e.g., employees, partnering governments or agencies, and citizen technology advisory groups). In addition to understanding how their choices can create new policy, public managers also need to understand how their choices might fit within some of the larger technology policy issues facing govern-ments in general. Although this book is about how public managers can go about building new service capacity via enhancements in information management and organizational design and practices, readers should have a basic familiarity with the seven broad policy issues outlined below.

Service capacity refers to the ability of governments to provide services to citizens, businesses, employees, contract workers, and clients via electronic networks. Published reports on electronic government suggest that service capacities can relate to general information technology (IT) capacities or to the capacity to provide services to citizens online. For example, *Governing* publishes a performance report card on overall IT capacities in major American cities. The grades given are based on a mixture of interviews with IT managers and reviews of documents that are mulled over by faculty and students at the Maxwell School at Syracuse University. The grade is primarily based on IT strategic planning, training of staff and online services for citizens. An annual survey of digital government services produced by *Government Technology* focuses more systematically and in more detail on services to citizens provided online. This survey divides governmental services into eight functional areas:

- Digital democracy
- Higher education
- K–12 education
- Business regulation/Electronic commerce
- Taxation
- Social services
- Law enforcement and the courts
- Other initiatives

Each state's capabilities are rated in each area. *Government Technology*'s service capacity ratings have tended to focus on basic abilities to communicate with key government officials. However, in each area, new standards for excellence are emerging. These include the ability to conduct transactions (e.g., pay bills, fees, taxes), to manipulate data and related maps, and to receive actual services (e.g., instruction, licenses, counseling, etc.) online. More complete service capacity reports are sometimes available through the publication of IT audits or consulting reports. These reports suggest that moving from physical to digital government involves not just new funding but also the development of enterprise-level standards; improved hiring, management and procurement practices; and a balancing of the support for technology among the functions of government (as an example, see Georgia Office of Planning and Budget 2000). While similarly detailed evaluations of local governments' online capacities are rare, qualitative reports suggest that local governments' online service delivery generally lags behind that of state governments (O'Looney 2000a).

Many government services can be provided merely by installing software and networks. However, a number of transactions (e.g., construction permits, purchase orders, travel reimbursements, contracts and voting) cannot take place online without additional assurance that a person's statement is authentic and uncorrupted. *Electronic transaction law and infrastructure* lay the foundation for these assurances. Different government and business functions need different types of assurance and security. Most states, and now the federal government as well, have passed legislation enabling the use of digital signatures and records. Many governments also recognize certification authorities or bodies that certify the authenticity and integrity of documents that have been sent or stored electronically. However, as the market, standards and infrastructure for certification authorities evolve, the appropriate role for governments in this area will also likely change. Some governments may decide to become their own certification authorities, and most will probably have to conduct ongoing research to discover the most effective structures for managing the division of liability and responsibility among the parties to an electronic exchange of documents.

Network infrastructure and *citizen access* are closely related but distinct areas of concern. Networks must exist before citizens can access the Internet, but this says little about the type of network, its capacity or its ability to serve desired purposes. In the past, regulated competition among private telephone companies has provided the model for policy making with regard to establishing access to a network. However, this model is not fully applicable to digital networks. This is because, unlike an analog telephone network, which is essentially a "you have it or you don't" technology, one can have many different levels of access to a digital network. As such, the market will tend to provide some areas and groups with high-quality services while providing others with minimal or no service. The amount of access (or bandwidth) determines the quality of service, and to a certain extent, the service type (e.g., video demands higher bandwidth). If governments decide to go digital, they will be obliged to establish some level of universal service. A key policy question in the coming years will be how to determine that level within an ever-changing technological environment.

Decisions about bandwidth also have an economic development component. Providing poorer, more rural areas of the state with second-class access to digital networks may doom them to second-class development opportunities. For both access and economic development purposes, the model of road networks, which are provided directly by government, represents an alternative to market-based provisioning. Public provision of roads occurs both because of tradition and to establish greater equality of access and a more extensive network than might otherwise occur were roads to be built based on private collections or tolls.

Some states have instances of both public and private infrastructure provision. For instance, in Georgia most communities receive the access a telecommunications or cable company has chosen to provide to the area, but cities like LaGrange and Newnan have used public resources to develop a higher level of local network capacity and citizen access. These communities see public provision of network capacity both as an economic development magnet and as a catalyst for more online government, education, and intra-community business transactions. In addition to choices about public or private provisioning, full citizen use of networks will depend on a variety of policies for pricing, access to kiosks in public facilities and spaces, and employee access at work (see O'Looney 2000b).

When it comes to *citizen and employee access*, network access by itself does not ensure that citizens' (or public employees') electronic interactions with government and the larger community will be superior or even equal in quality to nonelectronic interactions. This is the case because citizen access can be achieved under any number of network management regimes and network architectures. Management regimes define questions of when, where, how, to whom, using what software, with whose permission, for how long, and so on. Network architectures embed these and other rules and policies into the nature of the network itself.

Each form of *network architecture* can have a different impact on the type, style, frequency, duration and content of citizen-to-citizen, citizen-to-government, government-to-citizen, employee-to-government and business-to-government interactions. A poorly designed network infrastructure can limit or create an imbalance in each or all of these interactions, thereby limiting online democracy. Even more important than network infrastructure are the choice of software and the implementation and enforcement of participation rules (i.e., the social architecture) that will govern online interaction. To date, governments have not struggled greatly with the design of the public areas of cyberspace. Key decisions in the future could include: How many people will be allowed in a government-sponsored chat room? Will government facilitate communication between citizens who have similar interests? Similar prejudices? Will governments personalize their Web sites or allow citizens to filter information? If so, in which areas? To what extent? Will public officials monitor and moderate online communications? Will citizens be allowed to participate anonymously? Create and answer polls online? Currently, the shape of a room or the use of a loudspeaker affects democratic processes in physical space. The architecture of the public part of cyberspace will have an even greater effect on democratic decision making and citizen participation in the future.

Intellectual property, privacy, connectivity and *knowledge management* are also aspects of digital government that are interrelated. As with enabling electronic signature law, establishing policies in these areas will impact the ability of both the public and the private sector to work electronically. On the one hand, intellectual property and privacy are needed to give people the assurance that their work product and their communications will be appropriately respected. When this is the case people will be more ready to participate in online work and communications. On the other hand, connectivity, or the ease with which people are able to contact and communicate with others, is also needed if online communications are to be broadly possible. Obviously, both of these sets of values are necessary for a knowledge-based society and economy (*Electronic Commerce Primer* 2000). Unfortunately, there can potentially be conflict between these two values. That is, one can ensure greater privacy by putting limits on connectivity (e.g., making it harder to find someone's e-mail address) or ensure greater connectivity by limiting privacy. Ideally, we would be able to discover public policies that would maximize these two public goods as much as possible.

Connectivity can be fostered by effective organization of information (e.g., online e-mail links and e-mail lists for people with particular interests or characteristics), but can be undermined by practices such as "spamming" or by establishment of a network architecture that enables the filtering of information at various points in the network. Spamming, the mass sending of unwanted e-mail, detracts from connectivity because too much time must be devoted to deleting unwanted communications. With the filtering of information, people may be unable or unwilling to connect because they have difficulty identifying or accessing resources. Some state governments have developed anti-spam legislation (most of which has been rejected by the courts). The debate about whether to build a filtering capacity into the Internet itself is ongoing. A filter can block information, but can also be used to help people find information. With respect to privacy, the federal government's policy has been to ask e-commerce firms to develop self-regulatory mechanisms. However, this approach is being reexamined in light of three developments: (1) the public's desire for privacy protection in the context of making online purchases. Without a sufficient level of privacy, they may not trust the system, which would undermine the growing e-economy; (2) a public policy need for greater privacy protection in order to implement a uniform sales tax mechanism; and (3) a desire for uniformity on the part of businesses that will have to meet the more stringent privacy standards of the European Community. With respect to intellectual property, there is a concern both that the Internet has undermined intellectual property rights (because it has become easy to reproduce and mass distribute perfect copies of digital media) and that digital encryption technology may in the near future provide a too perfect protection of intellectual property. If this occurs, the cherished and important right to fair use of intellectual property by those seeking to expand our knowledge would be undermined (Lessig 1999).

In each of the seven areas of digital government outlined, state, local and federal governments will have difficult decisions to make. Not only will policy makers need to agree on the general purpose and direction of the policy in question, but they will also have to choose the type of mechanisms for

implementing the policy. The choice to use market incentives, public provision, mandates or subsidies for particular types of network architectures,
efforts to establish norms, or the implementation of new laws and regulations may be as important as the choice about a particular policy direction
itself. Because cyberspace is still in its infancy, the decisions made in the
next few decades are likely to be some of the most important for the next
century.

THE ADVANTAGES OF BEING WIRED

The advantages of becoming wired are most evident in the management
and operation of large-scale governments. In particular, governments that
are responsible for service delivery in large geographic districts can use information technology to deliver these services with relatively small staff.
Moreover, as the number of units needing coordination or the number of
new personnel entering a system increases (i.e., factors that tend to increase
with increases in organizational size), the communication, standardization
and connectivity advantages of becoming wired become more evident. In
some instances, becoming wired can make regional or large-scaled governments or agency operations realistic for the first time. Relatively speaking,
wired organizations offer fewer advantages for smaller governments or those
that cover a small geographic area. In smaller governments, information
overload typically will not pose a substantial problem. It is often the case,
for example, that staff in smaller governments know their community from
lifelong experience and that the informal connectivity among citizens, government officials, businesses and nonprofit organizations is more than sufficient to meet the needs of all involved. Such governments (e.g., those with
a couple of hundred employees or less) may not need wiring, because they
are already connected through daily interaction and gossip. While a wired
organization may be less immediately relevant in these jurisdictions, in the
long run the informal communications that characterize small-scale governments can be a barrier to organizational improvement. Because there is little
or no design for information gathering, analysis or communication in such
systems, the same informality that can lead to rich exchanges can also lead
to unexpected communication blockages. For example, a new employee who
comes from a different culture or area of the country may not be included
in the informal communication loop through which business has traditionally
been done. Without an explicit design for organizational connectivity, it may
be impossible to judge why that person is unable to do their job or to correct
performance problems that have their roots in communication problems. In
the larger scope of things, the lack of a design for connectivity tends to make
it difficult to question the customary operations of the organization. The
lack of an explicit connectivity design means that the target for complaints
becomes a fuzzy one and that the remedies might also be fuzzy and unable

to be evaluated. In such informally organized governments, there are typically few mechanisms for innovation and improvement of past practices.

Hence, even for smaller governments, becoming wired could improve the clarity of the organizations' standard communications, control and operational processes. In my twenty years of conducting organizational needs assessments and strategic plans, no matter how small the organization, the need to increase communication and shared awareness is unerringly cited by participants in these processes. Becoming wired is about shared awareness among dispersed staff who are empowered to change their behavior in order to achieve the desired impact and who use technology to increase the pace of operations. However, we may not want governments to operate at the speed of light if they are not going in the right direction. Hence, in addition to helping people work faster, wired organizations are ones that build in learning and the ability to change course in midflight. To do this, wired organizations need to facilitate systematic analyses of how desired outcomes occur and the storage and retrieval of that information.

WHAT DOES A WIRED ORGANIZATION LOOK LIKE?

In the business world, there are numerous examples of wired organizations. Wal-Mart is famous for wiring each of its store's cash registers to a central distribution hub where real-time data on purchasing dictate the resupply of goods at every store. Through such large-scale, customer-centric resupply and interstore transfer of goods, Wal-Mart is able to satisfy more customers and to maintain low prices. Amazon.com uses information about millions of customers' reading preferences to provide reading recommendations based on a filtering of preferences of like-minded readers. The U.S. Army uses computerized battlefield simulations to give commanders experience (and tacit knowledge) about the time window they have for firing a tank cannon. Life insurance companies use expert systems to enable a single case manager to handle all the tasks involved in filing, checking and approving most claims. In less than an hour a single worker can now complete a process that once took two days and numerous approvals by workers in different units. Doctors are now using online medical expert systems to check their own diagnoses against other possible interpretations. When there is a discrepancy between the two, the system offers advice on additional diagnostic tests. Health maintenance organizations are requiring that affiliated physicians incorporate such systems (as well as systems that help control cost) into their routines.

In each of these cases, the existence of information technology made an innovation possible, but not probable. What was needed to make the possible innovation a reality was a new organizational arrangement. Wal-Mart had to allow more decentralized decision making before local managers could show how centralized logistics could support a business advantage. Amazon.com created the archetype for a new organization—a virtual bookstore—where there were few bookstore managers but a multitude of book lovers available to give advice. According to William Lescher (1999), the armed forces had to overcome a whole panoply of organizational obstacles to what he calls "net-centric warfare," including such attributes as the tendency toward "group think," the existence of monopoly providers of specific technologies, a zero-defects mentality, aversion to the risk of failure, an underemphasis on organizational prototypes, and leadership that does not support decentralized innovation. In the medical field, technological innovation did not effectively support diagnosis and treatment decision making until physicians had been organized into provider networks, had encountered questions about their decisions, and were paid for their services in entirely new ways (e.g., through capitated or diagnostically related group payments).

Local governments have not yet taken advantage of the full range of options offered in a wired organization, but there are nevertheless examples of governments adopting information technologies and associated organizational structures and routines to better sense, analyze, store and respond. One example is the use of geographic information systems to help orchestrate the deployment of law enforcement resources to combat crime. As with wiring in business settings, the effectiveness of this new technology did not become apparent until New York City adopted new practices such as community-oriented policing and commander-level peer review of precinct-level efforts to use the information generated by the system.

Unfortunately, attempts to use new technology to support improvements in government services and decision making are not always successful. At the same time that systems for case management were revolutionizing the workflow of insurance claim workers, similar systems that might have provided one-stop services for clients of human services agencies either failed or were never given serious support. In particular, the kind of support for organizational change needed to make these systems succeed was often not forthcoming.

The failure of the public sector to create wired organizations is particularly acute at the local level, for a couple of reasons. First, there is a major coordination problem: local governments must often coordinate multiple categorical programs that have state and federal involvement and funding. Even if one can succeed in adopting a new technology, it is often impossible to achieve the level of collaboration among the interorganizational stakeholders necessary to create the breakthrough improvements seen in the private sector. Second, as Joseph Schumpeter noted over sixty years ago, innovation rides on a wave of creative destruction. That is, most significant innovations will not be adopted unless earlier technologies and modes of operation are destroyed. In the private sector, this process occurs either through failures of outmoded businesses or direct cannibalization of existing business operations by upstart divisions. Because governments cannot die and because they typically do not allow divisional organization, the typical channels for creative destruction do not run through government. The alternative channel for change has been the political one. This channel, unfortunately, is a general one that does not always accurately reflect the need for change in specific operations.

WIRED FOR WHAT?

Becoming a wired organization is a grand goal, but not necessarily a strategic one. The promise of wired government is that government will also be more responsive, coordinated, efficient, effective and accountable. These attributes, rather than the wire that connects people and machines, represent the strategic goals of government. Unfortunately, using information technology to increase these attributes requires that there first be clear objectives or measures for the attainment of these and other strategic goals. As every student of public administration knows, agencies often espouse vague, conflicting goals or goals that have been displaced by practices that work in a different direction than the stated goal. Becoming wired may not help governments in any strategic way unless governments have a strategy in mind. When Henry David Thoreau first heard about the successful completion of the effort to string telegraph lines from New York to San Francisco, he remarked, "What if San Francisco has nothing to say to New York?" Obviously, Thoreau was suggesting that the new telegraph system was only going to be valuable if it was going to lead to important things being communicated. Unfortunately, the truism that "system should support goals" is often forgotten in the rush to be on the leading edge of technology. Forgetting this maxim, managers often support the construction of information technology systems that make things worse and waste resources. Information systems are in fact more than hardware; they are interlocking sets of personnel, skills, organizational forms, norms and processes. As such, they represent the epitome of rationalization. Most systems are designed for a single purpose, and they allow one to accomplish a complex task quickly and efficiently. Systems do particular things the *right way*—at least as far as the current physical and administrative sciences can specify a right way. The problem with the vast majority of systems is that even as they do a particular thing right, they can make it more difficult to identify the *right thing to do*. This paradox exists not only because of what economists call opportunity costs (i.e., there not being enough resources to do Activity A because they were spent doing Activity B), but because systems by their nature pull attention in a particular direction. In building a system for one purpose, there is less time to consider, study and plan to do another thing. Also, the finely specified routines for doing one thing or the expertise or technology needed to do that thing can get in the way of performing other functions well.

There is no one wired organization. Rather, there are many wired organizations. It is useful to identify a range of systems from very coherent to very incoherent. Some wired organizations are coherent in the sense that all the key parts—the architecture and the displays of the information technologies, the norms of the people staffing the organization, the organizational policies and processes, and the funding, incentives and performance measures—all promote the same goal. In some cases a coherent system will be desirable. This is typically the case when the function being systematized through technology is a routine one (e.g., bill processing) and one that does not involve much discretion. In such a case, the rationalization of the process that a coherent technology offers is generally commendable. In other instances, however, a coherent system can have deleterious effects. For example, we can imagine a system that is used to ensure that every citizen who comes to the government for help gets exactly the same treatment—one that has been programmed into the code of the systems used by government employees. Executive managers would receive reports on the number and type of deviations from the routine and on the employees involved, and would structure incentives and employee training to correct unwanted deviations from the standard operating procedure. While this would be a wired system, it would be one that would very much work against customized services for citizens.

At the other end of the spectrum, wiring can lead to incoherence. In such a case, one part of the system, for example the culture of the staff or the incentive system or the organizational routines, may be at odds with the technologies being introduced or with another part of the system. Wiring that occurs without sufficient staff training is generally acknowledged to be a poor investment. Incoherent systems can create fissures in an organization. In the business world, these fissures typically lead to business failure. In government, where the organization cannot fail in an existential sense, such incoherence will typically lead to greater than average inefficiency, large staff turnover, ditched technology, and high levels of duplicated or unused technology investment. Accounts of the performance of city and state governments in the management of information technology, as presented in *Governing* magazine (2000), are instructive. Low-performing governments typically had systems that could not talk with each other and that could not grow to handle tasks. The expectation that governments can grow a system across functions assumes both a level of consistency across governmental functions and a level of software sophistication that traditionally have not existed. The emergence of government information system strategic planning, on the one hand, and knowledge management applications, on the other, may change this situation.

In the middle between single-purpose coherent systems and incoherent systems (which are most typically represented by a number of single-function or single-department applications) are what one might call multipurpose satisficing systems. Such systems are appropriate for many public sector functions where the function itself must achieve multiple goals. As Herbert Simon points out in *Administrative Behavior* (1997), this is the peculiar predicament of government. At the level of the street bureaucrat, satisficing occurs through the judicious discretion of individual government workers who do their best to match specific contexts to numerous possibilities for slight to moderate deviations from standard operating procedures. To illustrate the differences between the coherent, incoherent and satisficing systems, we can imagine a financial reporting system. A coherent system might be perfectly programmed to provide an accurate forecast of tax revenues based on a carefully constructed analysis of the government's fiscal history, current collections to date, and the sources of the collected funds. The system would be operated by a specialist trained in computer modeling of tax revenue data collections. The incoherent system might be headed by an employee trained in personnel issues, and might be composed of data that were not formatted or stored in ways that would allow for needed data fields to be incorporated into a predictive formula. The satisficing system might be headed by a general public finance staff member with an interest in modeling, who is able to develop predictions that are "good enough" when supplemented by the collective wisdom of the government's fiscal managers, but who is also able to use the system to track bank deposits and accounts, or provide managers with an estimate of their current expenditures. While the ideal may be a completely coherent system that addresses all tasks, the reality is that the achievement of such complete coherence would be prohibitively expensive.

Wired organizations can be created to enhance judicious discretion or to eliminate it. Wired organizations can be used to enhance or undermine control by policy makers, managers or citizens, and wired organizations can promote more customer service or less, more privacy or less, and more transparency or less. In the upcoming months and years, public managers will have a chance to reshape their governments (and indirectly governance) in ways that may alter permanently the developmental path of public administration and democratic governance. It will be important not just that our governments become wired, but how they get wired and for what.

GETTING WIRED: HOW MUCH AND TO WHOM?

Answering the how much and to whom questions is key to becoming an effectively wired organization. Recently, a large group of private and public sector leaders gathered at Harvard's Kennedy School of Government to discuss the need for leadership in preparing organizations for a more connected world. The result of this discussion was the monograph *Eight Imperatives for Leadership in a Networked World* (2000). Included among the imperatives were the following:

• Form IT-related partnerships to stimulate economic development.
• Use IT to promote equal opportunity and healthy communities.
• Prepare for digital democracy.

If we accept these imperatives, the wired government will be one that connects to citizens, civic and nonprofit groups, and profit-making organizations. It will be one that forms partnerships with both corporations and citizen groups. It will receive more input and more of its operating orders through online mechanisms that support democratic decision making, and it will actively seek to ensure that the full spectrum of citizens can participate in an electronic community. While traditional managers may view these imperatives as too much too soon, for too little in return, three arguments suggest otherwise.

In the first place, although governments differ with respect to how much of their work depends on the flow and processing of information or on producing information-rich products or services, a strong argument can be made that the vast majority of government tasks are based on or incorporate information as a major component. Land and transportation planning, building inspections, human services, human resource development, processing of applications and permits, billing, procurement, accounting, tax administration, ordinance development, legal services, case management and disbursement of public assistance, program evaluation, contract management and regulation enforcement are all essentially knowledge management tasks. Moreover, if one follows the reinventing government model, governments are advised to focus on these "steering" tasks and to shed the remaining physical work or "rowing" tasks.

GOVERNMENTAL PARALLELS TO THE EMERGING BUSINESS MODEL OF THE NEW ECONOMY

A second reason for public managers to take the network imperatives seriously is that these imperatives already substantially impacted on the private sector economy. To the extent that there *are* parallels between government work and work in the private sector, applying the emerging business model for the new economy to government suggests that there are extensive opportunities to improve both governance and governmental services. For example, Don Tapscott et al. (1999) have argued that the evolution of a networked economy has created new opportunities for businesses to relate with customers and suppliers. These new opportunities have their counterparts in government. (See Table 1.1.)

The opportunities for government to create new value for citizens and key community groups are as diverse and plentiful as those in business. However, governments cannot take advantage of these opportunities without the

Table 1.1
Business and Government Opportunities in a Networked Economy

Business Web Innovation	Example	Government Equivalent
Negotiating prices with customers	Priceline.com eBay.com	Negotiating fees with citizens. Reverse auctions for government procurement.[1]
More convenience and better selection of goods and services through the aggregation	Amazon.com	Providing government services from multiple levels (e.g., local, state, federal) at one stop.
Creating new values through the promotion of alliances and sharing	America Online Open source code	Providing online forums for discussion of policy issues.
Integrating processes and customizing them to meet personal needs	Order of customized Dell computers	Use of smart forms that take information once, store it and automatically extract it for use in several places (e.g., to fill out a tax form or a hunting license).
Enhancing transparency and network capability to exchange and deliver value among multiple users of the network	FedEx's tracking of packages	Online fee tracking. Tracking of legislation and meeting minutes regarding specific issues.

[1]Pennsylvania's procurement office has sponsored a number of online reverse auctions. In these auctions, the potential sellers progressively bid down the price of a well-specified product or commodity. Pennsylvania uses the reverse auction technique for contracts related to items such as rock, coal, aluminum, construction, office furniture and salt. The reverse auction is Web-based and employs software from FreeMarkets Inc. (Walsh 2000).

Source: Tapscott et al. 1999.

development of adequate and appropriate policies. Specifically, governments will need to formulate balanced policies to protect privacy, mandate online public access to government records and proceedings, and establish the framework for government-citizen and public-private negotiations, partnerships and exchanges. For example, if governments are to follow the lead of wired businesses and set up systems for serving citizens at a negotiated price, they will first need to develop policies that define the limits of such negotiations and that overcome existing barriers to such new economy transactions. Similarly, use of smart forms, ones that draw information from multiple existing databases, will only work if citizens are willing to risk, and governments are willing to minimize the risk of, a loss of privacy that could result from an increase in government agencies sharing information. Governments that enact privacy policies and security measures in tandem with their efforts to integrate information from diverse records will be more successful than ones that do not. Similar measures will be needed to assure that when citizens use government online services for tracking legislation or public deliberations, they will not be watched by the government that they themselves are watching.

Public managers should attend to the network imperatives identified above for a third reason: readiness for future opportunities. Organizations need to reach a certain threshold of experience with information technology before they can successfully integrate data collection, information creation and communication into better decision making. Reaching such a threshold is difficult enough within any single organization, but is even more difficult within partnership efforts such as might be needed among several local governments (or agencies) in order to establish a new level of service to citizens. Groups of smaller governments or agencies should have a particular advantage in this regard since their efforts will often involve a more manageable number of people. But for small and large governments alike, successful partnership efforts will be founded on all the partners having similar levels of technical experience, skill and administrative support. In the early years of computerization, the levels of technological competency among governments and their agencies were so widely divergent that efforts to create partnerships could only occur through specially funded IT projects. Even in these cases, however, the efforts would often founder due to the differences in government or agency practices, the skills of the respective sets of employees, or the understanding and support of the respective managers in the participating organizations. Although these differences among agencies have not disappeared, the gaps among potential partners have certainly narrowed. Advances in technology and, more important, in the adoption of communications standards make it more likely that public bodies have reached the threshold where the benefits of information partnerships could possibly outstrip the costs. In particular, the mass adoption of the Internet as the standard for data transmission and display has made it possible to create multigovernment or multiagency applications that have a chance of surviving. In my own community, for example, I participated in an effort to create a common application form for social services programs. The initial and only marginally successful effort was based on the creation of a private dial-up system that was used to transmit copies of individual database records to participating agencies. As this system was built before the Internet, it was much less efficient than a similar system designed today would be (e.g., it required adopting a set of technologies that would not have other uses, and it required more time to set up and learn). Because of the Internet standards, a single technology can be used for multiple purposes, and experience in setting up and learning a system for one function will shorten the time needed to set up and learn a system designed to serve another function. Considering that most of the expense of business or government computer ownership is in training and usability issues rather than in the cost of the hardware, the ability of Internet standards to promote a piggyback effect is crucial. At a concrete level this means that workers who have home Internet experience will already know the basics of how to use Web-based forms to enter and receive data. As agencies adopt the Internet as the default medium for transmitting and receiving data, they do not need to spend as much on training or on the installation and maintenance of specialized networking software or hardware. Also, agency partners can share the same data and potentially expand or integrate the system with their legacy systems. (A legacy system refers to older, typically mainframe systems that have been used for a period of years.)

Even though the Internet has made it much easier and more efficient for diverse agencies, departments and units to connect and to share data, adopting an Internet standard is not sufficient for success. Rather, overcoming cumbersome technology is just the first step—and not even the most important—in implementing a new, information-based function, process or program. Typically, the more important steps in such implementation relate to administrative policies and procedures. In the case of the common social services application, for example, the easiest to use and most sophisticated technology will not succeed in a situation where the director of Agency A does not support her staff filling out those portions of a common application that pertain to Agency B or where the new task of completing a common application will be undertaken only after other tasks have been completed.

REFERENCES

The Digital State. (1998). Washington, DC: Progress and Freedom Foundation.

Electronic Commerce Primer for the Georgia General Assembly. (2000). Atlanta: Electronic Commerce Study Committee, March 14.

Friedman, T. (2000). *The Lexus and the Olive Tree: Understanding Globalization*. New York: Doubleday.

Georgia Office of Planning and Budget. (2000). *Review of Administrative and Financial Practices, Scope Area 1: Information Technology and Telecommunications Final Draft*. Atlanta: Georgia Office of Planning and Budget, February 14.

Governing. (2000). The Government Performance Project: Information technology. Found at http://www.governing.com/gpp/gp0it.htm. June 9.

Landsbergen, D., and G. Wolken. (1998). *Eliminating Legal and Policy Barriers to Interoperable Government Systems. Phase 1: Policy Barriers*. August 12. Washington, DC: Intergovernmental Enterprise Panel, Office of Information Resources Management, Department of Veterans Affairs. http://iep. fedworld.gov/.

Lescher, W. K. (1999). Network-centric: Is it worth the risk? *United States Naval Institute. Proceedings* 125(7): 58–63.

Lessig, L. (1999). *Code and Other Laws of Cyberspace*. New York: Basic Books.

Mechling, J., and T. M. Fletcher. (2000). *Eight Imperatives for Leaders in a Networked World: Guidelines for 2000 Election and Beyond*. Cambridge, MA: Harvard Policy Group on Networked Services and Government. March.

O'Looney, J. (2000a). Access: Making your community Internet-ready. *IQ Service Report* 32, 5. Washington, DC: International City/County Management Association, May.

———. (2000b). *Local Governments On-Line*. Washington, DC: International City/County Management Association.

Simon, H. A. (1997). *Administrative Behavior*, 4th ed. New York: Free Press.

Tapscott, D., D. Ticoll, and D. Lowy. (1999). The rise of the business Web. *Business 2.0*, November. Found at http://www2.actnet.com/pdf/2410671.pdf.

Walsh, T. (2000). Pennsylvania reaps millions in savings with reverse auctions. *Government Computer News: State and Local* 6(7): 36.

2
Electronic Government: Stages and Status

LEVELS AND AGES OF BECOMING WIRED

Data Processing

B. K. Brussaard (1988) of the Ministry of the Interior in the Netherlands tells the story of how the Netherlands attempted to cope with and manage the organizational impacts of technologies. The first effort of this type took place in the mid-1950s when an interdepartmental committee was formed to advise the government on the purchase of computer equipment. The only reason for this extraordinary step, Brussaard suggests, was that computers were extremely expensive. Because of the expense, only the most mass routine tasks could be chosen for computerization. Thus began the age of data processing where the chief goal was to incorporate information technology into many of the clerical and repetitive processing tasks of government. While the golden age of data processing has passed, local and state governments still gain tremendous economies from using computers to automate such tasks as processing bills, ordering goods and services, balancing accounts, writing utility reports and monitoring inventory status. In recent years, governments have taken the basic approach of data processing—the automation of a single task—and have created fortuitous linkages with other technologies. For example, water meter data can now be entered through radio wave communications, and citizens can fill out application forms for a specific service on the Web and have this information processed by a government computer system. With the lowering of the cost of computing, it is no longer necessary to gather representatives from various departments to decide how to allocate scarce computer resources. In fact, the "democratization of technology" has meant that almost any government employee with a good data processing idea can implement it without worrying that computer equipment will be a factor. This has led to the oft-noted decentralization of information technology.

Information Processing

While the microcomputer has pushed toward decentralization and a measure of IT entrepreneurialism, the PC revolution was hardly under way before government, or at least large governments, began to understand that computers could do more than simply automate routine tasks. This realization was evident in the interdepartmental meetings in the Netherlands during the 1970s and early 1980s regarding the use of information technology. Meeting participants at this point began to generate more and more nonconventional ideas for using computers. Specifically, it was becoming clear that data used for routine tasks, when combined with other data and with an understanding of people, procedures and workflows, could be used by management to inform decisions. As this insight was refined in the early 1980s, the council of ministers in the Netherlands (and numerous executive public managers elsewhere) came to the conclusion that information processing could no longer be the sole responsibility of the department for which the data were being processed. Rather, executive managers needed to make an effort to combine data collection and data storage and to ensure that systems could speak to each other and provide a common interface. Out of this concern managers tried to design systems that would give them meaningful information with which to make adjustments in the flow of work or in the way IT operations were organized. Efficiency of effort also dictated that new systems not duplicate systems that had already been developed in the government. In short, this was the period of the discovery of information and management information systems (MIS). As with the data processing line of development, the development of MIS has continued, even though it is no longer the area of prime attention. Hence, later in the 1980s and 1990s, when managers began to discover how useful statistical process controls could be in identifying workflow weaknesses, these techniques were incorporated into information systems to help further refine the staging and implementation of a work process.

Work Redesign and Reengineering

In the late 1980s and early 1990s, another new committee was formed to advise the government of the Netherlands. This time the interagency committee was given a much broader mission: to advise on the revision of organizational and administrative boundaries with a view toward optimal operation of the government—not just optimal operation of the information processing tasks in government. This systems approach later became incorporated into Hammer and Champy's *Reengineering the Corporation* (1993). In this work-redesign effort, information systems were seen as a partner to systems management and resource management activities, but one assigned a supporting rather than a primary role. Within this age of work redesign, new client/server technologies began to provide some of the benefits of both the individual PC and the mainframe system. Hence, while the debate about centralization and decentralization continued, it became less important than the implementation, by whatever means, of principles such as including information processing in the real work or organizing around outcomes rather than tasks. (See Table 2.1 for Hammer's reengineering imperatives.) The most desirable system was the one that best fulfilled these mandates. Although the track record of reengineering efforts has been mixed, when reengineering was appropriately and successfully applied, it tended to create very dramatic improvements in productivity.

In Chapter 3, I explain why work redesign efforts have failed in particular cases. The chief gurus of reengineering have offered a couple of reasons why work redesign is no longer the primary management technique for incorporating IT in organizations. Hammer, on the one hand, has suggested that too many reengineering efforts got mixed up with an excessive desire to downsize the organization as part of the effort to gain economies. Champy, on the other hand, has suggested that reengineering efforts did not put enough emphasis on the culture of the organization. He nevertheless believes that the reengineering approach of changing the process first in order to change the culture is the correct one. Champy is quoted as saying, "I am a believer in changing what they do first and getting them to experience the physical nature of the change. Then it is more likely—but not guaranteed— that you will be able to change how they think. At the same time, if the culture and fundamental behaviors don't change, nothing sticks. Even with big things that companies do, you'll slide back" (Karlenzig 2000, p. 1).

Work redesign efforts have come under many different rubrics (e.g., systems engineering, business process design), but the emphasis is generally, as Champy suggests, on using technology to embed changed procedures, behavior, job responsibilities and workflow in fairly radical ways. Champy argues, probably correctly, that reengineering is a more powerful model for organizational change. However, good ideas for reengineering do not just appear full-blown in the heads of managers. This is one of the areas where knowledge management can make a contribution.

Knowledge Creation and Management

If work redesign is about changing processes, knowledge management is about understanding and putting to use the current best practices being employed by workers, managers and staff. These best practices can occur in

Table 2.1
Levels and Ages of Information Technology

Level or Age	Features/Concerns	Example
Data Processing	Incorporation of information technology into a single task or hardware resource so as to automate that task.	Development of single process mainframe Merging of address records with a mailing label printing application
Information, MIS, and Statistical Control	• Incorporation of standards for data exchange across processes • Concern for efficiency of data base development • Incorporation of information feedback loops for refining a process • Embedding analysis or statistical routines so as to identify weak links in a production or service chain. These analyses use time-based observations to identify opportunities to improve quality in a product or service.	Development of electronic data exchange standards (EDS) Development of general use mainframes MIS used to identify high absentee rate in the accounting department Statistical process control is used to: • Identify excessive inventory of unused parts in a vehicle repair facility • Identify the point in a process where defects are most likely to occur and under what circumstances • Identify problematic wait times or queues in a process or service Organize quality teams around desired outcomes
Work Re-Design Sub-areas: • Systems Management • Document Management • Enterprise Resource Planning	Using information technology to allow fewer people to complete an entire task that includes a number of functional processes that span multiple departments, usually through: • Organizing around outcomes rather than tasks • Having those who use the output of the process perform the process	Work redesign is used to enable a single case manager for multiple human service programs to: • Determine eligibility • Provide intake • Identify appropriate resources and referrals • Troubleshoot problems • Incorporate information from diverse sources

Table 2.1 (continued)

Level or Age	Features/Concerns	Example
	• Including information processing in the real work • Enhancing access to central databases • Linking people who are working on parallel activities • Putting decision points where the work is performed and building control into the process • Capturing information once and at the source (Hammer 1990; O'Looney 1993).	• Assess appropriate fees or charges • Order needed materials and resources • Determine if more expertise is needed and coordinate with the providers of expert services A classic work redesign will enable one or more empowered workers to provide one-stop services to citizens
Virtual & Enhanced Space	Using collaboration-focused information technologies to create virtual work- and decision-making spaces that span the limitations of physical space. Virtual space is used to enable dispersed persons to work as if they were in close proximity. Because information technology can enable enhancement or a stronger ordering of particular aspects of this space, those who design or make the rules for the virtual space have much more control over the nature of the work or decision-making environment than has typically been the case in public space. The key levers that are controlled by the designers and rule-makers of virtual space include:	Virtual space is used to enable the expansion of participation in town council meetings. Council meetings are designed to occur over long periods of time with scheduled times for voting. Citizens are allowed to participate through e-mail and group discussion forum postings. Even citizens who are out of town during the meeting are able to join in.

Table 2.1 (continued)
Levels and Ages of Information Technology

Level or Age	Features/Concerns	Example
	• time and place of meeting • the media available to those inhabiting the space • the rules for membership and interaction • the number of people who can be in the space • the rules for expulsion from the space	
Knowledge Creation and Management (see McCartney 1998; Maeil Business Newspaper 1998)	Using information linkage and processing technologies to bring the right information to the right people in the right quantities, so as to enhance the decision making and innovative capacities of human beings. Knowledge management typically involves automating the gathering, analysis and arrangement of information from disparate sources based on contextual understanding of clients, geography, decision needs, and business processes so as to identify (based on historical and new information) current and emerging best practices and the value of alternative options. Common knowledge management tools include search engines, data mining applications, and expert systems. Knowledge management processes will typically support double-loop learning or learning to identify the capabilities and faults of one's approaches or tools.	Combining citizen satisfaction survey data with information about the location of the citizen's home so as to identify common problems that are geographically based. This information could then be used to help prevent further dissatisfaction through pro-active remediation. For example, a receptionist could use this information combined with caller ID and phone-number-to-address software to identify callers who are from a particular area and to ask them if they have experienced a problem (e.g., a water quality problem) that has been associated with citizens in a particular area. In this way problems that could be larger than they first appear can be identified and solved early on. Also, it may be that the identified problem is being caused by a nongovernmental organization. In this case the receptionist can use the communication opportunity to inform the resident of this fact.

conjunction with existing standard operating procedures (SOPs), but just as often they may occur despite the current SOPs. As will become clearer in the next chapter, knowledge management is a somewhat expansive concept that is often defined to include approaches and techniques that were evident in earlier models or ages of IT. Nevertheless, at the heart of knowledge management is the idea of harvesting what you already know and putting the insights to work throughout the organization.

Knowledge management is probably most effective in areas where a government has broad experiences that can be applied to numerous individual situations. For example, American oil companies are now being asked to reenter Middle Eastern countries from which they were previously expelled, partly because these global firms have experience with oil exploration and extraction in thousands of different circumstances around the world. Now that oil is harder to extract in the Middle East, the broader and synthesized experience of these global firms can be beneficially applied to the new oil exploration and extraction problems facing Middle Eastern countries (Friedman 1999). The clearest government parallel to a global multinational firm is the U.S. government. Like the global firm before the application of knowledge management techniques, the federal government has massive unused or underutilized archives of knowledge that could be applied to thousands of situations in local communities across the country and the world. Similarly, the aggregate knowledge that state governments have would rival that of the federal government. While larger governments or groups of governments are more likely to benefit from knowing and applying what they know, nearly every organization has knowledge that is not being systematically utilized. In social services, for example, a vast amount of "system knowledge" is needed to effectively negotiate the system to better serve a client. It is often the case that an experienced social or healthcare worker will know who to call, who should be mentioned in the conversation, which buzzwords to use, which legal reference to cite, which day to present something to a judge, how to find free pharmaceuticals, and which service codes will raise the suspicions of program reviewers. For the most part, this system knowledge is not taught in social work classes and is difficult to keep up with even for the most experienced workers. In fact, the best knowledge in these organizations is highly distributed and short-lived. In order for every social worker to maximize their effectiveness, systems need to be in place for identifying and sharing new knowledge, while discarding and eliminating knowledge that is no longer valid.

The movement from data processing to work redesign to knowledge management can be illustrated in the development of a hospital database at Salt Lake City's Intermountain Health Care Center. In the 1960s, the development team first started building files by practice area for such departments as the laboratory, the medical records department and the radiology division. From a pure data crunching perspective, the individual hospital divisions could process data most efficiently, but only for purposes that were particular to each division. While such processing was a major advancement at the time, the discrete, division-level health information systems did not really begin to affect the quality of health care until they were redesigned in the 1970s, 1980s, and 1990s. This redesign involved three major thrusts. First, with the introduction of a client/server architecture, the system began to supply patient data where they were most needed—in the hands of nurses and doctors. In this way, nurses who had good and complete data could perform their jobs more effectively as well as take on greater responsibility for care (i.e., workflow and work organization could be improved). Second, the system was redesigned so as to automatically capture and organize patient data from many sources—from emergency room visits to routine clinical checkups. Some of these data would not have been accessible or captured under a traditional charting system. Third, the developers of the system began to incorporate analysis of more and more data. From this analysis the system was able to provide medical information in the form of alerts and reminders to nurses and physicians. That is, it began to act as an intelligent knowledge base—one that served as a second or third opinion or as a nurse with an infallible memory providing needed reminders to busy physicians. Today, the knowledge system includes such things as warnings for possible drug interactions and an antibiotic computer consulting routine that is more accurate than the average physician (Taylor 1996).

The movement from data processing to information systems to knowledge creation and management can also be illustrated by following the development of an idea from data to information to knowledge. Data are essentially simple, unqualified facts. For example, the fact that property taxes at 124 Main Street have not been paid is a piece of data. Data processing might aggregate the delinquent taxes for individual districts or jurisdictions. When pieces of data are combined in ways that allow one to know the context of data, one arrives at information. For example, when we know that the property at 124 Main Street is owned by Jim Smith, that it has been delinquent for two years and that Mr. Smith also owns other pieces of property with delinquent taxes as well as properties where taxes have been paid, we now have information. Only when we begin to be able to answer the questions of "how we know" something; "why that something is the way it is" and "why we know what we know" do we begin to have knowledge. For example, it may be that property tax bills for some properties were never sent to Mr. Smith. We could learn that Mr. Smith failed to be sent important notices by checking the mailing lists for all notices that were sent. If this were the case, we would act in a particular way. However, it may be that Mr. Smith is in financial trouble, in which case we would react in an entirely different manner.

Knowing the process that led us to declare Mr. Smith's taxes delinquent provides another path to knowledge. In the tax office, this kind of knowing why might be something like: "Before declaring a tax as delinquent and beginning the process of a public sale, you first need to send three notices within a month's time, including two by certified mail. If you receive no response, you need to obtain approval from the tax commissioner to begin a public sale process." Knowledge of this type allows one to act in strategic and intelligent ways within the context of the organization's goals (Beyond expectations 2000). If, for example, one were to experience a rise in tax delinquency rates, the knowledge of the "declaring delinquency" process might lead one to pursue particular possibilities (e.g., that the taxpayer did not have sufficient time to acquire the needed resources) but not others (e.g., that the taxpayer failed to receive any notice).

Electronic Public Space

While the contributions of data processing to work redesign knowledge management can be easily described, the development of electronic public space is still too new to fully depict the possible costs and benefits. The mere existence of electronic public space or virtual public space will not necessarily create any change in government organization or administration. However, the potential for such change is strong. This is the case because historically the creation of new space tends to occur simultaneously with attenuation in the use of older spaces. That is, people only have so much time to devote to activities within any one space. In addition to there being an economy in the use of public space, the new electronic public spaces are likely to embed new capabilities while possibly eliminating older ones. Electronic public space encompasses a host of new technologies such as online public forums, virtual public meetings, electronic rule making, Internet voting, personalized government Web portals, intergovernmental or government-with-citizen chat rooms, and virtual reality spaces and simulations. It is unlikely that governments will choose not to adopt or build at least some of these technology-based public spaces. However, the choices of where, how and to what degree these new spaces will impact our lives as citizens (or netizens) will be important. Such choices will likely have major implications for democratic governance, citizen participation and electronic service delivery. I will address this issue as part of a larger discussion in Chapter 5 of how some information technologies may have unknown consequences for our political and public management cultures.

IT LEVELS AND AGES: FEATURES AND CONCERNS

The type and degree of change in public administration will depend on the level or levels of wiring that a government chooses to implement. In each period of its development, IT has made important contributions to governmental operations and services. Historically, it has been easier for governments to take a data processing approach. This approach, for example, is particularly congruent with a stovepipe organization such as might emerge under a commission form of local government (i.e., one where each commissioner is responsible for a particular fiefdom of government departments and functions). In addition, the data processing level of IT, with its employment of simple but reliable and secure hardware, meets some of the high-priority interests of government. However, if we accept the premise that governments need to become smart, we must also conclude that they need to become wired and to employ the higher levels of IT to redesign work and manage information, knowledge and virtual space.

While there is extensive overlap in specific technologies and organizational change practices among the levels of IT infusion identified in this chapter (i.e., data processing, information processing, work redesign and knowledge management), each has a particular focus, one that would tend to lead public managers to see organizational change in a somewhat different light. Overall, one can think of the levels of becoming wired as running the gamut from dealing with the most routine, decided and concrete tasks to those that are unique, evolving and abstract. At the far end of this spectrum is the area of IT-enhanced knowledge production and management. At this level, work will always involve high levels of creativity, personal insight, and professional judgment and discretion. These are not the tasks at which information technology has traditionally excelled. Understandably, governments and businesses have not yet extensively employed information technology in this way. Nevertheless, advances in artificial intelligence, natural language processing and complex simulations are beginning to change the outlook for opportunities at this level.

THE PUSH FOR ELECTRONIC GOVERNMENT

For most of the history of public administration, information technology has been a low priority among public managers. However, as the Internet has developed to support new electronic commerce and business strategies, the push for similar changes in the public sector is becoming stronger. Citizens and businesses throughout the developed world are making their opinion clear: they want to conduct transactions through the Internet. Governments as diverse as the state of Utah[1] and the Home Office of Great Britain[2] are waking up to the fact that citizens want twenty-four-hour access to public services, information, fee payments and application processing. They also want to purchase goods online and enter into binding contracts with both businesses and government. Of course, citizens desire to complete these transactions with the least amount of trouble and the greatest amount of security and privacy. Finally, citizens want this new level of service to be provided at the least cost to themselves in either their capacity as consumers or in their capacity as taxpayers. The growth in citizens' desires to conduct their personal and professional business online is, of course, a direct result of the growth in the use of the Internet by both businesses and private individuals. On the business side, Forrester Research predicts that expenditures by businesses to design, develop, market and implement e-commerce applications will reach $64.8 billion in 2003. This prediction represents a compound annual rate of growth of 83 percent.[3] For e-business to grow as expected, governments will need to do their part to use technology as an efficiency driver. As recently as 1999, it was estimated that 90 percent of government services were delivered face-to-face.[4] When businesses and citizens are prepared to move at the speed of light, but government is only able to move at highway speed limits, the growth process will be impaired. Hence, the increasing calls for electronic government are not surprising.

Electronic government (e-government) generally refers to government's use of technology, especially Internet-based technology, to enhance the access to and delivery of government information and service to citizens, businesses, employees, consultants, and other agencies and governments. A truly wired government would be one that emphasized the delivery of information and services via electronic networks. However, as will become clear in succeeding chapters, becoming a wired government and building the infrastructure for e-government also will involve efforts to change internal technology, and organizational structures, processes, practices and culture. This larger effort to become wired, however, is likely to be driven by the initial desire to deliver information and services electronically.[5]

A highly capable e-government would enable citizens to communicate and transact business both with elected representatives (digital democracy) and with agency and program workers for purposes such as applying for program participation, registration, permits and licenses, filing and paying taxes, completing surveys and requesting customized information. E-governments would also support workers and contractors who telecommute, and allow for electronic management of employment relations (e.g., personnel benefits, travel and expense reimbursements, leave request, etc.). Finally, e-government includes the capacity to streamline ongoing business operations such as procurement, budgeting, payments, personnel, routing, and client intake and case management through electronic means.

BASIC CAPACITIES FOR ELECTRONIC GOVERNMENT

The capacity to conduct electronic government demands a number of both technology- and management-related capabilities, including but not limited to the following:

- The existence of a base information technology infrastructure within a department or service unit. This base might include computerized records and the hardware and software that enable staff to access and manipulate these records.
- A sufficient level of expertise in the particular technologies being used.

- Sufficient and consistent budgets for acquisition and maintenance of information technology and training in its use. Departments frequently use budget surpluses to purchase new technologies but lack adequate funds to support ongoing training in and maintenance of these technologies.
- A public that expects and is able to access services electronically.
- Leadership that is willing to risk being on the developmental edge of new technologies.
- The existence of a network.

RESOURCE AND MANAGEMENT CAPACITIES

In the private sector the management of technology is guided by profit incentives that determine the type, amount and distribution of technology across various functions and departments. In contrast, in government there are few such cues for guiding decisions about the introduction and management of information technology. It is not unusual to find discrepancies between per-worker information technology spending in technology-leading departments and per-worker spending levels in technology-lagging departments.[6] As such, within local, state and federal governments there is a tendency for some departments to get far out in front of the developmental curve, while others fall far behind. This disparity is often the result of differences in the ability of different departments to muster the human, technological and administrative resources needed to stay on the developing edge of new technologies. Agencies that get ahead of the developmental curve will likely combine three characteristics:

- Access to discretionary funding or to funding explicitly targeted toward technology. For example, law enforcement agencies often use the proceeds from fines to purchase and maintain new technologies. Similarly, the federal government sometimes supports the introduction of new information technologies in state government departments in conjunction with programs that are federally funded but state administered (e.g., the JOBS systems for public assistance programs).
- A critical mission that is data intensive. High-end information technology services tend to be clustered in departmental units that have a mission that depends on the effective processing of information. For example, law enforcement agencies use data in nearly every aspect of their work, from criminal investigation through release of prisoners. A loss of paperwork or key information at any point in the process can completely undermine the mission. On the other hand, a landscaping department can typically maintain grounds effectively (but perhaps not optimally) with only minimal amounts of computerized information processing.
- An information technology entrepreneur as a key leader in the department who ensures that information technology receives sufficient funding and attention and who includes information technology knowledge and expertise as key criteria in the hiring, training and promotion of employees. Such a leader would also work to maintain a critical level of information technology capacity in house, rather than

allowing the department to use contractors as the primary means of employing information technology.

Although there are dynamics that will always make some agencies or governmental units more technologically advanced than others, an important task for executive managers is to address discrepancies in technology funding that put specific agencies at a disadvantage and that hinder the completion of strategic missions.

Although in small governments IT-related management tends to be centralized in one or two positions, in larger governments, IT management involves many functions and issues. Chief among these management practice areas are the following:

1. Level of Control of IT (e.g., government-wide, divisional, regional, etc.)
2. Role of IT Function or Position in the Overall Government
3. IT Strategies, Plans and Policies
4. Financial and Performance Management of IT
5. Project Management
6. Procurement
7. IT Human Resource Management
8. Application Development Management
9. Maintenance/Change Control
10. Data Center Management
11. Network Management
12. End-User Computing Management
13. Relationship Management
14. Information Management[7]

AGENCY-LEVEL TECHNOLOGY POLICY AREAS AND INFRASTRUCTURE CAPACITY

In addition to resource and management capacities outlined above, governments that want to provide information and services electronically often need to develop policies as well as the standards, practices and infrastructure through which policy is realized and embedded.

Table 2.2 outlines many of the key areas of government technology activity and identifies some examples of collaborative policies, standards, practices and infrastructure needs. While it is possible and often useful to make valid distinctions among technology policies, standards, procedures and guidelines, for simplicity the items in Table 2.2 combine some of each. In general, policies represent more abstract statements (e.g., the government will make all data accessible), while standards are more concrete (e.g., NT

Table 2.2
Key Areas of Government Technology Policies

Area	Collaborative Policies, Standards, Practices, and Infrastructure
Access control and security for the different types of services (e.g., government-to-government, government-to-business, government-to-citizens)	Government provides for a single sign-on that identifies the user of the system and allows for transfer of this identification across systems.
Encryption/Confidentiality	Government establishes a government-wide encryption standard (e.g., will use an encryption key of at least 40K).
	Government sets privacy standards for all agencies that include:
	Notice and Opt-In: Citizens are notified of the personalization service and must explicitly give the government permission to perform the profiling and customization (opt-in) to receive personalized service. They can also opt-out at any time.
	Limited Access and Customization: The full profile is only available to the citizen, who is given an opportunity to correct any false information and to adjust profile data elements. Citizens could also opt to have some personalization services but not others, and could limit the time in which personalization services would be activated. Citizens could choose the level and type of information that they want to be used in the development of their profile.
	Security: The full profile would not be accessible to government personnel or anyone other than the citizen. Government personnel would only be able to access the limited information that they currently access to perform their current duties.
Certification Authorities and Authentication	Government contracts with one or more certificate authorities to provide digital certificates for government employees. Government policies require that persons needing the highest level certificates identify themselves in person at a designated agency.

Table 2.2 (continued)

Area	Collaborative Policies, Standards, Practices, and Infrastructure
Integration of IT Architecture • Operating system and platforms • Messaging/e-mail • Databases • Communications/network protocols • Geographic Information Systems	Government adopts standard operating system for desktop use and for new back office servers (e.g., Windows for desktops, Unix for servers). Government establishes long-term plan to move all local area networks into Intranets.
Integration of Development Languages	Government identifies 1–2 languages for development of customized Web applications (e.g., Visual Basic, Java).
E-Commerce (credit cards, Internet checks, bill delivery/payment)	Higher level government develops a single e-commerce infrastructure for all agencies and sub-governments.
Audit and Capacity Update Standards Processing capacity Rates for data processing	Government sets government-wide policy for processing capacity and efficiency. Government uses a commercial service to assess the state's rates on a periodic basis and establishes and maintains rates that reflect true costs (KPMG 2000).
Archiving Record Retention	Government identifies levels of mission critically related to record archiving and specifies the number and type of backup systems needed for each type.
IT Acquisition	Government selects a cost-benefit analysis software tool, requires its use for requesting funding for technology projects, and trains staff to use it (KPMG 2000).
Web Design	Government identifies key Web design components that are mandated as common across all agencies Design to support the predominant types and versions of browsers. Develop web-based presentations to use HTML 4.0. Design for accessibility (e.g., use The Access Washington Styleguide section on Universal Web Design) (Source: *State of Washington User Interface Guidelines— Version 1.0—Recommended by the Digital Government Steering Committee*).

Table 2.2 (continued)
Key Areas of Government Technology Policies

Area	Collaborative Policies, Standards, Practices, and Infrastructure
Inter-networking Standard	Government set TCP/IP as standard.
Information Management	Governments mandate that electronically stored information should: 1. Be secured against unauthorized manipulation and/or destruction. 2. Be considered public unless explicitly and authoritatively classified as confidential. 3. Be designed and managed in such a manner as to protect availability and recoverability. 4. Be designed and managed to maximize reuse and sharing. 5. Be designed and managed to allow/maximize public access. 6. Conform to format and identification standards. 7. Be cataloged in a state meta-data repository. (*Source*: State of Arizona, Government Information Technology Agency, Statewide Information Management, Policy Date Effective: 12/09/1998)
Data Exchange	Government develops a set of XML data catalogs for use by government agencies and partners.
Help Desk	Government establishes a one-stop help desk for all staff needs.

will be the preferred network operating system). Procedures generally deal with how the government will go about doing things like setting policies or standards, while guidelines tend to involve a mixture of policies and standards that are not backed by a strong mandate or penalties for deviating from the recommendations. (For a good example of the sorting of these, see Arizona Statewide Policies, Standards and Procedures Listing, at http://gita.state.az.us/PSP/default.htm.)

The level of governmental efforts to provide information and services online can be traced in governments' budgets, policies and initiatives. The following sections address these measures at the federal, state and local levels.

BUDGETS

According to forecasts by the Gartner Group, spending by federal, state and local governments on digital government is likely to quadruple between 2000 and 2005. The public sector will spend approximately $1.5 billion in 2000, but is expected to spend $6.2 billion in 2005 (General Accounting Office [GAO] 2000). More short-term trends at the state level are difficult to interpret due to the extraordinary level of state spending on information technology as part of the Year 2000 remediation efforts.

More in-depth research suggests that public sector investments in information technology are much more substantial than the data on the purchase of hardware, software and consulting suggest. For example, in a study of spending on information technology by county governments, it was estimated that in 1991 more than $31 billion (or about 23 percent of county budgets) was spent on information technology and the personnel needed to operate these systems. The study's authors report that several components of information management costs are hidden because they are not identified as separate line items in program budgets. Even though county government IT budgets had already reached a level representing over a fifth of the entire government budget, the authors of the study noted that only 34 percent of the top county executives had implemented a planning process for information management (Fletcher et al. 1992).

GOVERNMENT-WIDE POLICIES AND PRACTICES

At both the federal and state levels interest in moving forward with electronic government can be tracked through the hundreds of bills, oversight hearings and legislative proposals on topics such as Internet taxation, privacy, computer security, consumer protection, open access and competition.

Federal Policies

In addition, some federal agencies are being directed by statute to put in place greater electronic capabilities for information and service delivery. These include:

• Electronic Signatures in Global and National Commerce Act took effect October 1, 2000. This bill provides that a signature, contract or other record relating to a transaction will not be denied legal effect, validity or enforceability solely because it is in electronic form; and that a contract relating to such transaction may not be denied legal effect, validity or enforceability solely because an electronic signature or electronic record was used in its formation. However, both citizens and governments will need to consent to the use of electronic signatures and records to make an electronic transaction a binding one.

- The Clinger-Cohen Act of 1996 (also called the Information Technology Management Reform Act of 1996). This act requires the General Services Administration to provide government-wide online access to information about services and products available under the multiple award schedules program (Sec. 5401, P.L. 104–106, 40 U.S.C. 1501). The Clinger-Cohen Act also was designed to address problems related to federal IT management. It requires federal agencies to focus more on the results achieved through IT investments while concurrently streamlining the IT acquisition process.

- The Fiscal Year 1999 Department of Defense (DOD) Authorization Act required DOD to establish a single, department-wide electronic system for ordering supplies and materials (Sec. 332, P.L. 105–261, 10 U.S.C. 2451 note).

- The Electronic Benefit Transfer Interoperability and Portability Act of 2000 requires the Department of Agriculture (USDA) to establish a national standard of interoperability and portability for electronic food stamp benefit transactions (P.L. 106–171, 7 U.S.C. 2016).

- The Government Paperwork Elimination Act of 1998 requires federal agencies to develop, wherever practicable, electronic systems for submitting, maintaining and communicating information (including electronic signatures) in support of the delivery of government services. The deadline for compliance is October 2003 (Title XVII, P.L. 105–277, 44 U.S.C. 3504 note).

- The Privacy Act, which requires agencies to protect the confidentiality of records containing personal information and is now applicable to protecting personal information gathered by agency Web sites, will enhance the ability of governments to customize or personalize their delivery of information and services to citizens via the Internet (P.L. 93–579, 5 U.S.C. 552a; OMB Circular No. A-130, Appendix I, "Federal Agency Responsibilities for Maintaining Records About Individuals").

- Public Law 105–220 amended Section 508 of the Rehabilitation Act of 1973 to require federal agencies and states that receive federal funds to acquire only electronic and information technology (IT) that is considered to be accessible to persons with disabilities unless it would create an undue burden. Enforcement begins August 7, 2000. Accessible equipment is equipment that allows persons with disabilities to access and use information in ways and amounts that are comparable to what is available to people without disabilities. Source for more information: Center for IT Accommodation, the General Services Administration (http://www.itpolicy.gsa.gov/cita/index.htm).

- P.L. 106–107, Federal Financial Assistance Management Improvement Act of 1999, requires federal agencies to offer grantees an electronic grants process within eighteen months and to simplify grant application and reporting requirements.

State Government Policies

At the state level, the number of bills and laws related to electronic delivery of services is too large to catalog. Some of the more frequently mentioned areas of legislation related to electronic government include:

- Numerous state versions of electronic or digital signature acts. These acts vary in terms of the requirement for the use of specific digital technologies and in the involvement of the state in the development and regulation of certificate authorities.

- Numerous state laws that outline the development of statewide information technology departments, authorities, strategies, task forces and policy boards.[8] The policy charge in this type of legislation is similar in many respects. For example, many of these statutes provide for:
    - establishment of standards for procurement of technology resources
    - development of technology enterprise management and technology portfolio management
    - establishment of standards for information technology plans and the interoperability of statewide data systems and exchanges
    - setting of technology policy
    - establishment of architecture for state technology infrastructure
    - establishment of technology security standards
    - establishment of policies necessary to ensure the legal authority and integrity of electronic documents
    - establishment of centers for innovation
    - operation of technology empowerment funds and centers

- Model or uniform state law: The National Conference of Commissioners on Uniform State Laws (NCCUSL) has adopted two new sets of model acts that are related to establishing a legal foundation for e-commerce. On July 29, 1999, the NCCUSL (by a vote of the states of 43–6) promulgated the Uniform Computer Information Transactions Act (UCITA) for consideration by the various state legislatures. At about the same time, the NCCUSL also approved and recommended for enactment the Uniform Electronic Transactions Act (UETA).[9] In addition, when (or if) the NCCUSL finalizes recommendations for revisions to the Uniform Commercial Code (particularly Article 2), these revisions would also play a role in laying the foundation for e-commerce and e-government.

Basically, the Uniform Electronic Transactions Act (UETA) deals with all electronic "transactions," defined very broadly. The focus of the act, however, is on the procedures of the transaction. The Uniform Computer Information Transactions Act (UCITA) focuses on the substantive aspects of contracts involving computer information. However, there are numerous areas of overlap between UCITA, UETA and the federal Electronic Signatures in Global and National Commerce Act, including:

• Recognizing the equivalency of electronic records and writings.
• Recognizing the validity of electronic signatures.
• Recognizing that contracts can be formed by electronic agents.
• Recognizing that contracts can be formed by interaction of an electronic agent and a human being.
• Recognizing that a person is attributed with an electronic act if the other party can prove that the act was the result of the person or his or her agent.
• Recognizing that parties are not required to use electronic commerce.

The Uniform Electronic Transactions Act, however, also specifies such things as:

• The consequences if a change or error in an electronic record occurs in a transmission between parties to a transaction.
• The necessary and appropriate or acceptable procedures for electronic notarization and acknowledgment.
• The provisions that will satisfy the requirement that a record be retained when the record is an electronic one.
• Rules defining whether and when a contract may be formed by the interaction of electronic agents of the parties when no individual is aware of or has reviewed the electronic agents' actions or the resulting terms and agreements.
• Rules for defining when a message has been officially sent and officially received.
• The assignment of authority to a particular governmental official to direct the acceptance and distribution of electronic records by governmental agencies. Currently, some state laws tend to distribute this authority across agencies. Concentration of the authority could more quickly clarify the conditions under which agencies will be able to or need to accept electronic signatures and related transactions.
• How records that have or need to be copied or transferred among parties will be treated.

The Uniform Computer Information Transactions Act (UCITA) addresses electronic commerce issues that the UETA, as a procedural statute, does not. In particular, it identifies:

• how terms of an electronic contract are established;
• the meaning of "conspicuous" in an electronic user interface context;
• when an on-screen click is adequate to establish a contract;
• what state's law applies to an electronic contract that crosses more than one state;
• the effect of a choice of forum clause;

- the warranties that attach to published information;
- the default rules for information obtained by contract online;
- how changes in ongoing contracts are made;
- how contract terms are decided as between electronic agents; and
- the remedies that are available to parties who contract under UCITA terms.[10]

There has been considerable controversy regarding the parts of UCITA that involve the enforceability of what are called "shrink wrap" contracts for software. These are the implied contracts that are made when a consumer purchases a piece of software from a vendor but is unable to know what the contract entails or the true nature of the software product until it has been loaded on his or her computer. Because UCITA would provide less protection for dissatisfied consumers than is the case under existing contract law, states have been very slow to adopt it.

Local Government Policies

For the most part, local governments have not attempted to establish broad policy for electronic delivery of information or services. Instead they have concentrated on more administrative policies related to such issues as employees' appropriate use of Internet services or the need to respond to citizen e-mail within a certain specified period. Chapter 9 outlines a number of these administrative-level policies. One of the exceptions to the general disinclination of local governments to attempt to create broad policy has been in the area of Internet network competition.

Specifically, a number of local communities—from Broward County, Florida, to Fairfax, Virginia, to Portland, Oregon—have attempted to require that cable systems allow "open access" for Internet subscribers. This would allow a subscriber to contract with the Internet service provider (ISP) of their choice. Cable companies that also operate as an ISP would obviously prefer that Internet access through a cable modem remain a bundled service. While public managers might not see efforts of local governments to open up the cable Internet systems to competition as relevant to their administrative responsibilities, they need to recognize that the long-term impact of keeping the cable systems closed to competition may be substantial. This is the case because without competition there is a danger that cable companies will attempt to build networks that do not conform to the open standards of the public Internet. Already, for example, it may be impossible to stream video over some of the cable systems. The threat to governments is that when or if a government decides to build a citizen-serving application, there is the potential that even though the application is built to Internet standards, it would not work on the cable network. Hence, even though local governments involved in the lawsuits against the cable companies were most likely acting out of a desire to support local Internet service providers, they were unwittingly becoming involved in an area of major concern to theorists of cyberspace.

As of July 2000, the Ninth District Court of Appeals had decided that cable systems were essentially forms of telecommunication systems and therefore not subject to regulation by local governments. Rather, these systems, if they were to be regulated at all, could only be regulated by the Federal Communications Commission (FCC). While the Federal Communications Commission chairman has stated that the FCC will not require cable operators to open their networks to competitors, he has also indicated that the FCC might revisit the issue.[11] As of this writing, AT&T has agreed to work to open up its cable lines to competing ISPs. However, it is unclear as to whether the Supreme Court will agree to rule on an appeal to the decision of the Ninth District Court of Appeals.[12]

PRACTICES AND ACTIVITIES

Federal Level

At the federal level, the following activities highlight the strong interest in electronic government:

Through a series of presidential memoranda, President Bill Clinton directed agencies to provide "one-stop access" to government information and services and more efficient services and accountability, and to promote and work to establish the larger social benefits and potential of information technology. Specifically, agencies are challenged to provide easy public access to government information on the Web, to develop online forms, and to make the provision of public assistance and other benefits available through secure and confidential online transactions.[13]

The Federal Electronic Commerce Program Office, co-chaired by the General Services Administration (GSA) and DOD, has been established to provide leadership, coordination and reporting on government-wide electronic commerce implementation.

The Interagency Acquisition Internet Council has been charged to promote ways of using the Web in streamlining the federal acquisition process, and the Interagency Electronic Grants Committee (IAEGC) has been established to promote the development and use of Internet-based information technologies in federal grants and grant reporting procedures (GAO 2000).

Electronic Tax Administration (ETA) or the filing of tax returns over the Internet is expected to account for 26 percent of IRS returns in the year 2000.

The General Accounting Office has established a whole category of information system reports and has commissioned numerous reviews and examinations of electronic government issues at the federal level (e.g., on the use of the Internet to improve rule making and the implementation of e-commerce programs at individual agencies) (www.gao.gov).

The National Science Foundation has established a digital government initiative (www.nsf.gov).

The federal Chief Information Officers (CIO) Council is supporting the Information Technology Information Processing Systems (I-TIPS) for use by federal agencies such as the Departments of Housing and Urban Development, Treasury, Labor, Energy and Agriculture. I-TIPS is a Web-based decision support and project management tool for managing information technology investments.

State Level

It is increasingly common to find state governments using the Web to support basic transactions such as filing and paying taxes, issuing permits and licenses or license renewals, conducting intake into service programs, and filing applications. (See Appendix C for a list of services provided by Georgia, the state rated the highest for the development of e-commerce services in government.) Many states now provide legislative information, vital record information, labor and education information, and online college applications. A large number are also planning to develop online procurement and contracting systems. A smaller group of states are working on both the common applications and more specialized ones. States that lead in the area of electronic government include Georgia, Florida, Virginia and Washington.

In Georgia (http://www.sos.state.ga.us/):

• businesses can search online the corporation and trademark databases, and reserve a corporate name or obtain an annual registration form to be filed for an existing entity.
• physicians, nursing home administrators, physical therapists, low voltage contractors and architects can renew their licenses online.

In Florida (http://fcn.state.fl.us/gsd/) citizens can:

• complete job applications online.
• send a complaint form to a government agency.
• search for holders of business and professional licenses.

Virginia allows citizens to renew driver's licenses by logging onto the Department of Motor Vehicles' Web site, checking the accuracy of the personal information currently in the state's database, and paying the renewal fee with a credit card.

Washington State provides a number of unique Web information and service systems, including the following (for a complete list, see http://www.wa.gov/dis/e-gov/plan/applications.htm #Government to Citizen):

- Fastrack: Enterprise Financial Reporting System. This system provides Web-based access for requesting, viewing, printing and downloading of agency financial, budgetary and monitoring data.
- Uniform Medical Plan Online. This application provides the ability to access full benefits information and to enroll online.
- E-mail lists. Citizens subscribe to free e-mail lists for up-to-the-minute state government news and information.

Because a digital signature infrastructure has yet to be developed, certain types of activities (e.g., online submission of travel vouchers, binding contracts, etc.) will be difficult to conduct over the Web. Washington State has taken the lead in facilitating the development of digital signature infrastructure. In May 2000 the state chose a Salt Lake City firm, Digital Signature Trust, to provide all public entities in the state with digital certificates to use when doing online business with government. The digital certificate will certify the identity of the person who creates and sends an electronic document, payment or other data. By attaching a digital certificate, public employees (and eventually citizens) will be able to use e-mail or the Internet to send legally binding documents. Workers, for example, will be able to send purchase orders over the Internet without having to follow up with a hand-signed document. Digital certificates should be able to help Washington and other states reduce paperwork in government-to-government and government-to-citizen transactions (Locke 2000).

Local Level

While numerous state governments and their departments have the resources and technical capacity to implement a high level of e-government services, the situation at the local level is much more uneven. Some local governments such as the city of Boston and the city of Seattle have been able to develop a high level of electronic government services without private sector assistance. On the whole, however, local governments appear to be much more likely to turn to outside vendors (e.g., EZ-gov) to develop the technology for electronic cash transfer transactions. Some specialized local government innovations include:

- Web-enabled local government planning and economic development geographic information systems (see Ontario, California, as an example).
- Online procurement systems (see Orange County, California).

- Smart Permit System for online building permits and plan review (city of San Carlos, California).
- Street Beat information system—city of Rochester's daily reports on the status of city streets and public works and related services.
- Comprehensive collections of online forms and transactions (New York City and city of Boston).
- Extensive Technology Planning (Chicago: http://www.ci.chi.il.us/Planning/CITE/index.html).

While all of these innovations required substantial participation by in-house IT staff, the more technology-intensive innovations, such as the city of San Carlos' Smart Permit system, are the product of a partnership between local government and one or more technology vendors.

Unfortunately, except for large local governments or governments strategically located near a technology center, development of sophisticated e-government services will be difficult if not entirely beyond the capacity of most local governments given current budget limits. In these cases, local governments will need technical assistance, particularly with applications that involve online financial transactions. North Carolina's state government has taken steps to address this situation. Specifically, the state's E-Commerce Workgroup has recommended that the state "build a single statewide infrastructure that enables E-Commerce and simplifies the interactions of citizens and businesses with government." As this workgroup's report on electronic commerce argues, "Right now, numerous agencies are independently pursuing opportunities for E-Commerce. While these efforts are laudable, they involve a great deal of overlap in knowledge, processes and technologies. The result is unnecessary effort, higher costs and varying approaches for each interaction with the state" (State of North Carolina 1999, p. 13). Washington State is also working on making state-built infrastructure available to local governments. On June 26, 2000, the state announced the development of an Ultimate Purchasing System as one of Washington's top digital government projects. The system is designed to manage $1 billion in goods and services and be usable by state agencies, cities, counties, school districts, nonprofit organizations and others (http://www.wa.gov/dis/).

DIGITAL GOVERNMENT—INTEGRATED MANAGEMENT STRATEGY AND TACTICS

Creating a wired government, like all substantial challenges, demands effort that is both strategic and tactical at the same time. The preceding discussion has hinted at the nature of the wired government challenge and potential responses, and much of the remainder of the book will address these issues in more detail. The remainder of this chapter briefly explores one strategic challenge—project management across divisions and functions—and one tactical challenge—electronic commerce for government—as examples of the scope of effort needed to successfully respond to the challenge.

A Comprehensive Project Management Strategy

Project management is foremost about managing change in an organization, whether the change is mandated by external factors or motivated by internal factors related to improving organizational effectiveness. I hereby direct the Electronic Government Implementation Division to work to ensure that project management is consistently applied to the initiatives included in this executive order. (State of Virginia, Office of the Governor 2000)

As the above quote from Governor Gary Gilmore suggests, developing a wired government is primarily a management function—one that involves an effort that cuts across initiatives at many levels and within all the divisions of government. Table 2.3, which was developed by the Department of Information Services for use in the state of Washington, helps illustrate the broad scope of an effort to manage the development of the next generation of information technology applications across functions of state government. While the table includes some jargon that the reader may not be familiar with, what is important is the main idea: governments need to look at both the internal activities (e.g., travel vouchers, leave requests, interagency payments) and the external activities (e.g., tax filing, licenses, etc.) and to craft policies (built on paper) and infrastructure (built in silicon) that will enable the realization of a comprehensive statewide impact—rather than a series of narrow, uncoordinated, local efforts. The table also suggests that governments need to play a dual role as a provider of mission-critical infrastructure and as an incubator of new applications and technology. Traditionally, governments have been organized to play the first role but not the second.

The Tactics of Electronic Commerce in Wired Governments

As the outline of the state of Washington's plan for the next level of wired government in Table 2.3 suggests, developing an electronic commerce capacity is a key tactical element in the overall strategy. Terms such as Internet commerce, online transactions, electronic commerce, electronic business and cybertrade are often used interchangeably and with no common understanding of their scope. With respect to some of these definitions, there is no government parallel to private sector activity. However, if we define e-commerce as any transaction completed over a computer-mediated network that involves the transfer of ownership or rights to the use of goods or services, government parallels to private sector activity abound.

The following example suggests some of the complexity of measuring the e-commerce/e-government phenomena. Jane Doe, a local government worker, logs onto her computer, accesses the "Statepublications.gov" Internet site, and identifies a title of a state government publication that she wishes to purchase for her local government. Jane pays with a local government credit card that is reserved for online purchasing. The latest version of the book is transmitted electronically from a state government office to a local printer who prints a single copy of the book from the electronic version once the credit card account has been debited. Jane is not charged sales tax as part of the transaction, but is notified of the amount of use tax she potentially owes.

This example of e-commerce in government seems simple enough, but it may involve the use of additional electronic processes as well as incorporation of supporting government processes and infrastructure. These processes could include:

- Jane's accessing the Internet through a state sponsored online network;
- the state government's use of electronic listing of its publications and cooperative agreements with Web search engines and publication cooperatives. These are needed to enable Jane to find the publication title on the Web;
- the local government's ability to employ electronic procurement and payment to obtain the book from the state government publisher;
- the private sector printer's reliance on the state's electronic signature act to ensure that the contract with the state for printing services (which was negotiated and completed via a secure e-mail connection) is enforceable;
- electronic authentication of the credit card information Jane provided;
- electronic processing to obtain payment from the local government's bank;
- electronic processing of inventory and accounting of a sale on the part of the state government;
- electronic identification of the appropriate goods category that her purchase represents and search of a database of state and local sales (or use) tax rates;
- electronic calculation of taxes (or exemption from taxes); and
- electronic customer support to e-mail Jane an acknowledgment, order number and expected delivery date.

This example of how electronic commerce might take place between two governments in the near future is a bit more complicated than it might need to be, but not much. For example, although the example outlines a sales or use tax accounting mechanism that is not currently in place, such a mechanism will be necessary if state and local governments are to be able to tax electronic commerce as they currently do ordinary retail transactions. The other electronic steps in the example, however, are all part of current best practices among firms that do business via the Internet. Public managers will

Table 2.3
Outline of State of Washington's Plan for Next Generation Application Development

The Digital Government Portfolio

NEXT GENERATION AGENCY APPLICATION DEVELOPMENT

Internal - Government to Government (G2G)			*External - Government to Citizen (G2C)/ Government to Business (G2B)*		
Travel Voucher	Procurement	Leave Requests	Joint Tax Filing	Master License	License Tabs
	Interagency Payment				

Policy (Built on paper)		Infrastructure & Applications (Built in silicon)	
Collaborative Policy	*Statewide IT Policy (ISB-Specific)*	*Statewide IT Infrastructure*	*Agency Specific IT Activities*
			Applications Academy
	Security Policy and Procedures	Security Architecture	Security Plan and Interface
	Authentication	Authentication & Single Sign-on	
Subscriber Registration		Directory Services	
	Access Control	Access Control Services	
Encryption/Confidentiality	Encryption	Encryption Services	
	Certification Authority	Certification Authority Services	
Integration Architecture	Messaging Infrastructure Standards	Messaging Infrastructure	
E-Payments		E- Payment Services	Payment Interface
Credit Cards		Credit Cards	
Internet Checks	IT policies supporting non-proliferation	Internet Checks	
Internet Bill Delivery & Payment		Internet Bill Delivery & Payment	
		State Financial EFT Capability	
	IT Acquisition/ Investment		Project Design & Development
		24/7 Help Desk	
Audit Standards			
Digital Archive/ Record Retention		Digital Archive	
Agency Collaborative Evaluation	Internet Standards & Protocols	Software Component Framework	Tool Selection
	2000 Strategic IT Plan		

Table 2.3 (continued)

			Requirements Definition
Universal Web Design		AW Web style guide	
		inside Washington	

The Early Adoption Portfolio

INCUBATOR FOR BUSINESS TRANSFORMATION

Internal - Government to Government (G2G) | | | *External - Government to Citizen (G2C)/ Government to Business (G2B)*

Electronic A-19 Invoice (GA)*	Electronic Cash Tracking (ECY)*	Online Correction Form (DRS)*	ELF Tax Filing (DOR)*	Sno-Park Permit (Parks)*	WATCH (WSP)*	Internet Bid (GA)*

Collaborative Policy	*Statewide IT Policy (ISB-Specific)*	*Statewide IT Infrastructure*	*Agency Specific IT Activities*
Public Access (RCW43.105)		*Access Washington* Portal	Web, IVR, VC, TV
Disclosure & Privacy (RC42.17.260)		[Published Statement on Portal]	[Published Statement on Web]
		Pilot money manager infrastructure	
		Credit Card Services	Internet Standards & Protocols
		Secure access services (fortress)	2000 Strategic Plan
Electronic Authentication (RC19.34)		Pilot Certification Authority	
Software Exemption (RC84.04.150)		Collaborative Policy	Web-based Development Efforts
			Tool Selection (Forms)

The Foundation Portfolio

MISSION CRITICAL SYSTEMS, BEDROCK INFRASTRUCTURE

Internal - Government to Government (G2G) | | | *External - Government to Citizen (G2C)/ Government to Business (G2B)*

AFRS (OFM)*	Retirement (DRS)*	PayOne (DOP)*	EBT (DSHS)*	ACES (DSHS)*	GUIDE (ESD)*	One-Stop (ESD)*

Collaborative Policy	*Statewide IT Policy (ISB-Specific)*	*Statewide IT Infrastructure*	*Agency Specific IT Activities*
Portfolio Management (RC43.105)	IT Portfolio Management	[Implementation Continues]	[Phased Approach to Projects]
Year 2000 Liability (RCW4.24.650)	Year 2000 Compliance	[100% Certified]	[98% Certified]
Information Technology (43.105)	Standards		
	Host level computer OS	System/390 & UNISYS 2200	Vanilla Project
	Distributed "client/server" OS		
	Database systems		
	E-mail	Enterprise electronic mail directory	Migration to Microsoft Exchange
	Telecommunications wiring	Broadband standards-based	INPHO (Health Network)
	Inter-networking standard	(TCP/IP) Backbone Network	
K-20 Education (E2SSB 6705*)	Network transport/ electronics	K-20 Network	Phase I & Phase II
Justice Integration (RCW10.98.160)	PCN/ Livescan	Justice Information Network	Justice Information Blueprint
GIC Strategic Plan	*de facto*	GIC Clearinghouse	Coordinate Data

*Intended to be illustrative, not exhaustive.

Source: State of Washington, Department of Information Services, internal memo.

increasingly need to understand these processes and the supports and policies that make them workable. For this sample transaction to have occurred, both the local and state governments would have needed to change their traditional business operations, make considerable new investments, and be willing to manage supplier and customer relationships in totally new ways.

Some governments have gone so far as to mandate through state law that government agencies develop a specific set of e-commerce solutions for government agencies. For example, Utah's 1999 Digital State legislation (Utah Code, 63D-1-105) requires that the appropriate state entities shall allow the following services to be transacted through the Internet by July 1, 2002:

(a) application for and renewal of professional and occupational licenses;

(b) renewal of driver's licenses;

(c) application for hunting and fishing licenses;

(d) filings for income tax, sales tax, court documents and Uniform Commercial Code;

(e) registrations for products, brands, motor vehicles, corporations and businesses; and

(f) submission of an application for unemployment, welfare and health benefits.

Additionally, the Digital State Act requires that the state system of public education, in coordination with the Utah Education Network, make reasonable progress toward having the following services available through the Internet by July 1, 2002:

(a) secure access by parents and students to student grades and progress reports;

(b) e-mail communications with teachers, parent-teacher associations, and school administrators;

(c) access to school calendars and schedules; and

(d) teaching resources that may include teaching plans, curriculum guides and media resources.[14]

SPECIFIC COMMERCE-RELATED E-GOVERNMENT INFRASTRUCTURE

In addition to government employees having access to a network such as the Internet, developing e-commerce capabilities in government requires additional infrastructure (and the practices and policies to support the use of this new infrastructure). This additional infrastructure has two basic components: a financial (credit card) transaction component, and an electronic or digital signature component.

Financial Transactions

Because of the federal Electronic Fund Transfer Act[15] and the limit it places on consumer liability, the legal infrastructure for electronic financial transactions is already well developed. If a local or state government simply wants to enable citizens or businesses to pay their bills and fees via the Internet (and does not need to automate the collection and input of account data into government data systems), low-cost payment systems can be purchased from third party providers. For example, a government could contract with the Yahoo Internet company to collect fees for up to fifty services or items. The charge for this service is only $100 per month. To support payments for up to 1,000 services or items, the cost is $300 per month.

Alternatively, some governments will need to direct the data input into their own servers and databases or to verify the identification of the person involved in the transaction. These governments will generally require their own secure server system. The cost for such systems vary depending on the degree to which the transaction from consumer input to accounting to management report is automated. Table 2.4 outlines three basic levels of e-commerce and one complementary capability.

Electronic Signature Component

While many government services can be provided to anyone willing to pay for them, a number involve the government or its contractors, employees or citizens in transactions that require more validation (e.g., as to the exact terms of or parties to the transaction). In instances where the government is a purchaser, it will need to be sure that its online payments go (and are credited) to the individuals or firms who are involved in the transaction. In addition, the government will need to be sure that the public employees making agreements on the part of the government are authorized to do so. Finally, the government will need to be assured that the persons with whom the government is transacting business are who they say they are and are similarly authorized to conduct business at the level specified. Transactions such as transmittal of contract offers, employee or consultant requests for travel or business expense reimbursements, contractors' requests for large payments, and requests for public assistance all fall into this category.

A set of technologies and enabling legislation provide the means of assuring the integrity of online transactions. With the passage of the federal Electronic Signatures in Global and National Commerce Act, all states now have enabling legislation that is relatively flexible. That is, this legislation allows parties to agree to use whatever level of electronic security and identity and document authentication they see as necessary or sufficient to meet their needs. It should be recognized that broad enabling legislation may not

Table 2.4
Levels of E-Commerce in Government

Level 1:
Transmission of credit card number. This level assumes that the local government is already accepting credit cards for bill payments. What is added is the ability to view one's bill or fee amount and transmit one's credit card number and authorization to deduct the appropriate amount via a secure network connection. A feature of the Internet called the secure socket layer, or SSL, allows data such as credit card numbers to be transmitted in an encrypted fashion so that they cannot be read by someone who is listening in on the Web connection. If the government has contracted with a vendor to provide this service, the vendor simply transmits the credit card number to the local government billing office for further processing.

Level 2
Authorization and capture. At this service level, a credit card number is securely transmitted to the government as in Level 1, but two additional processes are completed—"authorization" and "capture" of the credit card transaction. The authorization request is the encrypted electronic message that is sent from the local government's Web site through a special accounting software (e.g., CyberCash's CashRegister) to the financial institution that issued the consumer's credit card. If the financial institution recognizes the card number and if the amount is within the card's limits, the institution will authorize the movement of funds. "Capture" is the action of submitting a credit card sale for financial settlement. When the government requests the capture of a transaction, the government's acquiring financial institution will credit the amount requested and authorized by the citizen's bank to the government's deposit account. At this service level the charge to the customer's account for a product or service ordered via the Internet is automatic, and the government is simply notified that its account has received new funds that are linked to account or bill numbers of the ordered services. Level 2 eliminates the work of government clerks who would otherwise be involved in submitting credit card transaction requests to their credit card merchant account. However, staff are still responsible for updating customers' accounts to show that their bills or fees have been paid. The cost of Level 2 type systems can run anywhere from $300 to $800 in setup fees and $30 to $40 in monthly fees, plus $.10–.20 per transaction.

Level 3
Completed business transaction. This level includes the capabilities outlined in the prior levels and adds to these an ability to update the government's databases (e.g., for accounting, budgeting, etc.) in real time. This automated updating completes the streamlining of the business transaction such that staff do not have to spend time on any individual transaction. In addition to creating savings in personnel costs, being able to complete an entire transaction online allows the government to provide receipts to citizens or, in the case of licenses and certificates, to provide an actual working license or certificate for immediate downloading by the citizen-customer. At this level data from a completed credit card capture or charge are used to update a customer's current account record. The customer's new account data can then be viewed by the customer (e.g., on the government's Web site), indicating that they have been fully credited with paying for the service.

be sufficient to allow public managers to proceed with setting up an electronic transaction infrastructure. Specific state or local legislation or policy may place barriers in the way of electronic transactions. In Ohio, for example, the need to have a valid signature on motor vehicle registrations has prevented the state from building an online motor vehicle registration renewal system (Byerly 2000). Even in cases where the enabling legislation might make it possible to complete transactions electronically, a requirement that citizens use a specific type of electronic signature can effectively limit the electronic transaction option to a small set of citizens. For example, if Ohio required that citizens wanting to renew their motor vehicle license had to purchase, install and use a commercial-level digital signature certificate, the number of citizens willing and able to do so would be much lower than if citizens only had to provide an identity code such as a Social Security number as part of their renewal application. In cases where some proof of identity is needed (e.g., on the part of the person who will receive a government payment or enter into an agreement with the government via an electronic network), public managers may be the persons making the call as to what level of assurance of identity is needed. Whereas an e-mailed statement that someone is who they say they are stands at the low end of the spectrum of identity assurance, digital certificates[16] stand at the high end of this spectrum. Individuals (or governments) purchase these certificates from firms that act as a third party between a message or certificate sender and the receiver. This third party essentially backs up the identity statement being made by the person sending the certificate. Such certificates come in different levels, which represent different levels of third party backing of the certificate. The higher-level certificates cost more, but may be necessary in cases, for example, that might involve the transmittal of substantial amounts of funds or the signing of important contracts. In between e-mail assurances and digital certificates are a variety of password and machine recognition procedures that provide moderate levels of assurance that someone is who they say they are.

In addition to citizens, vendors, consultants and employees potentially needing to acquire and use digital certificates, governments will also have to learn to use and accept these certificates as well. Technically speaking, once the certificate is purchased, the technology for recognizing a digital certificate is relatively cost-free. This is the case because the major Web browsers include a capability to read digital certificates on an individual basis (i.e., in which a government employee uses a Web browser to read the individual message or transaction process). When one needs to process large numbers of transactions where identity assurance is required, recognition of a digital identity is more expensive to develop. For example, if one wanted to automatically pay hundreds of bills based on a vendor's electronically presented invoice, the government would likely want to operate its own secure Web server. In addition to the operation and maintenance costs of this server, the government would likely incur costs for customized computer programming and ongoing security audits to ensure against unwarranted payment.

As suggested above, public managers will likely have a substantial amount of discretion when deciding what level of identity assurance to accept as sufficient for the completion of electronic transactions. The challenge for public managers will be to identify what level of identity assurance is the most cost-effective with respect to different types of transactions (e.g., transmitting a contract offer/acceptance; requesting that a utility be turned on or off; completing a public benefits application; requesting a zoning change; or employees requesting a reimbursement for travel). Cost-effectiveness is important because making identity assurance more of a sure thing is not cost-free. Higher levels of digital certificates both cost more and involve more hassles (e.g., one must travel to the offices of the certificate authority and present identification). As it becomes more difficult and expensive to assure online identity, fewer people will tend to use online service options, and the ability to move to a paperless transaction is thereby undermined.

Typically, when public managers are faced with discretionary decisions of this type, they will look to parallels and to how other governments or other public managers have addressed the same or similar situations. Unfortunately, few public managers have any experience at all with identity assurance systems, and those that do tend to have experience in only a narrow area of interest. Moreover, the basic parallel to be drawn with respect to electronic identity—requirements for written signatures on documents—often provides little guidance, because these requirements were often simply enacted as a pro forma element of a reporting requirement rather than as an element that was understood to be legally or procedurally necessary. Essentially, in many cases a signature requirement was called for because it would provide the document with a certain level of seriousness, and it was cost-free. In the electronic environment, the cost of requiring a high-level digital signature may outweigh the benefit, particularly if the benefit is merely a ceremonial one.

One of the first experiments with a digital certificate in the state of Georgia may help illustrate this point. The experiment involved a report that state-regulated banks regularly provided to the state's Department of Banking and Finance. After having initiated the digital certificate technology, the department realized that it was probably unnecessary to require such a high level of identity authentication. They could easily check an ID number or a machine transmittal number to ensure that the report came from a particular bank. The department's key insight, however, was that in the case of this particular report, there was no incentive for anyone other than the bank itself to submit a report. Hence, there was little or no likelihood of a fraudulent report being submitted. And even if this were to occur, the financial risk to the state would be minimal since the existence of two reports from the same institution would have triggered an investigation into the anomaly.

In making judgments about the level of identity assurance needed, public managers should ask themselves the following questions:

- What is the legal foundation for the current requirements for a written signature? (For example, is there also a requirement for a notary or witness? Are there legal penalties involved for a fraudulent statement? If so, how severe are these penalties?)
- What incentives are there for persons to misrepresent their (or their organization's) identity?
- What risk would the government experience were it to allow a lower level of identity assurance?
- Are there early warning signs for these risks that would allow the government to experiment with a lower level of identity assurance? Can the risks be managed in another way (e.g., through the purchase of insurance, through example prosecutions, etc.)?
- What technologies do the best job of providing the needed level of assurance that someone (or some document) is who (or what) he or she (or it) purports to be?
- How much difference is there between the costs (technical, administrative, practical) among the alternatives?
- What are the long-term benefits to government and its citizens, employees and partners of achieving different levels of electronic transactions?

In answering these questions, a public manager should be able to identify both long- and short-term strategies for developing identity-based e-commerce applications. Development of this infrastructure will not occur in a timely manner if public managers fail to take the following steps:

- Identify *all* the benefits of the development of the needed infrastructure. Public managers who only count the benefits to the government itself, and do not count the benefits that will accrue to employees, citizens and partners, will be likely to underinvest in the infrastructure or require unnecessarily high levels of identity assurance. While requiring a very high level of assurance will reduce government risk, it does so by imposing the financial cost on citizens, employees, and government partners, vendors and consultants. While this strategy may have some short-term benefits, it will essentially result in the government failing to maximize services to its constituents.
- Identify and test the full range of potentially workable identity assurance mechanisms. Governments will need to experiment (and share their results with each other) if they are to discover the best mechanisms for the range of transaction types.

Exploring a Specific E-Commerce Capability: Accepting Electronic Payments

The preceding discussion described two basic components of electronic commerce—a financial transaction component and an electronic identity or signature component. Now we will look a little more closely at one aspect of the financial transaction component, specifically, an electronic financial transaction activity in which a number of governments are investing: acceptance of bill, fee or tax payments via the Internet.

Once a government invests in the infrastructure that allows citizens and others to make payments to the government electronically via credit cards, the transaction fees charged by the credit card companies typically become the major ongoing cost for government e-commerce.[17] These merchant account costs are typically figured as a percent of gross sales or payments that are run through the account. With small accounts, the total fee percentage can be over 4 percent. With larger accounts, the percentage decreases, particularly when the merchant account transacts millions of dollars of business. To recoup these costs, governments (or third party service providers) offering e-commerce services will typically charge a fee for the added convenience of being able to pay online with a credit card. In some states, such as Alaska, public managers will find it difficult to self-finance online transactions that involve the government as a credit card merchant because state law prohibits governments from passing credit card fees on to consumers (Byerly 2000). For small charges, such as parking tickets, the convenience fee will usually be a flat rate, while for larger items, such as property taxes, the fee will normally vary according to the size of the bill. Some governments or their e-commerce solution providers charge fees that run as high as 10 percent of the payment or sales. The difference between the convenience fee (paid by the citizen) and the transaction fees paid by governments (or their e-commerce solution providers) represents potential profits or opportunities for lower service costs. In setting fees, public managers will need to consider different strategies and strategic trade-offs. Some state agencies, such as Michigan's motor vehicle agency, have chosen to strategically promote on-line vehicle registration. Managers of this agency believe that the long-term benefits of automating the registration process online will compensate for the state's absorption of $1 million in credit card fees (Byerly 2000). Governments that insist on self-financing will need to examine some specific trade-offs between the path of developing e-commerce capabilities in house and that of outsourcing the development and management of these systems. Several questions need to be considered in this regard.

In the first place, will the merchant account fees that the government pays be higher or lower than the convenience fees that vendor providers of e-commerce services will charge citizens? If, for example, the government has an existing credit card merchant account and is processing millions of dollars in payments, the case for outsourcing e-commerce solutions is likely to be weak, all else being equal. The weakness of the case for outsourcing is due in this instance to the likelihood that the government will be able to negotiate competitive transaction fee rates. Although transaction fees are not the entire cost of an e-commerce solution, they represent the highest ongoing cost. Small governments with fewer gross sales/payments are much less likely to be able to obtain competitive transaction fee rates. Moreover, if e-commerce solution businesses grow in size and scope, these private sector firms should be able to offer transaction fee levels that are substantially lower than those of all but the largest single government or government agency. When and if this occurs, these firms might be willing to negotiate convenience fees that are equal to or lower than those that the government would have to charge to cover the credit card transaction costs.

Because the e-commerce solutions business is still in its infancy, a more effective short-run strategy for small governments would be to join with other small and medium-sized governments to negotiate with e-commerce solution firms. Such partnerships are already being established in the procurement areas of e-commerce. For example, the Houston-Galveston Area Council of Governments' (H-GAC) Cooperative Purchasing Program has traditionally helped several hundred local governments purchase products such as cars and light trucks, fire apparatus, radios and heavy equipment. H-GAC researches specifications, manages the bid process and recommends awards to the board of directors, who represent the local government partners. Under a new agreement with Bank of America, H-GAC will receive electronic payment and other financial services as well as related support services (Business Wire 2000). Such cooperation on e-commerce solutions should enable the participating governments to achieve savings under certain conditions. The key condition is having a certain level of uniformity in the transaction processes. The more the transaction conditions differ among governments, the less effective a single or cooperatively developed solution will be.

Whether the public manager is considering joining a government e-commerce solution cooperative or not, the issue of uniformity is still relevant to the decision to outsource the development of governmental e-commerce. That is, vendors of e-commerce solutions will tend to provide competitive pricing for solutions such as shopping cart or procurement software where the functions are fairly generic. For example, NIC Commerce, a firm that provides e-commerce solutions, has implemented a commercial off-the-shelf (COTS) system for procurement in twelve federal agencies, including NASA and the Department of Justice. However, when an agency needs a more customized system, commercial developers are likely to charge much higher prices. Often a function will appear to be fairly generic until one begins to analyze the entire process that is potentially amenable to automation. Table 2.5, for example, compares the requirement differences between a generic parking ticket payment system that has been developed for a number of governments and those of a parking permit system for the University of Georgia. This comparison illustrates why customized systems often cost several hundred thousand dollars, while generic systems can be implemented for much less.

Table 2.5
Comparison of Generic Parking Ticket Payment System and Customized Parking Permit System

Generic Parking Ticket Payment System	Customized Parking Permit System
User provides the key information (e.g., citation number) to identify the payment that needs to be made. Payment made by credit card only.	System must access employee and student enrollment, status, and housing databases to see whether the person qualifies for a parking permit and to allow application only for those permits that the person is qualified for.
	System must check for existing permits.
	System must display current data about the vehicle and allow the user to change some data items.
	System must allow for purchase of permits in future semesters, but not allow for multiple purchases of permits in a single semester.
	System must allow for multiple payment procedures (e.g., credit card, payroll deduction, etc.).

Another question that public managers need to ask regarding the decision to outsource is whether their government has the in-house IT capabilities or the political will to create and maintain these capabilities. The answer to this question is crucial. Obviously, a government cannot create its own e-commerce applications without skilled programmers, but the key to making governmental e-commerce cost-effective in the long run is to be able to spread the development and infrastructure costs over numerous applications. Hence, governments that have a good track record with respect to keeping skilled IT personnel and maintaining high-quality infrastructure over time are more likely to find in-house systems building the more cost-effective strategy. Alternately, those who have not been able to maintain and upgrade capacities in this area may be putting their government's reputation at risk if they decide to attempt to develop e-commerce on their own.

A final question that public managers need to ask regarding the decision to outsource is whether there are specific legal or procedural restrictions that might make government-provided e-commerce more cumbersome than private provision. In Florida, for example, state officials who want to accept credit card payments are required to make full disclosure of all credit card fees. Because of the difficulties and risks involved in meeting this requirement, state motor vehicle agency managers decided to employ a private sector payment processor rather than create an in-house capacity to accept credit card transactions. However, there is an effort in the state to change this regulation to make it easier for state government agencies to build their own e-commerce capacities (Byerly 2000).

Organizing for Government E-Commerce

Regardless of the most appropriate technical strategy, many state agencies and local governments will need technical assistance, particularly with applications that require financial transactions. As suggested above, North Carolina's state government has taken steps to address this situation by proposing to build a single statewide infrastructure that enables e-commerce among and between citizens and governments at all levels. Utah's eUtah initiative is another example of how states are beginning to outline a statewide strategy for building an e-commerce infrastructure across a large number of different government activities. Georgia similarly has developed a mechanism to support state agencies engaging in e-commerce. Specifically, Georgia has set up the GeorgiaNet Authority to assist state government agencies in the development of e-commerce/e-government applications. However, the GeorgiaNet Authority does not support local governments in the state that are interested in offering online transactions. Other states such as Connecticut, Massachusetts and Pennsylvania have developed electronic malls that allow online purchasing by participating state and local government agencies from private sector vendors, but these services have not yet been extended to transactions that involve citizens or businesses making payments to government.

Extending the type of assistance provided by GeorgiaNet Authority or eUtah to local governments could jump-start e-government efforts across the state and make more efficient use of existing technical resources. In this regard, states should consider following North Carolina's example in developing a common information technology architecture for all governments in the state as well as specific plug-in technologies for e-commerce/e-government that can be used by all government entities within the state.[18] Similarly, the state of Washington's strategic plan for digital government is designed to change the focus of citizens' interactions with government from multiple points of contact with multiple government agencies to a single point of contact that is organized around the life events of citizens and businesses (State of Washington 2000).

Washington's plan is to have multiple state agencies, legislative and judicial branches, K–20 educational institutions as well as selected parts of federal and local governments integrated online into a single enterprise for delivering services to citizens in the most convenient manner possible. The full extent of assistance that Washington State plans to provide to local governments is still unclear. In mid-2000, the state had implemented an electronic mall or procurement system that could be used by local governments as well as a system for online reporting of revenues, expenditures and fund balances for counties and cities.

Development Cycles in Home Rule States

In terms of establishing the vision of one point of entry into government for citizens, federalism will likely present substantial barriers. States that have a tradition of home rule are particularly vulnerable to the costs involved in having to build multiple systems. It should be recognized that the "problem" presented by federalism is better described as a dilemma: while federalism can stymie efforts to spread development costs across multiple jurisdictions, it can also promote more experimentation and healthy competition among governmental units. The trade-offs of home rule have been experienced again and again in my home state, Georgia, which is a strong home rule state. Typically what occurs is that a sophisticated local agency will develop or acquire an information system before the state develops its own system. Over time, employees of the local government or agency will train on the local system and help customize it to their individual needs. Later the parallel state agency or government will become aware of the potential for better operations offered by a statewide IT system. The state will then go through a systems design and development process that will often take three or more years. By this point, other local governments or agencies have also developed their own systems and customized them to their needs. The result is that by the time the state has its system ready for implementation, a number of local governments or agencies are unwilling to adopt it even when the state-developed system carries no cost. This process of state- versus local- or field-level development has occurred in areas as diverse as motor vehicle registration, family and children's services case management, public and behavioral health management information systems, and systems of juvenile justice administration. Even though Georgia has recently passed new legislation that establishes a Georgia Technology Authority, it is uncertain at this point whether the authority will have the power or even the knowledge of the local development activities to better manage systems development resources across the levels of government in the state.

NOTES

1. In Utah this conclusion was reached through a 500-person survey and reported in *Electronic Commerce: How Are Utah Businesses Doing?* (Utah Governor's Office, 1999). Reported on by *CIO News*. See http://www.cio.state.ut.us/Docs/CIONEWS/cionews799.htm.

2. *Modernising Government: A Home Office Report Presented to Parliament by the*

Prime Minister and the Minister for the Cabinet Office by Command of Her Majesty (London, March 1999). Found at http://www.citu.gov.uk/moderngov/whitepaper/ 4310.htm.

3. Forrester Research, Cambridge, MA, press release, November 2, 1999.

4. KPMG's survey of top public executives, cited in *Southern Growth: Proceedings from the Annual Conference on the Future of the South*, Fall 1999, p. 15.

5. For definitions of e-government, see Mesenbourg 2000.

6. Examination of North Carolina's budget for new information technology, for example, suggests that information technology spending is heavily weighted toward criminal justice related systems. See Statewide Projects at http://www.state.nc.us/ irmc/irmcmain.htm. Also, in one comparison of two Florida departments that were on opposite ends of the information technology developmental curve, the leading department was spending $8,602 per agency employee on information technology while the lagging department was spending only $1,765. In addition to this fivefold difference in technology capitalization, information technology support was similarly uneven, with the leading department having 4.5 times as many support personnel per worker as the lagging department.

7. List adapted from KPMG 2000, p. 5.4-2.

8. For examples of state government activities, see State of North Carolina (1999, p. 13); North Carolina's Statewide Technical Architecture, at http://www.state.nc.us/ irm/techarch/archfrm.htm; SB 465 Georgia Technology Authority, at http:// www.ganet.org/cgi-bin/pub/leg/legdoc?billname=1999/SB465&docpart=full.

9. Uniform Electronic Transactions Act, drafted by the National Conference of Commissioners on Uniform State Laws, Denver, Colorado, July 23–30, 1999. Uniform Computer Information Transactions Act, drafted by the National Conference of Commissioners on Uniform State Laws, Denver, Colorado, July 23–30, 1999. November 1, 1999 Draft.

10. Series of papers on UCITA Issues, by Carlyle C. Ring, Jr., Chair of Committee to Draft UCITA, and Raymond T. Nimmer, Reporter of Committee to Draft UCITA. http://www.nccusl.org/pressrel/UCITAQA.HTM

11. FCC Press Release, "FCC Chairman Kennard shares goal of local governments to achieve open broadband access," August 11, 1999.

12. For update information on the Portland case, visit http://www.mhcrc.org.

13. Presidential Memorandum on "Electronic Government" and Presidential Memorandum on "Use of Information Technology to Improve Our Society," December 17, 1999.

14. Found at http://www.le.state.ut.us/%7E1999/bills/sbillenr/SB0188.htm.

15. Electronic Fund Transfer Act (15 U.S.C. 1693).

16. Digital certificates are essentially encrypted signals that ensure that the person sending a message or a transaction request is very likely who they say they are. This probability is based on the fact that before a digital certificate can be issued, the person requesting the certificate needs to show proof of identity. From that point on, it is incumbent on the person who has been issued a certificate to keep it in a secure place and not otherwise make it public. While digital certificates typically use very secure encryption technology, the processes used by certificate issuing authorities (CAs) to check a person's identity can vary tremendously. Most certificate authorities issue different levels of certificates indicating the degree of identity checking that has occurred.

17. There are actually two sets of fees that must be paid to complete an e-commerce transaction: the credit card company fee and the payment processor's fee. Currently, credit card companies charge more for online or over-the-phone payments than for in-store credit card payments, in part because the in-store payment includes a written signature. Currently, the fees paid to the payment processor (e.g., CyberCash) are more likely to be negotiable or based on volume discounts. Personal conversation with Jordon Burton, Senior Vice-President at Ezgov, Inc., July 17, 2000.

18. See North Carolina's Statewide Technical Architecture at http://www.state.nc.us/irm/techarch/archfrm.htm.

REFERENCES

Beyond expectations: How leading companies are using Lotus Notes to jump-start the 1-Net revolution. (2000). Found at http://www.lotus.com/services/consult.nsf/.

Brussaard, B. K. (1988). Information infrastructure for intergovernmental use. In *Governmental and Municipal Information Systems*, ed. P. Kovacs and E. Straub. New York: North Holland.

Business Wire. (2000). E-commerce solution to be installed for the Houston-Galveston Area Council of Governments. Charlotte, NC, July 6.

Byerly, T. (2000). In the slow lane. *Government Technology* 13(8): 50–66.

Electronic Fund Transfer Act (15 U.S.C. 1693).

Fletcher, P., S. I. Bretschneider, and D. A. Marchand. (1992). *Managing Information Technology: Transforming County Government in the 1990s*. Syracuse: School of Information Studies, Syracuse University, August.

Friedman, T. L. (1999). *The Lexus and the Olive Tree*. New York: Farrar, Straus, & Giroux.

Gurstein, M. (2000). *Community Informatics: Enabling Communities with Information and Communications Technologies*. Hershey, PA: Idea Group Publishing.

Hammer, M. (1990). Reengineering work. *Harvard Business Review* 90(4): 105–14.

Hammer, M., and J. Champy. (1993). *Reengineering the Corporation*. New York: Harper Business.

Karlenzig, W. (2000). Business process reassembling: James Champy has designs on reengineering the new economy. *Knowledge Management*, June. http://www.kmmag.com.

KPMG. (2000). *The Georgia Office of Planning and Budget, Information Technology and Telecommunications*. Final Draft, February 14. Atlanta: KPMG.

Locke, Gary. (2000). State's new digital government plan takes citizens from "in line" to online for one-stop services. Press release, May 16.

Maeil Business Newspaper. (1998). Knowledge management, knowledge organizations and knowledge workers: A view from the front lines. Dr. Yogesh Malhotra's interview with *Maeil Business Newspaper*, February 19.

McCartney, Laton. (1998). Getting smart about knowledge management. *Industry Week* 247(9): 30–37, May 4.

Mesenbourg, Thomas L. (2000). Measuring electronic business definitions, underlying concepts, and measurement plans. Bureau of the Census. Found at http://www.ecommerce.gov/ecomnews/e-def.html.

NASIRE. (2000). *Report on State Information Technology Organizational Structures (June 2000)*. Lexington, KY: National Association of State Information Resource Executives.

North Carolina's Statewide Technical Architecture. Found at http://www.state.nc.us/irm/techarch/archfrm.htm.

O'Looney, John. (1993). "Redesigning the work of education." *Phi Delta Kappan* 74(5): 375–81.

State of North Carolina. (1999). *E-Commerce: A New Way of Doing Business. Preliminary Report of the E-Commerce Work Group of the Information Resource Management Commission*. Raleigh: State of North Carolina, February.

State of Virginia. Office of the Governor (2000). Governor Gilmore issues executive order implementing e-government. May 24.

State of Washington. (2000). *The Digital Government Plan*. Olympia, WA: Information Services Board.

Taylor, Steven T. (1996). Point-of-care reengineering. *Enterprise Reengineering*, June: 1–2.

United States General Accounting Office. (2000). *Information Technology Investment Management: A Framework for Assessing and Improving Process Maturity*. Version 1. Washington, DC: GAO, Accounting and Information Management Division, May.

3
Information Technology and Government Business Processes

It was suggested in Chapter 2 that there is no single right approach to using information technology. Rather, each approach has its potential costs, benefits and appropriate uses. This chapter takes a closer look at the use of IT as part of an effort to redesign or reengineer public sector business processes. As the reader no doubt knows, millions of words have been written about business process reengineering and related areas.[1] Within this literature it is possible to identify numerous stages and tasks involved in conducting a process rengineering or work redesign activity. However, for our purposes, the reader need only be familiar with the general idea behind some of the more important stages in the process, including:

- strategic planning
- business systems planning
- identification of processes for improvement
- development of performance measures for processes
- identification of projects designed to boost process performance

From the broad stages in any work redesign effort, a well managed public agency that was planning on deploying new information technology would likely first have:

- developed a strategic vision and objectives that are aligned with customer and stakeholder needs and priorities;
- composed a business plan that identifies services and functions the agency must perform to achieve outcomes defined in the strategic plan;

- identified a management oversight process that assigns accountability for the implementation of the business plan; and
- established a way to monitor the implementation of the business plan.

Most important in this pre-implementation stage is the need for the agency to stay focused on the business values that are sought and not be sidetracked by the glitter of what is possible through technology. That is, public managers will need to emphasize business solutions and enhanced customer satisfaction over technical capability or sophistication. While technology may enable managers to dramatically change a business process, the changes need to be prioritized based on their expected net benefit rather than on attractiveness to IT managers or technicians.

While technical capability should always be secondary to business solutions, it can be a driving force in itself for modernization efforts. A recent study conducted by the Human Resources Technology Council (HRTC) of the federal government's efforts to revamp information systems used in human resource management identified both technical and administrative factors driving the development of new information systems. These factors include the following:

- The age of existing systems. HRTC found that the average age of human resources systems reviewed was 15.9 years.
- The changes in technology. HRTC reported that the majority of the older human resources systems were developed in a mainframe environment, which does not facilitate changes or user-friendly interaction. Technological advancements should allow agencies to benefit from a client-server environment which can be more easily changed, is less expensive to operate, and allows for more direct interaction between the system and end-users.
- Restructuring of the work performed in human resources organizations. Agencies having to do more with less are eager for technologies that can be quickly adapted to automate manual processes. Also, as human resource organizations become more decentralized, the technological architecture needs to be congruent with the organizational structure.
- Responsibility for personnel actions. Modern human resource departments tend to delegate more authority to program and field offices, have looser regulatory requirements, and allow employees and managers to take some personnel actions (e.g., changing benefit plans) that do not need to go through human resource management specialists. These managers and employees need to have access to databases and other IT tools and technologies that will facilitate their making these decisions on their own (HRTC 1997).

ENTERPRISE OR ORGANIZATION-WIDE ARCHITECTURE PLANNING

Once a strategic plan is in place, it typically becomes obvious that information technology will be needed to support strategic objectives that cut

Table 3.1
NIST Enterprise Architecture Model

Architecture	Action
Business	Drives the information architecture
Information	Prescribes the information systems architecture
Information Systems	Identify the data architecture
Data	Suggest specific data delivery systems
Data Delivery Systems (Software, Hardware, Communications)	Support the data architecture

Source: NIST Special Publication 500-167, Information Management Directions: The Integration Challenge, September 1989.

across the entire organization or enterprise. (Information technology managers use the term "enterprise" to denote the entire spectrum of activities or functions of the entire organization.) At the federal level, this need has been formalized in Executive Order 13011 (July 16, 1996), Federal Information Technology, which established the Chief Information Officers (CIO) Council as the principal interagency forum for improving practices in the design, use, sharing and performance of information resources. Once an enterprise-wide approach to information technology is adopted, public managers will find themselves involved in discussions of IT architecture. The term "architecture" encompasses a number of design structures that can be ordered hierarchically. In this regard, the National Institute of Standards and Technology (NIST) has developed the most widely accepted model for IT architecture. (See Table 3.1.) The hierarchy outlined in the table is based on the notion that an organization operates a number of business functions, such as personnel compensation; that each business function requires information from a number of sources; that each of these sources may operate one or more information systems, which in turn contain data organized and stored in any number of data systems. In the case of a small government agency, this ordering may seem too complex, while in cases where there are numerous business or information systems levels, the model may appear somewhat simplistic.

When charged with developing a Federal Enterprise Architecture Framework, the federal CIO Council faced a dilemma that is common to public managers who are attempting to take an enterprise approach to systems development in their agency or department: taking a conventional business process analysis approach would require substantial investment of time and dollars just to describe the baseline of the systems and structures currently

Figure 3.1
Cross-Functional Processes

FUNCTIONS	Acquisition	Receiving	Inventory	Assembly	Order Taking	Delivery
	Activity1 Activity2	Activity1 Activity2	Activity1 Activity2	Activity1 Activity2	Activity1 Activity2	Activity1 Activity2
PROCESSES	→ →	→ →	→ →	→ →	→ →	→ →

in use in the federal government. And it would require even more time and resources to then design an ideal architecture for the entire enterprise, and still more resources to develop and acquire systems in line with the target architecture. While this classic systems analysis stance might be desirable in many circumstances, the federal CIO Council rejected it, fearing that it would result in "paralysis by analysis" (CIO Council 1999). As an alternative to developing a fully integrated enterprise architecture, the CIO Council decided to take a segment approach to the design of the IT architecture. This approach was designed to promote the incremental development of architecture segments within a structured enterprise architecture framework. That is, the Council understood that it would be impossible to build one all-encompassing system. Rather, it would be beneficial to focus on a small number of major business areas such as grants or common financial systems. The practical approach taken by the CIO Council was dictated by the incredible complexity of systems within the federal government. For less complex organizations, development of fully integrated systems is more feasible.

THE BUSINESS PROCESS AND BUSINESS FUNCTIONS

The importance of improving a process is not always clear to the public or private managers, who are not always expected to think in terms of processes. In fact, if they do so, they are likely to be criticized. Instead, new managers are more likely to be given responsibility over a function rather than a process. To realize the importance of this distinction it is necessary to have a clear understanding of the meaning of these two terms.

A process refers to a complete workflow unit running from external suppliers to a set of value-adding activities, tasks and operations and ending with internal and external customers or reviewers. A process will typically involve numerous different functional activities (e.g., design, budgeting, requisition, purchasing, accounting, inventory, assembly, integration, quality control, packaging and marketing). Traditionally, newly minted managers are hired to perform in one of the functional areas, rather than being assigned responsibility for a whole process. By its very nature, process management requires that public managers take a cross-functional perspective in order to improve the entire process. As Figure 3.1 suggests, a process approach demands that managers examine the activities within functional areas and that they pay particular attention to how activities in one functional area relate to activities in other areas. The process in Figure 3.1 is a simplified linear one in which the hand-off points and interfaces are fairly explicit. In the case of many government processes, these points of interface will be more complex and fluid. In such cases, a business process analysis should lead one to identify potential opportunities to clarify the relationships among the functional divisions in the organization. Only after identifying when and how things are handed off to a related division can one think about how to redesign the entire process.

Looking at processes rather than functions has become an important task for managers in part because of the success developed economies have had in making functions more efficient. That is, because over the last one hundred or more years much attention has been given to functional specialization and to making specific functional activities as efficient as possible, there may be fewer opportunities for implementing further efficiencies within functions than across functions (or in improving processes). For example, organizing around functions can result over time in situations where in some functional areas resources may be underutilized, while other areas cannot keep up with the workflow because of resource deficiencies. Or it might mean that the hand-off points between functional areas are not well defined or regulated. Or it could mean that there are unnecessary duplications of effort or levels of processing.

Knowing when a process is working well is often more difficult than knowing when a function works well. This is the case because a process can involve many multiple criteria for performance (e.g., one or more criteria for each activity or functional area). An orientation to a process will often involve a public manager in making decisions about the proper resource allocation for the greatest quality boost for the citizen or consumer within budget restraints. Hence, efforts to improve, redesign or reengineer a process will often require the participation of executive-level leaders to ensure that a new process is at least given a chance to prove its worth. However, because executive-level leaders rarely understand the details of a process and are only infrequently able to ensure the wholehearted acceptance of change, developing a new process is also highly dependent on acceptance by the people who will be doing the work.

USING INFORMATION TECHNOLOGY TO IMPROVE A PROCESS

The role of information technology in a business process improvement effort can vary substantially. In some cases, the introduction of technology is a large part if not the entirety of the improvement process. This would be the case, for example, at NASA, where the mission of sending robots to Mars will involve the creation and coordination of numerous interconnecting technologies and systems. Similarly, when a store sets up a self-checkout system, the process improvement effort is centered on the introduction of the technology. In other cases, technology will only have a minor role in changing the process. For example, a process improvement might involve having a single clerk perform both the intake and eligibility determination functions in a welfare office. Because of the process improvement, the clerk can now use the same information system that was previously used by two or more clerks. As such, the technology did not necessarily contribute substantially to the process improvement effort. However, even in less technology-dependent process improvement efforts, information technology can play a key role in providing important course-correcting feedback. That is, information technology can help public managers identify how well a process improvement effort is meeting key process improvement benchmarks.

More particularly, information technology can be used to improve a process along the four major process benchmarks identified by the Department of Defense in its Framework for Managing Process Improvement (1994).

Specifically, information technology can be used to:

1. Identify how and to what degree a process, product or service *conforms to standards*. Conformance to standards depends on there being a norm or best practice measure. In government, a standard might involve protection of privacy, delivery time, accuracy of accounting, or conformance to public laws, rules and regulations. Public assistance systems for food stamps or Medicaid that help caseworkers reduce their error rate represent information systems that are primarily oriented to conformance to standards measures.

2. Identify how and to what degree a process, product or service *fits the intended purpose*. Measures of the fitness of a particular process with respect to its purpose can come in many forms. Some measures would likely involve tracking how stakeholders experience a process. Generally, when stakeholders experience satisfaction with a process, it is likely that the process fulfilled at least one of its purposes. However, a process may bring pleasure or satisfaction to a stakeholder, but not actually meet its original objectives. In both cases, technology can be used to help track, for example, how citizens experience a process and how effective a new process might be. For example, if we imagine that a government allows citizens to apply for, register and pay for recreation programs online, the government might ask citizens who use the service to estimate the amount of time the online service provision has saved them in comparison to their having to interact with two or three different government departments. However, if one of the purposes of the new process was to reduce the error rate in registrations, governments may also want to use technology to measure whether there was an increase in the error rate. If such an increase were discovered, the government might yet choose to keep the new online registration system because of its other virtues, but the fitness of purpose analysis would have alerted public managers to the need to address the undesirable impacts of the new process. What this description suggests is an important difference between classical data processing approaches and work redesign approaches. Whereas in the former, technology was used to make a process more

efficient, in the latter, technology is often used to reshape a service or process to make it more responsive to both citizen and governmental needs.

3. Identify and track the *time it takes to complete a process*. Here information technology can be used in the service of Tayloristic concerns related to time and motion. The difference is that now computers can take the place of people with stopwatches and can tirelessly and continuously identify areas for possible improvement. Process time measures look at the length of the process cycle and at throughput. Furthermore, process time within a constrained budget (such as is typical in the public sector) can serve as an acceptable surrogate measure for process cost. By focusing on reducing the time it takes to complete a process—a task that is often easier than tracking process cost—public managers can often achieve the complementary result of reducing process cost.

Information technology is rarely used effectively to track all three of the types of time that are consumed in a process. That is, public managers may concentrate on tracking the operations time or the time that is actually used in transforming inputs into outputs. Or managers might focus on the time where no value is actually being added to the product or service. Here, the measure might include the amount of wait time; time spent attending meetings, developing reports, or filling out travel or procurement forms; or time spent in managing staff, in complying with regulations, or in planning or budgeting activities. Finally, managers might focus on the time it takes to ensure the quality of a product or service. This would include time spent on error detection, inspection, rework, problem determination, problem solving, prevention and training related to quality issues. The total quality management movement, for example, would often focus on this use of time with an eye on moving from quality inspection and rework toward embedding quality into the work itself so as to prevent quality-related problems.

Obviously, there can be merit in using technology for reducing all three types of process time. Depending on the circumstances, managers will want to focus more on one type of process time than another. However, over a period of years managers should consider all three types of process time both independently and as a composite. Such an approach should enable managers to discover the greater opportunities for improvement.

4. Identify and track the *various costs of a process*. An examination of process costs involves consideration of where resources are consumed within each function, activity and subactivity in the process. Information technology can be used to track the different types of costs (e.g., variable, fixed, semi-variable and semi-fixed). Information technology can also track costs associated with production factors, such as labor and the different types of labor (temporary, part-time, telecommuting), equipment costs and operation time, and facility and equipment deterioration costs, as well as costs that might not be integral to a process but that are unavoidable nevertheless. While the use of information technology to track costs is not new, the use of activity-based cost accounting methods is still fairly rare in public management. But such methods produce dramatic improvements in business processes. (Brimson 1991)

PRINCIPLES OF PROCESS IMPROVEMENT

Improving a business process involves any number of steps, depending on the strategy being used. The identification of benchmarks is key because these benchmarks establish the goals of the process improvement effort. Once goals are identified, it is often useful to develop principles for process improvement. The specific principles to be followed will vary depending on the nature of the work and the individuals and functional units involved. For example, the following list of principles was developed by the Army Corps of Engineers in its effort to improve the use of technology in its business processes across units (Spivey, n.d.). I have provided some explanatory comments based on a reading of the case study.

- *Data must be separated from applications.* Here, the notion is that the data should be structured such that the adoption of any new application in any of the units would not negatively impact the usefulness of the data.
- *Data are captured at the source.* The idea here is that data will be more accurately recorded when entered by those who gather them.
- *Data must be shared by all.* This concept was central to the business modernization effort because in realizing this principle it was necessary for each unit to give up the idea of owning the data. To replace the data ownership idea, the Corps attempted to develop the idea of data stewardship. This proved to be one of the more difficult principles to implement because of a natural tendency for people to think they own data because they have entered them into a system. To move toward the data stewardship concept, staff had to be shown that data could be shared with substantial benefit to other units and to the organization as a whole.
- *Data must be captured only once.* The idea here is that entry by multiple people or units is undesirable because it results in duplication of effort and increased likelihood of errors in data entry.
- *Collect only minimal essential data.* This principle is based on the idea that systems often get overbuilt, in that many of the added system functions do not contribute to improving the business process. Rather, these functions are included simply because it is possible to include them. Overbuilt systems can result in a less efficient process due to increases in the time and effort involved in data gathering, entry, analysis and reporting.
- *Users must direct development.* While this principle is part of the conventional wisdom of systems development, it should not be followed blindly. That is, if current users direct the development in ways that reinforce an existing process that is inefficient and in need of reengineering, the result is not likely to be satisfactory. Hence, this principle should probably be restated to indicate that users should direct the development of a system once *all* the stakeholders have agreed on the key requirements of the new or improved process.
- *Improve information quality, timeliness and access.* While this principle is an obvious one, it is not as simple to implement as might appear. This is the case because in designing or redesigning any process, certain trade-offs exist among desirable char-

acteristics such as quality, timeliness and access. For example, one can surely increase information quality by having more people review the information. However, this will lead to a decrease in the timeliness of the information. Similarly, as access to information is increased in the form of being able to see and make revisions to the information, there may be a decrease in information quality since some inappropriate changes will be made. Because of these trade-offs, managers will need precise understanding of the impact of a change in timeliness, quality or access on the business process. In some cases (e.g., emergency management), timeliness may be the most important quality, while in other cases (e.g., the issuing of food stamps) an improvement in quality of information may be of primary importance.

GETTING FROM THE CURRENT TO THE DESIRED PROCESS

Once benchmarks and principles have been identified, managers need to map out two sets of processes—the current process and the process as they desire it to be. Each of these steps can be difficult if the organization is attempting to reengineer all the business processes at one time. The Corps of Engineers, for example, discovered as they began to outline their business processes that many were interrelated, including design management and construction management, finance and accounting, planning and programs management, and operations and maintenance.

Once these existing processes were outlined, the Corps developed a number of models for what they desired in each of several of the business processes. However, in doing so they realized that they had made a mistake, as their goal had been to understand how various pieces of information worked together to move the organization forward. As a consequence of this realization, the Corps managers chose to redraw the models as a single command model. In doing so, they discovered a need, for example, to build a database of databases so that they could keep track of what information was being gathered where and for what purpose. Building the overall model and database of databases, however, better positioned the Corps to fulfill its principles, particularly with respect to capturing information once at its source.

A FRAMEWORK FOR DEVELOPING IMPROVED IT ARCHITECTURES

As the example above suggests, public managers will need to be very deliberative in moving from current to desired business processes. A useful tool to assist in this deliberative effort is a model or framework of enterprise architecture planning. While a number of models are available, the most widely accepted is John Zachman's, as outlined in his article "A Framework for Information Systems Architecture" (1987). Zachman's framework (see

Table 3.2) has been adopted by the federal government's CIO Council and by many state technology councils.

Zachman's framework is essentially a matrix that links different views of stakeholders in an IT development process with the task-related questions of who, what, when, where, how and why. The architectural views go from the abstract and strategic perspective of the planner, who is concerned with the overall size, shape and relationships that will exist in a system, to the most detailed view of the systems development subcontractor, who creates the specifications for actual code programmers. In between these two extremes are the views of the following:

- The owner of a business process or model, who is concerned with the daily routines of the organization and how these relate to each other.
- The designer of the system, who must determine the data elements, the flow of the system's logic, and functions that the system will perform in support of a business process.
- The builder of the system, who is charged with actualizing a system's logic and functions within a set of applications, platforms and tools. A builder must be able to match the information systems model to the available technical resources (e.g., programming languages, input/output [I/O] devices, etc.).

The key to effective use of Zachman's framework is to ensure that all the cells in the matrix are completed to the greatest level of detail possible. By making all the cells explicit enterprise-wide, public managers can obtain some assurance that the parts of the overall system will be related or integrated with each other in such a way as to produce desirable results. If the cells are not made explicit, there is a danger that the system will be designed in a way that will lead to problems down the line. For example, filling in the framework cells appropriately would force project managers to conceive of data as independent from functional processes or instructions. If this separation is ignored, the resulting system could be plagued with the problems that have long been associated with systems that kept data and process united, that is, to change either the data or the process, one often had to rewrite the whole program (CIO Council 1999).

Zachman's framework also forces planners or IT project managers to develop models that are logically independent of application or technology constraints. This characteristic should enable public managers to change their choice of specific technologies without substantial disruption or excessive cost.

Table 3.3 presents a more detailed view of the key cells in Zachman's framework. This view allows a general public manager to get a sense of the various tasks involved in implementing a complex IT project.

Use of the framework for IT architecture can help provide both management and financial benefits. On the management side, the existence of an

Table 3.2
Zachman's Framework for IT Architecture

	Entities (what)	Activities (how)	Locations (where)	People (who)	Time (when)	Motivation (why)	
Planner							Scope
Owner							Enterprise
Designer							System
Builder							Technical
Subcontractor	Data	Function	Network	Organization	Schedule	Strategy	Components

Source: Adapted from John A. Zachman, "A Framework for Information Systems Architecture," *IBM Systems Journal* 26(3): 276–292.

Table 3.3
Detailed View of Key Cells of IT Architecture

	Entities (What)	Activities (How)	Locations (Where)
	Data Architecture—Definition of the major kinds of data needed to support the business.	*Applications Architecture*—Definition of the major kinds of applications needed to manage that data and support the business functions.	*Technology Architecture*—Definition of the technology platforms needed to support the applications that manage the data and support the business functions.
Planner	**List of Business Objects** (things, assets, concepts that might be of interest)	**List of Business Processes**	**List of Business Locations**
Owner	**Semantic Model** (things, assets, concepts that are significant to the enterprise)	**Business Process Model**	**Business Logistics System**
Designer	**Logical Data Model** (fully attributed, keyed, normalized entity relationship model)	**Applications Architecture**	**Systematic Geographic Deployment Architecture**
Builder	**Physical Data Model** (model of the table structure in a relational database system or class/hierarchy model in an object-oriented system)	**System Design** (object-oriented notation logical data flow)	**Technology Architecture** (actual hardware and systems software at the nodes and the lines)
Subcontractor	**Data Definition** (e.g., field size, type, language required for implementation)	**Programs** (supporting software components such as operating systems, databases, etc.)	**Network Architecture** (specifically the node addresses and the line identification)
	Data	Function	Network

Source: Adapted from CIO Council 1999.

appropriately elaborated framework helps public managers to identify over-looked or missing information that could streamline a business process or an overlooked opportunity to expand service delivery in new ways or to new areas or groups. The latter might occur, for instance, were a public manager to see that nothing was elaborated in the network cell. In such a case, the manager could potentially identify opportunities for distance education or shared processing across an open network. Similarly, an IT blueprint allows managers to more quickly identify the nature of the existing knowledge base and to build IT solutions that optimize the use of this existing resource. On the cost-saving side, a framework can highlight areas for potential savings. Used appropriately, for example, such a framework should enable one to see where it might be possible to reuse an improved business redesign model or an application, or at least large sections of program code. Moreover, the systemwide view should help one to identify areas where interagency or interdivisional sharing of the development cost for new software makes economic sense.

Although managers should not expect the development of enterprise architecture to be cost-free or even affordable within any one annual budget cycle, industry studies suggest that recurring operations costs will typically decrease as more of the desired enterprise architecture is defined, understood and implemented. One demonstration IT cost study suggested that data residing in a single sharable database are likely to have more than forty-three times the value of the same data residing in forty-three redundant databases. Redundancy, the author of the study argues, can diminish the value of a system because of the multiple costs for data capture and interface development. On top of these costs, one must also add the costs of identifying which data points are inaccurate in a set of inconsistent data (English 1999).

INFORMATION TECHNOLOGY INVESTMENT MANAGEMENT

Public managers seeking to improve a business process need to be able to leverage technology to assist in their change effort. Achieving such leverage, however, is often more difficult than it first appears. This is the case because government agencies, particularly large ones, are often involved in a number of technology design, development and acquisition efforts. Some of these efforts will overlap, some will act in a complementary fashion, while others will tend to undermine or interfere with other efforts. Because of this complexity and potential for poor or even negative returns on technology investment, government executives have increasingly called for reviews, audits and improved management of technology investment. At the federal level, the General Accounting Office (2000) has developed a highly detailed select/control/evaluate model as a preferred approach to federal IT investment management. The model is based on a cycle of IT investment that includes

Table 3.4
Fundamental Phases of the IT Investment Approach

Select Phase: How do you know you have selected the best projects?
• Screen
• Rank
• Select

Control Phase: Are the systems delivering what you expected?
• Monitor progress
• Take corrective actions

Evaluate Phase: How are you ensuring that projects deliver benefits?
• Conduct reviews
• Make adjustments
• Apply lessons learned

---

a technology selection phase, a systems control phase and an evaluation phase. (See Table 3.4.)

While the cycle of investment will generally occur in every government, the GAO believes that the cycle activities will become more effective as a government department matures in its abilities to handle and integrate a larger scope of IT projects and investments. The GAO outlines five stages of maturity in this regard. (See Table 3.5.)

The key tasks at lower levels of maturity involve recognizing the need for and taking corrective action when a project is having trouble meeting its scheduled production or cost milestones. As a government department matures, it should be able to learn from past decisions and better manage the root causes of implementation problems—and do so across a wider range of related projects (i.e., across the IT portfolio or collection of projects).

According to the GAO, successful governments follow a disciplined process for tracking and overseeing each project's cost and schedule milestones with an eye toward improving project outcomes over time. This tracking in turn requires the creation of an IT asset inventory to ensure that the entire group of stakeholders has some basic information about the government's IT assets. Sometimes this involves a simple inventory of the location, cost and ownership of the assets, while at other times it involves more complete details about data fields, structures and designs for interoperability.

As the government creates its IT investment portfolio, it will need to keep in mind that a portfolio is more than a collection of projects. Instead, the GAO suggests, the portfolio should include a conscious, proactive look at how the organization as a whole expends its limited resources on IT, a list of beneficial impacts these investments are expected to have on government

Table 3.5
Maturity Stages in IT Investment Management

Maturity STAGES	Critical PROCESSES
Stage 5: Leveraging IT for Strategic Outcomes	Investment Process Benchmarking
	IT-Driven Strategic Business Change
Stage 4: Improving the Investment Process	Post-Implementation Reviews and Feedback
	Portfolio Performance Evaluation and Improvement
	Systems and Technology Succession Management
Stage 3: Developing a Complete Invest-ment Portfolio	Authority Alignment of IT Invest-ment Boards
	Portfolio Selection Criteria Defini-tion
	Investment Analysis
	Portfolio Development
	Portfolio Performance Oversight
Stage 2: Building the Investment Foun-dation	IT Investment Board Operation
	IT Asset Tracking
	IT Project Oversight
	Business Needs Identification for IT Projects
	Proposal Selection
Stage 1: Creating Investment Awareness	IT Spending without Disciplined Investment Processes

or its constituents, and a baseline for continuously searching for investments that will more effectively or efficiently fulfill the government's mission. Hence, an IT portfolio should include an ability to organize and easily find lessons learned and recommendations gleaned from earlier reviews of tech-nology or process change implementations. Additionally, when the govern-ment has reached Stage 4 maturity, it should be able to plan for an orderly succession of IT projects (e.g., "de-selecting" the most obsolete, high-risk or low-value IT investments, while selecting the most leading edge, low-risk or high-value ones). At Stage 5 the government is generally doing most of its IT planning in conjunction with strategic business plans rather than as an ad hoc activity.

Managing Other IT Development Issues

Managers of IT projects must attend to a number of other issues, including the following:

Credibility

While managing the actual productivity of an IT investment should be of primary concern, ample anecdotal evidence suggests that, in addition to managing the actual investment, public managers need to be adept at managing expectations about new information technology and its capabilities. The key here is being able to maintain the credibility of a project until it comes online and proves its worth. This credibility management may at times call for boosting the application's supposed benefits; however, in most cases it will involve downplaying the revolutionary nature of the proposed system and being very conservative in terms of forecasting the project completion date and budget. In addition, large projects need to be assessed for the level of risk involved.

Balance between Unified Approach and Independence

Since PCs have begun to be used in governmental organizations, there has been a tension between the development of a unified organizational approach to information technology and systems and the freedom to develop unique, customized IT solutions to particular problems. Mainframe systems by their very nature tend to support and maintain centralized control. PCs, on the other hand, tend to provide a flexible platform for experimentation by individual program managers. While the independence that PCs afford has been touted as a boon to the economy in general and to small business development in particular, its value to public sector organizations has been more suspect. For example, in 1993, Norris and Kraemer (1996) conducted a survey comparing information technology in cities that used only PCs with cities that used mainframe or central computer systems. They did not find that PCs added to the speedup of automation of governmental functions. Rather, they found that central system cities were more widely automated, had more use for IT and more satisfaction with the technology, and were more likely to deploy leading-edge technologies than PC-only cities. The relatively poor performance of PC-only cities was traced to their reliance on ad hoc solutions, outsourcing or the use of so-called computer gurus. These findings do not necessarily undermine the idea of supporting more customized development; rather, they suggest that when executive-level public managers allow program managers to develop customized PC-based systems, they need to ensure that they dedicate sufficient resources to ongoing support and integration with other systems. Business firms that traditionally support mainframe systems tend to be larger and to incorporate more years of experience, on average, than firms that support PC systems. Moreover, the former have more of a tradition of support than the more development-oriented PC firms. Because of this difference, the centralized-IT-system cities may have had an advantage with respect to their including ongoing support resources into the system development process. As PC systems have matured and become more powerful and more client/server based, the differences between these systems and more centralized ones have probably narrowed substantially. However, the lesson of too much independence with too little support is one that is still relevant today.

Joint Development

Small local governments are particularly disadvantaged with respect to their ability to build, use and maintain sophisticated IT systems. While the solution to this problem would logically be the joint development of systems for use by a number of smaller governments, in reality this solution is rarely implemented. Joint development is hampered by the fact that few communities are in the same development cycle or have exactly the same needs at the same time. When joint development does occur, it may be the result of such things as a new reporting format or mandate for local governments to follow. Such appears to be the case with respect to financial systems developed in Wisconsin in the mid-1990s (Wisconsin counties 1995). Whether the joint development involves multiple governments or simply multiple stakeholders within one government or governmental department, it is recommended that public managers formally capture and document agreements among all stakeholders. By achieving and documenting an agreement up front, it becomes more difficult for stakeholders to wash their hands of the project when it falters (ITRB 2000b). Joint development agreements can, of course, be changed over time, but the formal agreement process should be maintained over the life of the system development project.

Bridging the Culture of Use between PCs and Mainframes

Similar to the issue of balancing centralized control and the independence afforded by PCs is the issue of how to manage networks that provide some of the control of a centralized system, but provide that control to a number of individual users. For example, the *Wall Street Journal* reported in 1994 that an Andersen Consulting employee made a computer error related to a directory of employee e-mail addresses. With the company's networks operating as they were supposed to, the new error-possessing directory structure was replicated in hundreds of other computers in the company's system. As a result, thousands of Andersen employees could not get electronic mail. To control for this type of error in the future, managers at Andersen and elsewhere had to learn to solve problems of ownership and access. These problems had originally been solved in the 1960s with mainframe technology, but that ability had been lost with the use of stand-alone PCs (Yoder 1994).

Recruitment of IT Talent

Government's experience of a shortage of IT workers is generally more severe than is the case in the private sector. No single explanation is available for this higher than expected difficulty in recruiting IT personnel into government organizations. However, the key suspected causes include a lower than average base salary and an impression that governments are using older systems. Assuming that government systems are older, were an IT person to join the government, he or she would likely be condemned to always be behind the curve with respect to IT skills development. The more successful governments have been able to overcome these weaknesses by directly addressing the source of the weakness and by emphasizing the advantages of government employment. Specific activities in this regard include the following:

- Offering flextime and job sharing, and being willing to accommodate special needs such as not having to work on weekends or time off to help get one's child to day care.
- Offering positions that do not require much travel.
- Ensuring that the department employs the most recent technology.
- Use of annual salary surveys to close the salary gap or at least not allow it to get wider.
- Use of more colorful and exciting job advertisements.
- Participation in coalitions of IT employers, colleges and technical institutes. The purpose of this participation is both to expand the possible pool of candidates and to reduce the potential for loss of IT personnel due to other employers targeting one's best employees. The theory is that if you get to know the other employers who are competing for IT talent in your area, they will be less likely to poach from your staff (Cunningham 2000).

Project Management

As the number of failed large IT projects has grown, a more intensive search for answers has taken place. Paul Wohlleben, former deputy chief information officer at the Environmental Protection Agency, for example, has noted that the government does not really have the number of seasoned project managers needed to head up large IT efforts. As a result, government agencies tend to turn to an in-house program manager or IT manager who has neither headed nor assisted in heading a large project before (Ferris 2000).

Similarly, the Information Technology Resources Board (ITRB), an intergovernmental body that advises agencies on how to salvage troubled IT projects, suggests a number of insights that can be tapped to improve IT project management, including the following (see www.itrb.gov):

- Unskilled project managers will often try to do too much on their own or with available talent. Instead, they should attempt to objectively match staff competencies with the tasks, but when a match does not exist, they should be sure to get the needed expertise.
- Consensus building skills among IT project managers are often as important as technology skills themselves.
- More successful projects tend to be ones that balance the mix of outsourced and in-house personnel.
- The scope of a project's requirements should be reasonable. Reasonable requirements will help stabilize a project and lead to an improved outlook for project success.
- Systems should be implemented incrementally, delivering, for example, in twelve months or less, some usable level of functionality in support of a specific business objective.
- Everyone should agree on what is meant by potentially vague terms such as architecture or standards.
- Progress and productivity should be monitored. In the majority of reviews it has conducted, the ITRB has recommended the establishment of a process for independent validation of progress.
- Progress should be visible to all. ITRB generally recommends that project managers establish a set of key progress indicators and publish them regularly to all project participants.
- COTS or commercial, off-the-shelf software should be assessed for its potential to serve the needed functions prior to investing in built-from-scratch applications or systems.

The Use of COTS Applications

Increasingly, government agencies are turning to commercial off-the-shelf (COTS) applications to fulfill requirements previously met through customized software development projects. Public managers are increasingly relying on COTS solutions because of (1) continued problems with software developers being able to complete work on time, or within budgeted appropriations; (2) the growing availability of sophisticated enterprise-level COTS packages for business processes; and (3) the extensive reviews in the trade press that have identified COTS solutions as less costly than developed software. The Information Technology Resources Board (2000a) suggests that while COTS applications may provide a solution, cases must be assessed independently. The ITRB suggests that a government organization take the following steps as part of this evaluation of COTS products:

- *Understand the COTS product.* Because a COTS application is commercially available, it should be possible to obtain hands-on experience with a system similar to the one you may implement. It may also be possible to prototype or pilot a package in the setting in which it will be used. If this is not possible, public managers in charge of the selection should at least visit or talk with others who are using the COTS software in a similar manner.

• *Examine the "gap."* Unless one is extremely lucky, COTS software will not be able to fulfill every one of your needs or desires. The gap between the business processes that would ideally be supported and those that actually can be supported by a COTS package may be large or small, but the ITRB argues that it is "imperative that you understand this gap *well before* the implementation begins *and* ensure your organization can accept this gap without degrading performance" (2000a, p. 2).

• *Incorporate lessons learned.* Other organizations have probably learned ways of more effectively incorporating COTS software into their business processes. Learn from these organizations, particularly ones that are similar to your organization.

• *Secure required resources (e.g., skills, time and money).* Make sure you have the resources needed to acclimate your organization to the new business processes supported by a COTS product.

• *Focus on the data and the interfaces.* In this regard ITRB recommends that managers work to develop documentation for the legacy databases and conversion routines early on in the process.

• *Involve functional users early and often in the implementation of the COTS product and associated processes.*

• *Validate performance and scalability.* Can the product support the number of users and geographic locations your organization plans to grow toward? Can it work on all the platforms that you currently use or hope to be using in the future?

• *Select mature products.* Using COTS products that have been successful elsewhere and that have an established network of vendors and other support personnel is obviously less risky than using products that do not have these supports.

• *Fully understand contractual conditions.* This may be the most important assessment step in that it will determine the potential for COTS to grow within the organization at a reasonable cost. In recent years, some governments have been hard hit by developers of Web-based or -enabled versions of COTS. For example, the vendor of one Southeastern city's financial management and administrative software package wanted an extra $20,000 to Web-enable each individual module for such activities as building permits, planning permits, taxes, parking tickets, and so on. These module expenses were on top of the cost of purchasing a starter kit for $20,000 that was necessary for any of the individual modules to be Web-enabled. Similarly, public managers should always ascertain who owns the license to the source code, what rights the government has with respect to being able to modify the source code in-house, and what is included in any software maintenance agreement.

• *Be aware that the cost of sustaining the effort is usually underestimated.* COTS may or may not minimize future costs related to adapting the product to new operating systems or to new hardware components or interfaces. While such costs may be lower than with a custom system, they nevertheless can be substantial.

NOTE

1. It is often useful to understand the relationships between (1) continuous process improvement, or an effort to reduce variation in the quality of products and services and incrementally improve work flow within a functional area; (2) business process redesign, which removes non–value-added activities from processes, improves cycle time, expands response capability and lowers process costs; and (3) business process reengineering, which involves a radical transformation of processes, often through the application of new technologies in order to achieve large-scale improvements in process efficiency, effectiveness, productivity and quality. Essentially, these terms differ with respect to the scope and degree of the change effort. When the gap between current performance and necessary or mandated performance is large, reengineering, with all its attendant risks, is called for. However, where all that is needed is a small, incremental improvement, or where visionary leadership is not available, CPI or BPR may be all that is needed or desired.

REFERENCES

Brimson, J. A. (1991). *Activity Accounting: An Activity Based Costing Approach*. New York: John Wiley and Sons.

CIO Council. (1999). *Federal Enterprise Architecture Framework Version 1.1, September 1999*. Washington, DC: Chief Information Officers Council.

Cunningham, C. (2000). Reeling in IT talent in the public sector. *InfoWorld* 22(20): 78–79.

Department of Defense. (1994). *Framework for Managing Process Improvement*. Washington, DC: Electronic College of Process Innovation, December 15.

English, L. P. (1999). *Improving Data Warehouse and Business Information Quality: Methods for Reducing Costs and Increasing Profits*. New York: John Wiley and Sons.

Ferris, N. (2000). The technology beast. *Government Executive* 2(4): 45–50.

HRTC. (1997). *Governmentwide HRIS Study*. Washington, DC: Human Resources Technology Council.

Information Technology Resources Board (ITRB). (2000a). *Assessing the Risks of Commercial-off-the-Shelf Applications: Lessons Learned from the Information Technology Resources Board*. Washington, DC: Information Technology Resources Board.

———. (2000b). *Practical Strategies for Managing Information Systems*. Washington, DC: Information Technology Resources Board.

Norris, D. F., and K. L. Kraemer. (1996). Mainframe and PC computing in American cities: Myths and realities. *Public Administration Review* 56(6): 568–76.

Spivey, D. (N.d.). *Engineering Management in the Information Age*. Washington, DC: Army Corps of Engineers.

United States General Accounting Office. (2000). *Information Technology Investment Management: A Framework for Assessing and Improving Process Maturity*. Version 1. Washington, DC: GAO, Accounting and Information Management Division, May.

Wisconsin counties share innovative applications. (1995). *American City and County* 110(10): 19.

Yoder, S. K. (1994). Technology. (A special report): The business plan—When things go wrong: The main strength of networks—giving control to individual users—is also its greatest weakness. *Wall Street Journal*, November 14:R16.

Zachman, John A. (1987). A framework for information systems architecture. *IBM Systems Journal* 26(3):276–292.

PART II
THE CHALLENGES OF
KNOWLEDGE MANAGEMENT

4

Knowledge Management: The New Frontier of Information-Enhanced Management

> The acquisition of knowledge is the mission of research, the transmission of knowledge is the mission of teaching, and the application of knowledge is the mission of public service.
>
> —James A. Perkins

Knowledge management may be a fad, but the underlying concepts of managing in ways that are based on knowledge rather than guesswork, instincts, or personal or political preference are as old—and as new in some contexts—as the scientific revolution itself. In this chapter, we look more closely at the ways knowledge management differs from earlier IT development concepts as well as how it fits with these concepts and with two of the major IT technology strategies of our time: enterprise resource planning (ERP) and customer (or citizen) relationship management (CRM). We then outline some simple knowledge management ideas and examine in detail how managers can impact the cycle of knowledge in their organization by using specific technologies (e.g., expert systems) during particular phases of the knowledge cycle. Next, we identify two core technologies—metadata and data warehousing—that need to be in place before attempting to implement ERP or CRM strategies. Finally, the future of knowledge management as an organizational reform strategy is assessed.

KNOWLEDGE MANAGEMENT DIFFERENCES WITH EARLIER IT ENHANCEMENTS

Knowledge management differs from the earlier stages of use of information technology in at least four ways. First, knowledge management focuses on a larger array of tasks, particularly decision-making tasks that have not traditionally been viewed as amenable to information system support. Second, knowledge management implies that human beings are responsible for continuously renewing the system and refining their understanding of key contexts for information. The emphasis here is more on effectiveness than on efficiency per se. This contrasts with traditional reengineering efforts that assume a given set of goals and contexts and identify needed changes in organizational design to achieve greater efficiency. Third, the role of front-line workers in a knowledge-centric system is different. Whereas workers in the earlier stages of IT-enhanced work (data processing, statistical control and work redesign) only need to understand their part in a work-process flow, workers in a knowledge-centric system need to have an overall understanding of their government's mission, goals, strategies, techniques and stakeholders, as well as how their individual work fits with these larger purposes and contexts. In knowledge management systems, front-line workers are encouraged to actively and continuously assess, provide context for and reinterpret the information archived in the information systems. A key distinction between a knowledge management system and a work reengineering, document management or enterprise resource planning system is that the former allows and encourages workers to record their own observations about processes, documents and techniques in their day-to-day use of the system. Thus, empowerment-oriented organizations provide a better fit with knowledge management systems than is the case with other types of organizations. Fourth, because knowledge management focuses on double-loop learning, or learning about how one learns, it helps to build in an expanded potential for continuous improvement. Yogesh Malhotra, a strong proponent of knowledge management, believes that the qualities associated with knowledge management approaches (i.e., continuous incremental change brought about by refinements in knowledge and understanding) help managers avoid the kind of implementation failure that many organizations are reported to have experienced in their efforts to radically reengineer work. Malhotra implies that "radical change" imposed top-down on the organization and its staff will necessarily create implementation barriers that knowledge management approaches do not. Malhotra's belief in knowledge management's superiority to earlier IT enhancement approaches is one that has not yet been tested. It can be argued, for example, that each of the levels of IT enhancement of work outlined here (data processing, statistical control, work redesign and knowledge management) potentially represents a valuable contribution to governmental performance and productivity in certain contexts. Where knowledge management has the most to offer is in work environments where judgment, discretion and customization of services and responses are highly valued. What makes knowledge management ever more important to government and the private sector alike is that as more and more of the routine work is automated, a higher percent of public service jobs require discretion and customized service delivery. These are jobs that can best be supported by knowledge management IT approaches.

MANAGING THE TENSION BETWEEN KNOWLEDGE MANAGEMENT AND WORK REENGINEERING

Public managers who want to establish leading-edge organizations are constantly in danger of leading their organizations prematurely in the direction of an unproven or inappropriate business fad. Blindly adopting a knowledge management approach could easily represent such a strategic blunder, particularly if the public manager does not understand the place of this approach within an overall effort to improve efficiency and effectiveness. John Seely Brown and Paul Duguid (2000), writing in *Harvard Business Review*, provide some guidance in this regard, suggesting that reengineering and knowledge management represent profoundly different but complementary approaches to business operational strategy. Reengineering, they argue, is a top-down process that is focused on the way routine tasks can be more efficiently organized based on knowledge that is explicit enough to suggest improved organizational patterns and workflows. Reengineering works well when the operational environment is fairly predictable. In contrast, the focus of knowledge management is on effectiveness, particularly within unpredictable environments where tacit knowledge is more important than explicit knowledge. Knowledge management, they suggest, works through identifying the existing improvised practices that people use to get work done. Brown and Duguid believe that management will always involve balancing the tension between innovative practices, "the way things actually get done," and processes, "the way matters are formally organized." The manager's role is to identify the practices that are working and then strive to have these "best practices" become routine processes. Unfortunately, there are a couple of common barriers to managing this tension.

First, managers typically identify jobs as either being routine or nonroutine. According to Brown and Duguid this ignores the tendency for all jobs over time to become less congruent with the designed processes of the organization. Managers who fail to recognize this are unlikely to be able to identify promising improvisational practices or to correct situations where management has assumed that a process is being followed. I personally discovered the importance of ensuring that processes and practices do not get too far out of line in a study that my colleagues and I did of part of the system of behavioral health in the state of Georgia (Bittner, DuBois & O'Looney 1998). One of the key issues we were asked to look at was the percentage of persons entering the public community service system who were eligible for Medicaid. When the data from the state's system were analyzed, the number of persons identified as eligible was far lower than had been expected. Moreover, when these management-oriented data were compared to the billing data used at the community level, it quickly became apparent that the former represented a gross undercount of those who were actually eligible. On further inquiry, we discovered that the local intake workers for the most part simply ignored the Medicaid eligibility input field since it did not have any operational impact at the local level. This practice was effective from the local point of view because it simplified data entry while not losing any data at the local level. Unfortunately, policy makers at the state level did not have access to the local data systems that would have enabled them to also know with accuracy the number of Medicaid-eligible clients. Moreover, because state-level managers had not looked intensively at the practices being followed among "routine" workers, they were not aware of the discrepancy between actual practices and official processes.

Second, managers not only need to understand the gap between paper processes and day-to-day practices, they also need to understand that people don't always fully understand their own practices. Brown and Duguid tell a story about Xerox service representatives fixing customers' machines. If the representatives were directly asked to explain how they went about deciding how to repair problems, they would talk about how they used the built-in error codes to diagnose the problem. However, when an anthropologist followed these Xerox service representatives in their daily routine, he discovered that their own individualistic view of their work was a very incomplete explanation. While using the error codes was sufficient to solve problems in some cases, it was often the case that the combination of new and old machinery and different user environments would create problems that were not diagnosable from the error codes. When a truly difficult problem occurred, the representatives would generally be found discussing the problem at breakfast. While eating, "the reps talked work and talked it continuously" (p. 76). Based on the Xerox anecdote, Brown and Duguid note that what may appear to be a highly independent function can actually be one that is very dependent on informal socializing, particularly socializing that involves the telling of "war stories" that outline the causes and effects of events within the work environment.

KNOWLEDGE MANAGEMENT: DIFFERENCES WITH TRADITIONAL GOVERNMENT APPROACHES

Knowledge management often involves gathering, linking and transmitting information from and to multiple stakeholders through organized processes so as to provide benefits to those involved. In the business world, for example, knowledge management supports customers, providing information and ideas about products and services. In some instances, knowledge management is used to link feedback from potential customers to the team developing new products and services. While knowledge management processes are explicitly designed, the knowledge management activities themselves may or may not be formal. The implication of the Xerox service representative anecdote, for example, is that knowledge management can mean supporting informal gatherings where exchanges of information take place. Whether a knowledge management activity is formal or not should be determined by a careful analysis of the specific circumstances in which knowledge in a particular organization is created, transmitted, understood and used. Just as in some instances the analysis might reveal a need to support informal exchanges, in other cases it might mean removing support for informal gatherings that provide little or no opportunity for knowledge creation or exchange.

Knowledge management is about getting the right information to the right people in the right quantities at the right time. This process will typically involve the gathering of more information than has traditionally been the case. Also, it commonly requires a higher level of cross-referencing, analysis and distillation.

Major Knowledge Management Strategies

While knowledge management encompasses numerous activities and tasks, two strategic areas of knowledge management activity have received considerable attention in the last couple of years. One is the area of enterprise resource planning (ERP), and the other is the area of customer (or citizen) relationship management (CRM). In many respects, one can conceive of these two major strategic areas as referring respectively to the management of internal and external affairs of the government. In each of these areas, public managers should understand the full array of knowledge management steps or processes (e.g., data capture, retrieval, use, display, etc.), the technologies that can be used in support of these steps (e.g., expert systems), and the administrative practices that help organizations to manage their knowledge better (e.g., the use of metadata).

Enterprise Resource Planning (ERP)

Enterprise resource planning systems are designed to knit together data from the full array of administrative functions, such as procurement, accounts receivable and payable, materials and work order management, personnel development and benefits administration, activities-tracking and budgeting, facilities management and document management. The goals of ERP include:

- A reduction in the need for employees to enter and correct data.
- Greater availability of information across departments and divisions.

- Information and data architectures that create a backbone for management information and decision support systems.
- An ability to support performance-based management and to provide ongoing reports on revenue and spending, project management, staffing and training, facilities use and project achievement.

ERP systems should help public sector program managers to more easily monitor and improve operations. The Federal Emergency Management Agency (FEMA) has installed an enterprise system that links together numerous functions such as emergency coordination, human services delivery, and emergency infrastructure support, as well as support for disaster mitigation. As a by-product of the linking of diverse types of information, the National Emergency Management Information System appears to be providing benefits payments to disaster victims faster and more accurately than was previously possible. The system includes the ability for mailed documents to be imaged and stored and retrieved electronically as part of a holistic case record. Because these records are available to all the claims processors at any time, the workflow is improved and victims can be kept informed of the status of their case (Laurent 2000).

While ERP systems provide the potential for numerous benefits, they are not always so simple to implement, particularly if there is a time constraint on making the transition. Recently, for example, a $112 million ERP project blew up in the face of Hershey Foods Corporation, which experienced a 19 percent loss of revenue due in part to the failure of its ERP systems (Stedman 1999). As with most complex information systems, ERP systems are more prone to failure the more complex they become. Unfortunately, the power of these systems comes, in part, from their ability to guide workers and managers through complex activities. As such, there is a certain necessary complexity. The wisdom needed in the development of such systems is akin to that employed in scientific theory building. That is, the systems (like scientific explanations) should be as complex as necessary to provide the information (explanation), but not more.

Because of the complexity of enterprise-level processes most managers will attempt to fit off-the-shelf ERP applications to their particular situation. A common problem with adopting prepackaged software is the tendency for a poor fit between the functionality offered by the application and what the adopting organization needs. A review of ERP implementation (Soh 2000) indicates that it is particularly difficult because of the need to

- match application modules with organizational functions and units
- standardize data across all modules
- adopt an underlying business model ("best practices") as it is defined by the software developer

- implement the application in a single time frame that may be unrealistic for some departments
- coordinate a large number of stakeholders
- educate these stakeholders as to the functionality of a system that is typically far beyond what has been the case to date.

More specifically, public managers should be aware of and explore the potential for different types of misfits between prepackaged ERP solutions and their own organizational needs. Such misfits are more likely to exist within the public sector because most ERP software has been developed for the private sector. Also, misfits are more likely to occur in areas where global standards have not yet evolved or where regulatory practices are likely to be different across jurisdictions. For example, Soh (2000) discovered that an ERP solution for hospitals in an Asian country presented more customization challenges with respect to patient care functions than with respect to financial and accounting functions where global standards exist. According to Soh, the particular types of misfits between ERP packages and organizational situations that managers should be aware of include:

- *Data misfits*: These exist when there is incongruence between organizational requirements and the ERP solution in terms of things such as the format of data (data type, allowed length, default values, etc.) or the relationships among data tables that make up the underlying data model. Incompatibilities of this type are particularly difficult for the nontechnical public manager to assess. However, public managers overlook this type of mismatch at their peril because data formats and relationships exist at the core of an ERP application. As such, seemingly minor changes can be prohibitively expensive to implement.
- *Functional misfits*: These occur when the ERP does not function in ways that are compatible with organizational functions. Such misfits can range from simple applications that control access in ways that disrupt the workflow to more complex incompatibilities between the way the ERP is designed to account for the flow of funds and the way the organization needs to make such an accounting. For example, if a system that has been built for the private sector is organized around insurance payments for medical care, it may not function effectively in an environment where bills are either paid for by individuals or are prepaid. Data validation procedures (i.e., where the system checks to see if the data entered meet particular parameters) also represent areas where prepackaged ERP solutions tend to break down. In general, public sector systems, in the human services area in particular, tend to be less tolerant of error and require more complex validation than is generally the case in the private sector.
- *Output misfits*: These occur whenever the ERP's default presentation of data (e.g., in reports, charts, tables, etc.) is incompatible with the needs of the organization. While output misfits are likely to be frequent, the cost of repairing them is relatively minor when compared to many data or functional misfits. For example, most of the better ERPs have flexible report writers that can be customized.

Because implementing an ERP can bring both benefits and headaches, public managers would be wise to allow for the time and effort needed to bring together the key players in the implementation process: key users, information systems (IS) or IT department personnel and the ERP vendor. Each of these players holds some piece of important knowledge (organizational requirements, existing IT infrastructure and software functionality, respectively) that needs to be integrated to make the ERP implementation successful. Typically, failed ERP implementations occur when managers do not make sure that potential users have a prominent role early in the development process. When these users discover major misfits, it may be too late in the process to fix them in a timely and inexpensive manner or too late to get the users to accept the system on its own terms. Involving key users early on can help avoid both of these undesirable cases.

Observations by experienced ERP consultants (Willcocks & Stykes 2000) suggest that overcoming the misfit between ERP applications and specific organizational needs will require leadership that

- appoints a project champion who is able to spend a considerable portion of his or her time on the implementation.
- sets a time frame of less than a year for completion of the implementation.
- manages the expectations for implementation such that staff understand that initial implementation will only be 80 percent of the deal, but will allow users to get a feel for the basic system capabilities.
- ensures that consultants are in support roles rather than in leadership roles and that in-house IT staff have up-to-date skills.
- encourages a variety of small multifunctional teams to work on different modules.

Citizen Relationship Management (CRM)

Private sector managers need basic knowledge management skills to perform what is called customer relationship management, or CRM. In the public sector, CRM could just as easily be said to refer to citizen relationship management. CRM relies on information technology to help managers and workers understand in a timely manner

- the size and scope of current citizen concerns.
- the speed and direction of emerging concerns.
- the breakdown of concerns among different constituencies.
- the underlying causes of concern among different groups.

With this information, managers should be able to respond in a more timely and appropriate manner to citizens' calls.

In a recent article about CRM, Cohen & Moore (2000) present the following scenario:

Mrs. M calls the mayor at home at 8:00 A.M. on Monday morning to ask why her garbage wasn't picked up by 7:30 A.M. as usual. When the mayor calls you at 8:05 A.M., you should be able to use the workstation at your desk while the mayor is on the phone with you to view a list of all of Mrs. M's previous calls to the locality for any reason, together with the locality's response to each call. You also should be able to e-mail this list to the mayor while you are on the phone so that he or she can view it and print it. Or the mayor should be able to look these up and print them out while you still are on the phone. These capabilities ought to be extremely helpful in putting the mayor and council at ease over the situation. (p. 10)

A basic CRM system will enable public service employees who receive communications from citizens to access substantial amounts of information about the citizen that already exist in one or more computer databases while the communication (e.g., phone call or e-mail) is being received. In this way, a public service worker can potentially identify other sources of concern or emerging problems. For example, if service workers can see data related to utility bills, taxes, fees, fines, tickets and the like, they will easily be able to identify when a citizen may be having multiple financial problems. These problems may be the root cause of an unrelated complaint. By working only on the concern that the citizen is currently presenting, the service worker could be ignoring the underlying problem that needs to be solved if the citizen's relationship with the government is to be stabilized.

In addition to providing basic information at the point of contact with the citizen, a sophisticated CRM system can assist a manager in analyzing complaints by type, locality, individual or unit service provider, age and occupation of complainant, and so on. The most advanced CRM systems use computer-telephony integration to create an automatic link between a phone call and the local government's data files. These systems, which have been in use in emergency 911 systems for some time to provide for automatic name and location identification, are beginning to be used for citizen relationship management systems as well (Cohen & Moore 2000).

The real power of a CRM system is based on the integration of the system with the response and work order processes in the agency. That is, the system should not just record data about the complaint, but should also record data about when the agency responded to the call, when the response was completed, which department(s) and personnel were involved in the response, what the government's response was, and how much it cost. By integrating CRM with office automation technology, the system should be able to generate a letter or automated e-mail response to the citizen by merging information from database files related to the call or the issue of concern with the word processing or e-mail application.

Next, where an enterprise-wide work order application exists, the CRM system should be linked to the work order application. Properly configured, the combination of CRM and work order applications enables automated assignment of the work generated by each citizen communication to a specific agency, department or unit. Similarly, the CRM system can be integrated with government geographic information systems that will allow a display of the data based on geographic values. CRM can also be integrated with citizen satisfaction assessment processes. For example, the system could be programmed to periodically produce a service satisfaction survey that is mailed out at a certain point in the call-response-action cycle. Using such a system, a manager could identify when and where particular responses might lead to increased satisfaction and at what cost. Analysis of this information could, in turn, lead to identification of responses that were more and more cost-effective. Surveys could also be conducted based on location or complaint-specific criteria (e.g., all those who complained about garbage pickup in the last year).

SIMPLE KNOWLEDGE MANAGEMENT IDEAS

While the processes described in Table 4.1 suggest a sophisticated information technology infrastructure, the real heart of knowledge management is a concern for information discovery, creation and exchange rather than the use of technology per se. In fact, as the following list of simple knowledge management ideas suggests, governments can often achieve the goals of knowledge management, that is, getting the right information to the right people, without implementing overly elaborate technologies.

- Create a virtual conference room where citizens are invited to collaborate and communicate with local government staff once a week using groupware, database and communications technology. The conference can provide an opportunity for citizens and staff to strategize about trends and developments that could impact government services (e.g., new recycling technologies, better communications, growth in demand, etc.). Each month the public manager in charge of government strategic planning synthesizes the best ideas aired in the virtual forum and presents them to the council or commission.
- Create an online database of citizen concerns and complaints ordered by variables such as department, work process, time of day, district, key concern, workable solutions, and so on. Make the database searchable and available to staff across all departments. Develop a summary report every month from the database.
- Create an online database of citizen and staff solutions to common issues (e.g., what to do when a water leak occurs on citizen property versus city property; how quickly the city will be able to respond to a request for building inspection and things that the builder can do to ensure that the inspection goes smoothly, etc.). Have staff gather and review new information about best practices from the database once a month.

Table 4.1
Traditional Versus Knowledge Management Interactions Among Key Stakeholders in Government

	Traditional	Knowledge Creation & Management
Citizens & Decision Makers	Government uses individual polls and surveys to identify trends in public opinion. Using this information, the government develops a public awareness campaign to help correct myths or misunderstandings about ordinances and policies.	Government uses cross-referencing of multiple polls and surveys with citizen participation data to more completely specify citizens' thinking on key issues. Government uses filtering technology to identify different citizenship groupings and the context (e.g., hot button issues, neighborhood concerns, newspaper articles, etc.) in which specific groups become active. Government develops a more targeted or "niche marketing" public awareness campaign that is context-specific to help correct myths or misunderstandings about ordinances and policies.
Citizens & Public Managers	Government uses individual polls and surveys to identify citizen satisfaction with existing services and citizens' desire for new public services. Using this information, the government takes action to improve existing service delivery and to develop the most highly desired new services.	Government uses cross-referencing of multiple polls and surveys with data on citizens' actual use of services and data on specific service qualities (e.g., wait time, quality of customer service personnel, etc.) to identify citizen satisfaction with existing services and desire for new public services within different contexts. Government uses filtering technology to identify different consumer profiles, their respective concerns and triggering points (for satisfaction and dissatisfaction). Using this information, the government takes action to improve existing service delivery through both customization and movement toward the central concerns of the majority of citizens.

Table 4.1 (continued)
Traditional Versus Knowledge Management Interactions Among Key Stakeholders in Government

	Traditional	Knowledge Creation & Management
Public Managers & Local Government Staff	Government uses individual polls and surveys to identify employee concerns and issues in order to create a more productive working environment.	Government uses cross-referencing of multiple polls and surveys with data on employee tasks, years in service, psychological profiles, work performance and other demographic factors to more completely identify employee concerns and issues. Managers use statistical software to track the effectiveness of different changes in the working environment on staff morale and productivity and to create best practices management policies that are customized to employee characteristics, station, and needs.
Citizens & Local Government Staff	Staff rely on standard operating procedures and basic customer service principles to guide interactions with citizens.	Based on profiles of key citizen group needs and concerns (see above), staff use any number of "best practice" procedures to provide a higher level of personalized service to citizens. Staff continually update the knowledge base to insure refinement of the customization process.

- Have staff scour the Web for sample ordinances, reports, evaluations, best practices, innovations, and so on, on key policy issues to create online, searchable repositories of these documents for policy makers. Train policy makers to use the repositories.

- Install kiosks in multiple public sites, including the sites where citizens would normally be receiving services. These kiosks would provide an alternative way to receive service when staff are not available as well as a way for citizens to register their level of satisfaction with the services they receive. In this way, citizens standing in line for services can choose an automated alternative or can choose to provide information on service satisfaction while they are involved in receiving the service. Having a feedback mechanism close to the service context will help ensure that the information is timely and not lost due to decisions to "just forget about" a particular instance of inadequate service.

- Have staff organize all e-mail correspondence into a large searchable archive. Develop relevancy codes for use by staff to better organize the correspondence for retrieval. Train staff to use the search tools for effective discovery of stored knowledge.

- Create searchable repositories of time-stamped minutes of meetings, e-mail, documents, notes on conversations, and so on—that is, of everything that goes into a decision or the design of a process or service—so that everyone can be up-to-date on the issues and can get a sense of the total context in which decisions have been made.

- Create an online database of expertise. The database would include information on experts among personnel within government, citizen experts, consultants within the community, and experts from regional or national organizations. Include an ability to provide feedback from government departments that have used particular experts or consulting firms.

- Create cross-department knowledge groups that are charged with identifying best "cross-cutting" practices and setting standards in these areas. Have these groups create center-of-excellence Web sites that provide tutorials and online courses as well as skills certification for the rest of local government staff.

The exact approach to knowledge management that a government should attempt will depend on the particular organization's needs and the technological and human capacities currently available (or that the government is willing to acquire).

Case Examples: Knowledge Management in Procurement

Federal Law Enforcement Training Center

In the mid-1990s, the Procurement Division of the Federal Law Enforcement Training Center reworked its purchasing system to make it into a strategic business activity. The division built a system that allowed purchasing agents to accumulate and communicate knowledge about the performance of vendors and contractors. The system was designed to help both in-house customers and suppliers to develop higher quality and lower costs over time. To create this system, the Procurement Division had to promote teamwork, trust and learning. Procurement agents became responsible for systematic learning about contract statements of work and associated performance measures. Over time, this learning about performance statements of work, quality assurance plans and past contractor performance allowed the division to move from cost-plus to fixed-price performance contracts and to realize savings of 20–40 percent (Electronic College of Process Innovation 1995).

Patent and Trademark Office

While knowledge management can involve sophisticated systems for archiving, analyzing and retrieving information, at the heart of knowledge management is the idea of "knowing what you know." A simple example of this is the effort by the Patent and Trademark Office (PTO) to automate the purchase process for transactions under $25,000. Under the old system, the in-house program office customer would route a paper requisition form to the procurement office for approvals, requests for quotations, and the selection and issuing of purchase orders. Using off-the-shelf financial software, the PTO built a system in which the program office customer develops a requisition on the computer network and then sends it out for approval and processing electronically, eliminating all paper. Before this system was developed, the data entry personnel in the procurement office did not know exactly what the program personnel wanted, why they wanted it, or the essential features of the desired good or service. Often, they made mistakes without realizing they had done so. With the new system, the electronic requisition form is filled out in the program office *by the customer*, the person who really knows and cares about the order. Customers no longer have to wait and wonder how their requisition will be translated by the procurement office. The customer is in control. Moreover, the system supports the program office customer shopping for goods, identifying necessary price quotes, and handling the entire process.

Although some of the success of the new system could be traced to the new software and network capabilities, associated administrative reforms contributed the most to the streamlining of the work process. Two administrative reforms in particular were key to this success. Each of these reforms grew out of a single knowledge management principle: allow people to know what the organization as a whole knows *and* allow them to act on this knowledge. The first PTO administrative reform concerned the ability of program personnel to complete purchases on their own. Once the system capabilities for doing checks, edits and reconciliation with the financial system were implemented, it became feasible to allow program personnel to complete an entire purchase process. The system had substantially reduced (but not eliminated entirely) the risks involved in such empowerment. The specific administrative reform took advantage of these changed circumstances by allowing program personnel who had received a modicum of training (five days) to complete purchases of up to $25,000 without having a third party stop the process. This new arrangement empowered those who had the knowledge. However, the particular administrative reform was also built upon management's more complete knowledge of its own operations. That is, the PTO's information systems allowed managers to show that procurement controls rarely identified sufficient savings on small purchases to justify the time spent in the review process. As a result of this reform, common procurement delays of four to six weeks for small purchases were eliminated.

The second major administrative reform associated with the implementation of an automated purchasing system was based on the idea that the new system had created an opportunity for purchasing officers to act as a virtual team in terms of customer service. Before the system was established, the progress of requisitions and associated paperwork was nearly impossible to track. Yet close to a third of the calls to the procurement office involved questions about the status of requisitions. Because the callers typically did not have the form number or the date handy, tracking down the requisition was difficult and time-consuming. With the automated system, which organizes all the approvals and forms together in one folder that can be searched based on any number of identifying characteristics, callers can now be helped by any of the available procurement agents. The system supplies a requisition status report and allows the agent serving the caller to prompt the reviewers with e-mail messages. However, to make this enhanced level of customer service possible, it was necessary to make a dramatic change in the culture and structure of the procurement office. Under the old system, procurement agents were separated into small- and large-purchase agents. With the new system, there was less need for small-purchase agents and more capability to provide quick responses to customers' questions—if every agent took up a position in the queue. Hence, PTO procurement managers decided to collapse the units of the procurement division into one and to make everyone a generalist contract agent. All agents are cross-trained in large and small purchases, and every agent is able to satisfy a customer because every agent has contract officer authority. Instead of procurement staff workers having to refuse a customer's request because it involves an area over which they have no responsibility (e.g., "I'm sorry, I only do computer purchases. You will need to talk to Mr. Jones, who is out of town right now"), they can now address customer needs immediately (Erwin 1995).

THE BREADTH OF KNOWLEDGE MANAGEMENT

Many kinds of knowledge can potentially be managed more effectively through the use of information technology. At a minimum they include the following:

1. Knowledge of general techniques. This knowledge can include general education skills as well as specific technology skills of machine operators, supervisors and performance managers. Knowledge of technique is often developed most effectively through formal schooling. However, while the return on general education is typically broad, transferable across tasks, and long-lasting, knowledge of specific technologies is more narrow and time-sensitive. For example, knowing how to use one vendor's specific software application (e.g., ESRI's ArcView) will only contribute marginally to the ability to use another vendor's application in the same field and even less to other vendors' applications for different purposes (e.g., AutoCad programs). In addition, knowledge of earlier versions of a software application may be of diminishing value as new versions of the software are published.

2. Knowledge of expertise. This concerns knowledge about who has what knowledge or how to find important knowledge. Searchable databases of experts are often developed to better manage this type of knowledge.

3. Process knowledge. This knowledge of an organization's tasks, techniques, processes and tools is highly amenable to knowledge management. Managing process knowledge is particularly cost-effective if the processes are already being documented through a flow of paper or electronic orders, accounts, records and the like. However, if a process is not already being documented, building a management system for process knowledge can demand substantial amounts of new resources employed in capturing and formatting process information for entry into the knowledge base. In many instances, the expected benefits of this type of knowledge management system are not justified by the set-up cost for the system. Process knowledge has become more important as organizations have moved away from *standardized mass production* approaches to *mass customization* models. Management of process knowledge in the former has less to contribute simply because the process is, by definition, standardized. As such, the business process (and the knowledge of the process) changes less rapidly, and attention to updating staff's knowledge of the process is less crucial. With mass customization of products and services, management of process knowledge is a central part of customer service. This centrality can be seen in the care and attention that Microsoft and other software manufacturers give to the development of their products' knowledge base for the process of application installation. The Microsoft product installation knowledge base contains millions of pages of information and represents millions of hours of service representatives' experience. The tremendous cost of developing this system for managing process knowledge is justified by the fact that, without it, millions of customers would not be able to achieve a successful installation of the software product they purchased due to undesirable interactions between the product in question and other software and hardware components of the customer's computer system. The knowledge base in this instance is tremendously large because of the complexity of the thousands of possible interactions among already installed and to-be-installed software and hardware products.

4. Customer/citizen/supplier knowledge. This knowledge concerns the interests of those with whom one transacts business or exchanges favors, information, services, prestige, funds or goods. Management of this knowledge is crucial for competitive advantage in the business world, but has traditionally been of less concern to public managers except as mediated by elected officials who translate citizen desires into policy.

5. Knowledge of organization and innovation. Among the categories of knowledge, this kind of knowledge is possibly the most tacit, and therefore the most difficult to systematize and transfer via computer-mediated communications. Knowledge of how particular groups work together, or of how certain groups are likely to adopt or not adopt a particular type of technology represents for managers the most valuable kind of knowledge. Extracting "lessons learned" from pages of reports, informal notes, meeting minutes, e-mail messages and the like presents the greatest challenge for knowledge managers. Improvements in natural language

processing and automated content analysis are necessary before we will experience much success in the management of knowledge of organization and innovation.

THE MANAGER'S ROLE IN THE KNOWLEDGE MANAGEMENT PROCESS

Managers are responsible for implementing knowledge management systems such as ERP and CRM in ways that produce positive results. When these results are not forthcoming, managers are likely to complain that the application is not effective. In response to a complaint of this sort about a CRM package, Scott Nelson (2000), a Gartner analyst, provides the following apt retort: "CRM is not a technology. It is a complex interplay of 5 things: strategy, tactics, processes, skill sets and technology. The latter reinforces and enables the former, not vice versa" (p. 1). Nelson suggests that managers first create a vision of the ideal interaction with the customer (or citizen), then develop strategies and tactics to support this vision. Finally, within the context of the strategies and tactics, managers should examine the processes used and the skill sets needed. Only when these steps are completed should a manager evaluate how well a particular package or CRM application will support the vision.

The most frequently implemented knowledge management systems tend to be in the area of ERP. Unfortunately, like other technology initiatives, ERP implementations do not always deliver on their promises. The failure of these systems to achieve significant benefits appears to be due in large measure to executives not fully understanding what they are implementing (Ross 1999). One of the common misunderstandings about ERP systems is that they will impose discipline and integrate organizational processes, when in fact the effectiveness of these systems is premised on an organization already having established cross-functional processes. A second misunderstanding about these systems, according to Ross, is the perception that ERP will produce improvements in traditional operating measures. Instead, it is more likely that ERP systems will have their most significant impact on processes that were previously unmeasured. By discovering such processes and measuring them for the first time, these systems can potentially have a positive impact on such things as quality or cycle time. The key, according to Ross (1999), is ensuring that employees at all levels of the organization can and do take advantage of the increased availability of data to make decisions that enhance the organization's capabilities or efficiency. In this regard, managers and employees need to become much more aware of how data can be used creatively to rethink current processes. Public managers need to train and empower public employees to focus on data through the entire knowledge management cycle from creation to use. To do this, however, public managers themselves need to become familiar with the individual features of the knowledge management process (Van Buren 1999).

Cycle of Knowledge Management

Because knowledge management is a reiterative process, however, there is no single starting point where one begins to build it into a business function. Rather, one can start at any point in the cycle of creating, capturing, storing, analyzing, representing, codifying, transmitting, interpreting, using and re-creating data, information and knowledge. The following outlines and briefly examines the key features of most of the identifiable steps in the knowledge management process.

Creating

New knowledge is typically generated within a specific context. However, within that context the knowledge generated may not appear to be new. In fact, to those who work within the specific context, the knowledge may appear routine. It is only when such knowledge is understood as having value in other settings that it can truly be said to have been created. The manager's task in this regard is to have in place a process that will lead to the certification or recognition of the newness of the knowledge with respect to the organization as a whole—even if the knowledge is old knowledge to some departments. The U.S. government's patent search process provides a model for certifying knowledge creation at the level of national technology.

Capturing

Capturing involves gathering and formatting the knowledge so as to allow for entry into an information system. The public manager's role in this process is to identify the necessary and desirable information to be gathered and to specify the gathering process and the data entry format for the information. In this regard, managers will want to look for opportunities to use existing information gathering activities as mechanisms for gathering additional information or to reformat existing information so that it can fulfill a knowledge management function in addition to its original function. For example, in many counseling or corrections programs, measures of clients' mental and emotional conditions are taken. Typically, these measures are stored in a chart that is used by therapists but rarely used by program managers. As a result, an opportunity to create a new level of knowledge is lost. Were these data to be collected as part of a program database, however, over the course of a few hundred cases it would become possible to begin to draw some conclusions about how certain program approaches work better with clients displaying certain mental or emotional conditions. Formatting the data is important in the process because the data needs of the therapist are likely to be much more detailed than those of the program manager. Hence, if the data were to be entered into the program database in the same format that it is currently used for client case records, it might result in knowledge that is unusable due to the excess of detail. In addition to developing appropriate data capturing and formatting in the first place, public managers will probably want to identify an acceptable process (i.e., one that is compatible with a knowledge management culture) for adding or subtracting items to the list of those to be captured or for changing information capture formats.

Arranging and Storing

Storage of information involves rearranging data into a variety of forms and providing enhancements to the information such as indexing, creation of metadata (or data about the data), cross-checking the data (i.e., for the purpose of making the data more accurate and up-to-date), and linking and cross-referencing information in different databases (i.e., for the purpose of identifying the universe of possible inquiries into the data). Nontechnical public managers are likely to need more assistance in this stage of the process because of the technical nature of some of the decisions. Managers should get the advice of persons with experience in large-scale (or enterprise-level) systems and in data warehousing. In particular, managers should ask a series of questions regarding the scalability of the choice of storage and processing systems. Scalability refers to the ability of a system to take on new tasks (e.g., completing queries across hundreds of tables, the processing of a multiple-part transaction without loss of data in cases where one of the transaction steps fails) and new records (e.g., to add thousands of new records or to archive historical records) while maintaining acceptable performance. Often when a system experiences problems with scalability, the problems will be blamed on technical errors such as a failure to predict and prepare for the number of records that the system was going to need to store. Looking more deeply into the situation, however, it is often discovered that scalability problems are the result of higher-level managers not adequately specifying the tasks that they want to automate. Recently, in working with a state-level department responsible for drought management, I helped to build an application that would enable public managers, elected officials and ordinary citizens to report problems with drinking water sources. The application quickly grew from a simple one-page electronic reporting form to a complete online updateable and queryable system for reporting on four different types of water source problems and one linked to existing and yet-to-be gathered data on drinking water sources and associated conditions. Whereas the initial system could have been built with a microcomputer database, the resulting system needed an enterprise-level database solution. It was not so much the fact that the final system was going to have that many more records than the initial system that led to a potential scalability failure with the original design as it was that the final system needed to be that much more capable. That is, most scalability failures occur when managers ask the system to do things that were not in the original design. Unfortunately, it is rarely the case that managers will fully understand what they want from a system until they begin to think through their processes and needs as they employ the system itself (or a prototype of the system).

Finding

As the amount of information available through networks (such as the Internet or a government intranet) has grown far beyond the levels that would enable human processing of all the available information, finding information that contributes to knowledge has become one of the most important knowledge management functions. The growth of Internet resources has put tremendous pressure on software creators to develop better information search engines. Although progress in this area has been substantial, finding the right information quickly will likely remain a challenge. The best that public managers can do may be to attempt to track progress in search engine arenas and implement the improved versions of these engines in their own systems. Currently, for example, the more sophisticated search engines can employ document (or Web site) usage data combined with user profile data to help direct specific users to documents (or sites) that have a higher probability of providing the desired information. These engines employ a number of probability functions to direct users toward sites that similar users conducting similar searches have found useful. Given the more constrained subject matter of an internal information system and the narrower interests of the users of such systems, the potential for building effective search engines and routines for these systems is fairly good.

Analyzing

Choices of specific data analysis techniques or approaches are nearly infinite. Identifying and discussing specific techniques is beyond the scope of this book. However, from a more strategic point of view on this issue, managers need to be aware of a basic choice continuum regarding the degree to which analyses will be preset as opposed to free-form. Each type of analytical system has its advantages and disadvantages. Preset analyses tend to favor provision of knowledge discovery capabilities to users who might otherwise not be able to exercise such capabilities. That is, the user of a preset or automated analysis can obtain knowledge even though he or she is not skilled in analysis. Systems that provide preset analysis tend to be easier for novices to use. Also, such systems tend to produce more communication about the results of analyses among users than would otherwise be the case. Essentially, users tend to have more common experiences with the system. On the other hand, preset analysis is limited to asking the same questions again and again. Such analysis is likely to be useful if one expects important changes in the underlying phenomena being measured. It is not useful, however, if what is needed is to take an entirely new look at the phenomena. In this case, free-form analysis is more useful. When a system provides users with the ability to perform free-form analysis, what this means is that instead of users being

constrained to getting answers to a number of preset questions, they are able
to ask any number of complex questions (or queries) that they might want
to pose. For example, where a constrained system would allow a manager to
report the number of service units per day by region, a more free-form
system would allow a user to ask how many service units were provided in
January in regions that had populations over 10,000 by staff who had over
five years of experience and college degrees. While such a capability may
appear to be an unadulterated good, systems with such capability tend to be
much more complex and difficult to learn than systems without it. The key
advantage of such free-form systems is that they enable experienced users to
initiate analyses that have a higher probability (than preset analyses) to create
new knowledge. There is no one best choice of system capability with respect
to the preset to free-form analysis continuum. Often some mixture of these
capabilities is likely to provide the most satisfactory solution. The most satisficing point along the continuum will be one that is aligned with the
organization's culture, the existing and emerging skills of the employees and
the threats and opportunities in the organizational environment. In some
cases systems are available (or can be built) that grow in complexity and
capability in accordance with these factors, but these customized systems
obviously cost more.

Representing

Representation of data can be as critical in the decision-making process
as the choice of analysis or data format. Public managers have an obligation
to both represent data in ways that lead to the clearest possible understanding and to prevent staff or others from using government data to create
misunderstandings, whether intentionally or unintentionally. This task is
larger and potentially much less manageable than may appear at first glance.
Once one concedes that any representation is an individualized simplifica-
tion—in the way that a Mercator map is—of a more complex underlying
reality, one is faced with a representation problem. Public managers, in particular, need to be sensitive to this problem, as they are more likely than the
average private sector manager to be accused of dictating a particular or
biased representation of data. While there is no perfect solution to this problem, public managers should spell out a reasonable process for developing
and refining guidelines for data representation. Given the nature of this
challenge, the process should include a mixture of statisticians, policy makers, government staff and managers, and grass-roots-oriented citizens. The
governing body, so as to make clear its expectations regarding data representation, should then affirm the recommendation of this advisory group.
The alternative ethical position—to display data in a wide range of formats
that project a wide variety of "truths" and thereby avoid the fallacy of the
single truth—is not ultimately a responsible one in that it suggests that all
representations are equally true. When all representations are considered to

be equally true, it is more likely that interest groups will seize on (and hide
behind the semiofficial character of) the one that is most congruent with
their individual point of view, thereby making consensus that much more
difficult. Although the former process of having a representative advisory
body make a recommendation may result in some loss of information (i.e.,
due to the imposition of a limit in the number or type of representations to
be sponsored by the government), the nature of the loss over a series of
decisions will probably not be systematically prejudicial. The essential fairness is based on the fact that the recommending body will essentially be
establishing policies from behind a veil of ignorance about future decisions.
Were members of this body to know what issues are likely to be debated in
the future (and therefore impacted in a particular way by a particular representation of data), they might be tempted to choose representation models
that would favor the outcomes they desire in the forthcoming decisions.
However, because they do not know the nature of the issues in the future,
the temptation to unjustifiably include a particular representation in the accepted set is minimized (see O'Looney 1997 for a discussion of the uses of
geographic representations in local government decision making).

Sharing

The value of sharing of information and information-based products needs
to be understood in light of the following:

- The sharing of production costs. This type of sharing is particularly desirable in
  cases where several organizations would otherwise be making substantial investments in producing the same information. Cost sharing has become particularly
  important in the world of geographic information systems (GIS), where a number
  of governments can save resources by sharing the production cost for a base map
  that can be used and built on by all the stakeholders.
- The sharing of the products among co-producers. The GIS community has also
  discovered that by formatting the underlying data in compatible ways, the community members can obtain GIS data sets from other members and incorporate
  the new information into existing systems so as to make them more valuable.
- The public sharing of knowledge. This refers to the "merit good" nature of information or knowledge products. For merit goods, the marginal cost of producing
  another good is miniscule and the value of open access to the product is large. In
  such merit good cases, it makes public policy sense to make the goods public ones,
  that is, paid for through public funding and available to all without substantial
  charge.
- The economics of networks. The theory of network economics suggests that the
  value of networks increases exponentially with the increase in the number of users.
  This idea can be grasped by comparing the value of the original telephone network,
  which had only a few users, to modern universal service networks, which connect
  nearly the entire populace. In the former, an individual user could only perform a
  couple of information functions (i.e., those such as diplomacy or banking that might

be undertaken by elite users). With a universal network, however, the number of functions is as large as the product of the number of unique configurations of users of the network. The key to this added economic utility is the fact that everyone has agreed to be part of the same standard network, rather than joining alternative networks or using other communications technologies. Network economics are also at work in the context of narrower or more organization-specific needs for knowledge sharing. As public managers consider building knowledge management systems, they may benefit from agreeing to standardize individual system elements in such a way that these individual systems can (if not immediately, then at some time in the future) be integrated so that more people can share in the use of all the individual systems. That is, these individual systems can begin to function as an integrated enterprise system rather than as a series of incompatible system components.

Transferring

Whereas *sharing* can be successful only in instances where the receiver of the knowledge can readily employ the knowledge, *transferring* of intellectual capital is necessary when the person on the receiving end of knowledge is not immediately prepared to use that knowledge. As such, transferring could include an education/training needs assessment, guided learning exercises, and techniques for instilling the tacit knowledge needed to make use of intellectual knowledge.

Using

The use phase in knowledge management is about:

- identifying appropriate contexts for effective use.
- discovering the points of leverage that will enable a new piece of knowledge to be incorporated into an existing process.
- identifying ways to ensure that old or abandoned knowledge will be effectively reused whenever similar contexts arise.
- identifying *all* of the situations where a piece of knowledge could be employed and exploiting the full range of employment possibilities.
- leveraging current knowledge by identifying potentially complementary linkages between knowledge in diverse parts of the knowledge base.

Learning to Learn

Learning to learn represents the most strategic phase of knowledge management, but is also somewhat difficult to define. In terms of specific management techniques, learning to learn involves:

- the promotion of activities that support creativity (e.g., encouragement of divergent thinking).

- identifying the available experts that can be consulted.
- identifying contexts where previous learning can inform current needs.
- understanding how to adjust the environment to better meet the identified "best environments" for learning.
- creating models of "best practices."
- creating knowledge-based asset accounting methods that assign value to the knowledge and monitor its development (Armour 2000).

THE TECHNOLOGY OF KNOWLEDGE MANAGEMENT

While not all of the phases of knowledge management can be facilitated or substantiated through an application of technology, efforts are being made to develop and apply technology to many phases. Most public managers are aware of how technologies such as spreadsheets, databases, optical character recognition and statistical programs can be used in the phases of knowledge management. However, public managers may be less aware of how some of the emerging technologies can be used to enhance knowledge management at different phases. The following discussion presents some examples of these emerging technologies.

Technology for the Finding, Capturing, Analysis and Retrieval Phases of Knowledge Management

The continuing refinement of Internet search engines represents one of the most visible knowledge management activities being automated. These search engines apply intelligence in four ways: (1) by sending out "bots" or small search programs to identify Web pages that have not yet been indexed; (2) by capturing and storing the information in these pages in ways (e.g., multiple indexed databases) that allow for quick retrieval; (3) by applying Baysian probability functions across the range of searched pages to make inferences about the meaning of the material on the Web page; (4) by retrieving the Web pages that, based on these probabilities, are most likely to contain material that the user wants—even if the page itself does not contain the search words that the user entered. The engine is able to perform this feat because the application code tells it, for example, that a page that contains the words "chief" and "executive" and "veto" and "federal government" is likely to be about the U.S. president even though the page itself does not contain the word "president."

Within a government, these sophisticated search agents can be used to do the following:

- Automate purchasing department functions such as identifying the lowest prices for regularly used items.

- Create a government news clipping service that brings recent articles about the government to the attention of public managers.

- Analyze the amount of material being created by various government departments on particular issues.

By adding further analysis routines, the technology could:

- Advise purchasing managers on the best time to purchase particular goods based on historical and trend pricing data.

- Advise public information officers on areas of government that have been particularly ignored or overexamined by the media.

- Provide executive-level public managers with information useful for assessing if the government as a whole is focusing on high-priority strategic goals or is instead attending to lower-level goals.

Technologies of the Analysis Phase of Knowledge Management

Expert Systems

Although some standard, off-the-shelf technologies can produce good analysis, the more complex or specific a process, the less likelihood there is that such standard technologies will be sufficient. Instead, public managers will want to consider developing and using a variety of expert systems or knowledge-based systems. It is not always easy to distinguish a conventional system from one that embeds expertise or intelligence because there is no clear line that defines these two. Rather, an expert system is one that

- tends to provide two-way interactions with users;
- explains its reasoning and terms;
- adapts to the needs of the user;
- analyzes data within a variety of contexts;
- uses a variety of heuristic reasoning, pattern recognition and probability analysis rather than "one calculation fits all" processing; and
- provides an ability to conduct what-if modeling.[1]

As off-the-shelf programs have become more sophisticated, they have incorporated more expert system capabilities. For example, the "assistant" that comes with Microsoft Word attempts to provide expert assistance based on a two-way dialog, while Microsoft Excel provides the ability to do some what-if analysis of spreadsheet data. For the most part, however, off-the-shelf software will not enable public managers to routinely embed knowledge into government processing of information and organization of workflow. Rather, it will be necessary to build a customized system. Well-designed systems should enable public managers to automate or assist current staff to perform such operations as:

- eligibility determination, problem diagnosis, referral suggestions
- spotting of false insurance, tax refund or worker compensation claims
- recognition of abnormal events (e.g., excessive sick leave, entry of zero work hours or bills, etc.)
- ensuring that case decisions or personnel actions conform with regulations or mandated practices
- analysis of performance indicators to identify patterns of practice (e.g., hospitals with the best record on child health care may be more likely to use a particular procedure or piece of equipment)
- spotting of budget anomalies
- identification of extreme performance and suggestions as to its causes
- handling of complex mechanical problems
- forecasting of revenues or benefits based on numerous what-if scenarios
- development of customized self-help legal forms and advice
- generation of potential solutions
- management of building environmental control systems (Shaw 1988)

Types of Expert System Knowledge

Ideally, expert systems would be refined over time to incorporate two important types of knowledge: (1) the most recent knowledge and practices of experts (i.e., the "if-then rules"), and (2) a more complete understanding of the knowledge domain. The knowledge domain or knowledge base is a set of hierarchical object and attribute relationships that enable the system to apply rules to particular circumstances. For example, in a tax auditing situation, the system might know that Joe is a training consultant, which is a particular type of educator. As such, the system could then identify and use certain facts that are stored about educators to audit Joe's tax return. One fact might be that educators are allowed certain deductions for their own continuing education. Another fact might be that the average amount deducted by training consultants on their tax returns is $2,000. Using these facts, the system would then apply certain rules to see if Joe's return deserved further attention (e.g., did his deductions for continuing education exceed twice the average of his peers?).

Expert systems have generally held the greatest promise of productivity gains in areas where expertise is in short supply. Public agencies, for example, that experience high rates of turnover are typically less likely to produce expertise through on-the-job experience. Such agencies are prime candidates for implementing expert systems. (See Part III for a discussion of expert system styles.)

Example Expert Systems

The Occupational Safety and Health Administration (OSHA) regulates workplace safety along numerous highly technical dimensions. Because of the complexity of the regulations, businesses and even OSHA employees themselves experience difficulty interpreting the regulatory guidelines and standards for facility safety and employee well-being. In addition, because these technical rules and regulations vary with time, changes in knowledge, and circumstances, business owners and OSHA officials need to be able to keep abreast of how these changes might impact particular workplace settings. The information needs to be prompt and accurate so as to place the least burden on business operations. Historically, OSHA was not particularly efficient in responding to requests for rule interpretation. Callers were often transferred among several OSHA departments before finding the answer to their questions. In 1995, OSHA began creating a series of expert systems to help employers (and new OSHA employees) learn how OSHA rules apply to a variety of circumstances. Currently, OSHA has developed expert systems to help answer questions about rules, standards and programs related to the following topics: asbestos; confined spaces; fire safety; hazard awareness; lead in construction; lead in general industry; lockout/tagout; online confined spaces; respiratory protection; safety and health programs; safety pays; and U.S. Department of Labor "elaws." Many professionals, trade associations and consultants, as well as the trade press, have contributed to the development of OSHA expert system tools, and the programs themselves have attracted wide use among business managers and consultants.[2]

In the area of human services, California's Merced has developed the MAGIC (Merced Automated Global Information Control) system to enable caseworkers to assist clients in accessing services and benefits from a number of social service programs with complex eligibility rules. Typically, it would take a considerable amount of time and expertise in a number of different program areas for a caseworker to assist clients to apply for participation across the spectrum of programs for which they are likely to be eligible. With the MAGIC system, caseworkers with only basic knowledge can help clients to determine eligibility and complete an intake as well as a number of required tracking, scheduling and reporting procedures. MAGIC is reported to assist caseworkers to become more productive by automating numerous processes and bringing to bear the knowledge of experts so as to reduce error rates (Kidd & Carlson 1992).

The IRS is also a dedicated user of expert systems. The Correspondex expert system, for example, is used to generate millions of letters to taxpayers each year. The system is reported to have reduced error rates by two-thirds, to have improved grammatical correctness, and to have increased the politeness of correspondence. The IRS also uses expert systems to identify returns that might be more appropriate for auditing than others (i.e., the Automated

Issues Identification System) or to send taxpayers the correct information via automated phone systems (Liebowitz 1997).

Technologies for the Learning to Learn Phase of Knowledge Management

Finding Available Experts

While searchable databases of experts and their specific expertise represent a first-order application of technology to a knowledge management process, this technology tends to be costly to maintain because someone must be responsible for identifying and cataloging the multiple and changing types of expertise that exist in an organization. A more advanced knowledge management approach to this same function would employ a "bot," or intelligent agent, to continually scour the documents in the files of all employees. The "ideas" in these files would then be indexed using sophisticated search engine technology. The result is a searchable database that is always up-to-date and that no one has to maintain.

Building Models of Best Practice

To build a model of best practice an organization will typically have to experience numerous failures and successes that are associated with various configurations of organizational structures and workflow designs. Unfortunately, an organization may experience massive failure while trying to accumulate enough experience to evolve a model of best practice. An alternative to this learning through failure is the development of learning through simulation. Simulation technologies are being used in many business situations to identify ways to optimize the flow of goods, parts or work activities in a production, distribution or sales process.

Technologies for the Use Phase of Knowledge Management

The use phase of knowledge management will often involve making routine the practices that have been identified as optimal in particular circumstances. As a large part of government is focused on constituent services, public managers should be particularly concerned with technologies that offer improvements in this area. Unfortunately, the most frequently used technology in this area—the automated answering service—has, in many cases, caused a decrease in the quality of customer service. Moreover, because very few government organizations have developed policies regarding rapid reply to e-mail inquiries, the introduction of this technology has also not led to an improvement in constituent services. Obviously, these technologies were not implemented in ways that resulted in increased service levels; rather, they were established to optimize the use of government staff time. Fortu-

nately, new developments in voice recognition and automated e-mail response may help rescue these flawed first-generation customer service
technologies.

Automated e-mail response technology is quite well developed. This technology uses natural language processing of an incoming e-mail message to
identify sets and patterns of key terms and phrases that have a very high
probability of being related to a specific problem or concern with which the
agency typically deals. Once the system has a large enough knowledge base
of all the key terms and phrases and patterns, a set of rules for automated
responses is established. Additionally, the organization using the system will
set probability levels to determine whether the person (or citizen) making a
request or expressing a problem will receive an automated response or will
instead be routed to a live worker who is responsible for handling difficult
cases.

Example: The pattern of phrasing in an incoming e-mail indicates that
Citizen A is probably opposed to the property assessment received on his
home. Assuming that the pattern meets the appropriate probability level that
the message is of a particular type, this citizen would receive a response that
details the method used for property assessment. In addition, if the e-mail
provided identifying information, the system could potentially go through
the specific steps that were used to assess the citizen's own property.

Technologies for the Representing Phase of Knowledge Management

Technologies for the representing phase of the knowledge management
process include both off-the-shelf software, such as spreadsheets that provide
charting of selected data, and more customized data visualization tools used
to help mine information and understand relationships in a data warehousing
operation. The new buzzword in analysis and reporting software is OLAP,
or online analytical processing. OLAP technology essentially provides multiple views of the different dimensions and combinations of dimensions of
business data. For example, within a few seconds OLAP software would
allow one to contrast a view of "amount of sales by salesperson by month
by region" with a view of "amount of sales by item by salesperson by region,"
and so on. It is possible to create these multiple views of data because of
underlying relational database technology that has been designed to allow
for the maximum cross-referencing of data fields. One firm offering OLAP
tools, Brio (www.brio.com), suggests that their system will simplify complex
analytic functions by using intuitive data navigation tools such as pivot tables
and interactive charts.[3] These tools allow for "ad hoc drill-anywhere" visualization, as well as predefined drill paths and drill-to-detail capabilities.
Drilling refers to the ability to reach further into a database (i.e., from the
more abstract categories, such as "total tax revenues," to the most concrete

item, such as "a check from citizen Jane Doe for $400 for property taxes on the property at 632 Main St.").

Similarly, IBM's Data Explorer, which is still under development as of this writing, provides tools for "manipulating, transforming, processing, realizing, rendering and animating data and allow[s] for visualization and analysis methods based on points, lines, areas, volumes, images or geometric primitives in any combination" (http://www.research.ibm.com/dx/faq.html).

More advanced applications now generate information landscapes from text data that allow users to see the density of ideas (visualized as mountain peaks) and their relationships visualized as the proximity of the various topical points on the landscape. These visualizations allow managers to better understand and interpret relationships and trends in large data sets. (See http://www.cartia.com for an example.)

Intelligent Agents and the Future of Government Service Delivery

Much of the knowledge management technology that is likely to transform organizations in the next decade is still in the lab. For example, researchers at Carnegie-Mellon University and the MIT Media Lab are developing systems that allow intelligent agents to communicate, share knowledge and negotiate exchanges. Agents are simple computerized routines that continue to perform a function as long as the conditions that activate an agent exist. An agent, for example, might check your electrical use and notify you when use exceeds a certain level, or it might roam the Web to see if any of your friends are online, or it might seek out the best interest rate among local banks. In the future, it is likely that people and institutions will use numerous agents to perform routine tasks. The services provided by agents will become more valuable as agents themselves communicate, particularly around functions that are routine. If, for example, governments and citizens shared such technology, it would be possible to further customize the delivery of services to citizens and the extraction of information from citizens. Example uses of this advanced technology in government might include:

- Automated notification and negotiation of government sales of surplus property.

- Governments automatically passing on new information that the agents for citizens suggest would be of interest (given recent indications of interest on the part of citizens, e.g., through their Web browsing habits).

- Governments' customized packaging of information and reminders based on information provided by the citizen's agent. These agents, for example, might track the citizen's bill, tax and fee paying habits and identify occasions when a reminder from the government would be effective and when it would be just 'junk mail.'

EVALUATING NEW KNOWLEDGE MANAGEMENT SYSTEMS

Because of its relatively short history, particularly in the public sector, there is little experience with evaluating the effectiveness of knowledge management. One company, Mitre Corporation, has touted its experience in evaluating knowledge management impacts. Mitre's experience in this area is relevant because, as a nonprofit firm that provides system engineering expertise to federal agencies, its benchmarks for success are service- rather than profit-oriented, mirroring those of a public agency. Mitre looked at a number of success measures and then estimated the dollar value of the benefits. A review of these benefits, as outlined in *CIO Magazine* (Young 2000), however, suggests that Mitre uses the term "knowledge management" to include numerous practice that, technically speaking, are more instances of work reengineering than knowledge management per se. One of the key benefits identified, for example, is the ability to move more administrative tasks onto a self-service basis. Using the new "knowledge management" system, Mitre reports that employees are able to update their own personnel records. A second measure of the system's success was the amount of time employees spent in managing documents. Because Mitre's system was designed to automatically translate all documents into HTML (the language of the Web) and to index the documents, staff time could be used for more productive purposes while the documents themselves became available through the entire company and worldwide through Intranet/Internet access. Mitre's system in this and other regards incorporates benefits of an enterprise resource planning system. These include the ability to track prices, identify the status of signed-out property, purchase and track goods online, and fill out electronic time cards. These capabilities substantially reduce the time that staff spend in performing these functions, but they do not represent any particular advances over enterprise-level work redesign efforts. Similarly, Mitre cites the cost savings from a reduced need for training new employees due to the system reducing turnover by making it possible for more employees to telecommute. Again, this capability is one that follows Hammer's work redesign principle, "Enhance access to central databases."

With respect to tasks that are definitely knowledge management functions, Mitre's system supports the ability of employees to search a knowledge base that includes information from most of the major functional areas and projects of the corporation. Now, for example, employees can get answers to their human resource questions without having to call on the staff of the human resource office. Hence, one measure of improvement can be a reduction in the per capita calls to the human resource unit. This measure assumes, however, that there are no other events—such as a change in benefits—that have led to either an increase or a decrease in the need to contact that unit. An alternative measure in these instances would be an assessment of the complexity of the calls that are made. That is, if the system is adequately answering routine questions, the human resource staff should be left with a higher proportion of complex questions that require innovative responses. More prosaically, managers can assess knowledge management systems by looking at the size of the knowledge base and the number of times the system is accessed. At Mitre, the audit team took this process one step further by analyzing the Web logs (all the documents are stored on a Web server) so as to identity the specific topics and Web folders that are used. The team could also look at the order of access to gain a better understanding of the typical patterns of navigating the information. Documentation of navigation patterns could suggest a better organization of the available knowledge for the future. Moreover, the system also allows the audit group to measure interorganizational collaboration. Employees were each given a Web page on which information about their skills, projects and interests was published. By tracking which employee homepages were accessed by whom and how often, the audit group could begin to get a better picture of how knowledge was being shared. In addition, employees are encouraged to publish information. Access of this published information (either within a unit or across units) is tracked, thereby providing measures of different types and levels of collaboration.

In addition to these direct measures of knowledge base size and use, public managers can always use survey methods to help identify the strengths and weaknesses of a new information system. Mitre, for example, found that 91 percent of employee respondents felt that the new system improved productivity. On the other hand, only 61 percent reported that they could find what they needed faster than ever before. The gap in these figures suggests one of the inherent dilemmas of knowledge management systems. As systems grow in size and in information capacity, improvements in the quality of the search engines and the human skill needed to find the desired information often cannot keep up.

Why Knowledge Management? Why Now?

Until recently, the need for knowledge management was not apparent for a number of reasons. First, with the exception of professional researchers, most employees and managers did not have much diverse information to manage. Instead a certain limited number of data points were identified as central, in part because they were the only data points available. One of the key values of knowledge management is the systematic approach that it outlines for capturing and distributing the undocumented knowledge of managers and staff. This documentation function is particularly important whenever worker turnover or retirement rates are high, whenever the knowledge base far outstrips the memory capacity of any one worker, or whenever there is a chance that a critical capacity will be lost because it resides in only one or two workers who may change jobs or be assigned more work than they can possibly do. While these challenging circumstances are not new, knowledge management can help governments to respond to them more effectively.

Second, the data that were available tended not to be real-time data. Hence, although these data could be used to chart progress, encourage change in control procedures, and provide the rationale for broadly redesigning work, they could not be used to actually inform work at the point of day-to-day decisions. Third, because of more limited data collection and because of the lack of enterprise-level systems (i.e., systems that collect and link data for a large spectrum of purposes across the entire organization), few efforts could be made to create new knowledge from existing information. Fourth, sophisticated information processing tools (e.g., for natural language processing, data mining, filtering and cross-referencing) had not yet been developed. For these reasons and because management was considered an art that could not be performed by a machine, knowledge management was not seen as a potential aid to organizational functioning.

In many fields, the conditions that kept knowledge management from being seen as a vital part of organizational development have disappeared. Knowledge management represents a second-generation development in that knowledge management systems are designed to address the problems created by first-generation information systems. First-generation systems store a great deal of data, provide immediate access to some data, and enable some linking of data across domains. In addition to gains in productivity, however, these first-generation systems also tend to produce information overloads as well as a glut of disconnected information. The excess of data fragments that is produced but not used could potentially contribute to organizational productivity—if the data were adequately analyzed, synthesized, massaged and communicated. This is the challenge for creators of knowledge management systems. Most of the creators of this next generation of systems recognize that computers cannot and should not replace human judgment, but they nevertheless believe that they can build systems that will help managers distill data fragments into information.

Knowledge management is in many ways about creating order out of the chaos of excessive information. As Virginia Postel (1998) has noted, methods of indexing and tracking information have become one of the most important ways in which we order reality. She argues that while a library of all the world's books, shelved randomly, is a treasure, using such a library would be an incredible waste of time. Similarly, the Web has frequently been criticized for being overly ripe with information that is useless because it cannot be found and its quality cannot be ascertained. Only as more intelligence has been built into new search engines has use of the Web been able to match its promise.

KNOWLEDGE MANAGEMENT FOR INNOVATION

While the core of knowledge management is about knowing what you already know, the ultimate use of knowledge management is to foster innovation. As such, knowledge management should lead to the generation of new ideas. According to Hargadon and Sutton (2000), managers can help foster the generation of new ideas. However, to do so they must first relinquish the image of innovation being the product of a lone genius. Instead of this romantic ideal of invention, managers should adopt systematized approaches that are designed to produce new ideas. These approaches, Hargadon and Sutton argue, can be employed by practically any organization. The key in this regard is recognizing that innovators use old ideas as the raw materials for new ones. Hargadon and Sutton call strategies for encouraging the recall and use of old ideas knowledge "brokering," and they call the system for sustaining innovation "the knowledge brokering cycle." At the beginning of the cycle, managers and staff are encouraged and assisted to capture good ideas from a broad spectrum of sources. This is the stage in which knowledge management tools and technologies for cross-referencing data and information play a large role. However, knowledge management is only an enabling factor, not sufficient in itself to foster innovation. Managers and staff need to be trained and encouraged to use the knowledge management tools in ways that will potentially provide for new insights. Although executive managers can encourage managers and staff to work with the available tools, the real key to making this stage of knowledge brokering work is the development of relationships among people with different points of view and expertise. Here, simple low-tech measures like seating arrangements and break times that encourage talking across specialty areas, posters listing old ideas from a variety of sources, and the strategic placement of knowledge mavens (people who love to tell what they have just learned) are as important as the implementation of new technologies or communication tools.

The second and third stages of knowledge brokering involve keeping ideas alive and finding new uses for old ideas. Progress during these stages involves exploring ideas in groups and using ideas in new or unique circumstances. Again, executive managers can encourage this process by building environments that promote purposeful play and exchange among people with diverse points of view. Information technology tools and applications can be the medium in which such play occurs, but play can also be encouraged through the layout of physical space that naturally fosters interactions or through the recruitment of people who are naturally playful. Information technology tools or media that are particularly effective in helping people to play with ideas include such things as simulation games, modeling applications and visualization programs. Simulation or modeling programs can be used to test out both individual and group generated solutions to problems and to discuss the factors that impact the process being simulated. Generally, simulations should allow players to understand, challenge and change the underlying assumptions of the simulation so as to test new ideas and relationships. Simulations have been most frequently and effectively used by the various branches of the military to test new approaches to warfare. However, transportation and health departments, law enforcement, environmental and emergency management organizations, and even human services agencies have used simulation programs to help managers and staff to better understand the dynamics of their work. (See National Center for Simulation, http://www.simulationinformation.com.)

The fourth stage in the knowledge brokering cycle, Hargadon and Sutton suggest, involves turning promising concepts into real services, products and processes. At this stage, managers may propose developing prototypes of information systems to test the new process, service or product within a low-risk environment before going to scale.

Different governments may need to focus on different stages in the cycle or on each stage equally. For example, large governments are more likely to be hampered by the inherent difficulty in moving ideas from one unit to another. These governments should consider developing internal consulting groups whose job it is to broker knowledge across the entire organization. Smaller governments, on the other hand, may need to bring in people from the outside to help staff understand how something they already know is being used in a different way in another organization. All governments can help encourage the exchange of knowledge among existing workers through activities such as brown-bag lunches, where one or two workers simply explain what they are working on and the techniques they are using or considering.

The Tactical Advantages of Knowledge Management

Knowledge management can provide decision support and leverage in a wide variety of situations. (See Table 4.2.)

KNOWLEDGE MANAGEMENT AND A FOCUS ON THE INDIVIDUAL CITIZEN

Knowledge management represents a new level of use of information technology to enable complex analysis and customized retrieval of information. A major impetus for the development of knowledge management in the private sector is the realization that 80–90 percent of a company's sales typically come from just 20 percent of its customers (Taylor 1999). Businesses realized that if they customized the messages for and treatment of these customers, they could reap tremendous advantages. Governments are obviously different because people do not generally get to choose to opt out of

Table 4.2
Critical Advantages of Knowledge Management

Without Knowledge Management	Knowledge Management
Content or Data can be:	
Unclean: Include mistakes that could be identified by cross-referencing with other systems.	Helps managers identify prevalence and individual instances of unclean data.
Out-of-date: More up-to-date information can be generated through cross-referencing or through analytical techniques that identify "unreasonable" information.	Example Advantage: Only one mailing is sent to an address, and the address is the right one for the purpose of reaching the targeted audience.
Unlinked and Unappended: Information is presented out of context. Relevant information that would make the data meaningful or improve the decision process or service delivery is not part of the query results.	Provides managers with supplemental resources that can be explored in cases where a manager needs to know more before feeling comfortable with making a decision. Links to additional information are provided or the additional information is included.
	Example Advantages: A social worker who is considering requiring that a client return to school would know that the client was responsible for a disabled home-bound relative and would adjust the requirement accordingly.
	Emergency response teams would know the number and characteristics of people who were caught in a building through the combination of land, utility and social service records.
Overwhelming: So much information is presented that it is impossible to digest.	Information is filtered so that one can obtain information at different levels of detail.
	Example Advantage: A city utility bill processor is faced with a possible mistake in a customer's bill sometime in the last two years. Instead of the system bringing back 24 months of bills and payments, it returns only those bills that differ from the expected bill given past usage in similar months, thereby sorting the important from the unimportant information.
Context-less: One does not know who else is aware of the same information.	Information about who else has accessed the document is available.

Table 4.2 (continued)

Without Knowledge Management	Knowledge Management
	Example Advantages: A plumbing inspector knows that the electrical and construction inspectors have completed their work and that once he has approved the plumbing he can also issue the occupancy permit. A social worker knows that the client's doctor has access to the social worker's most recent case notes, thereby making it unnecessary for the social worker to call the doctor to relate the same information.
Pattern-less: Patterns in the data are not identified or tracked.	Allows decision makers to understand the impacts of decisions on different groups or to identify where service needs or uses are greatest.
	Example Advantage: A government that wanted to insure that the overall impact of a series of decisions did not adversely impact any one group could do so. A knowledge management system would track costs and benefits to specific groups over time. Similarly, such a system could identify the profile of particularly high or low users of services or citizens who frequently or infrequently complain about service delivery.
Memory-less: Best practices are not identified or suggested by the system, or represent crude, rather than customized, advice.	Supports operational personnel by quickly identifying the best practices within very specific contexts and historical experiences.
	Example Advantages: Water pollution workers inventory complaints about water quality. The system analyzes all related complaints (e.g., by type of problem, area of problem, water system components involved, etc.) in specified time periods and provides suggestions as to possible systemic problems that should be investigated.

Table 4.2 (continued)
Critical Advantages of Knowledge Management

Without Knowledge Management	Knowledge Management
	Upon receiving a call from Mr. Jones, the city clerk is able to use a knowledge system to note that Mr. Jones has called four times previously about a similar issue. The clerk is also able to note that Councilman Henry is the representative who has had the greatest success in handling Mr. Jones' problems in the past. The system suggests letting Councilman Henry handle the call, but also suggests that Sarah Smith, an assistant city clerk, might have some success as well (because she possesses knowledge and interpersonal characteristics similar to those of Councilman Henry).
Produced at the wrong time: Knowledge or new information arrives at a decision maker's desktop whenever it is produced rather than whenever it is needed.	Knowledge (including access to tutorials and training) is provided in a just-in-time fashion such that managers and staff are continually learning in small chunks the information that they need to meet the next challenge.
	Example Advantages: A new member of the planning commission hears the term "transferable development rights" in a commission discussion. The member logs onto the city's knowledge management site and types in the term. She is prompted to identify (or test) her level of existing knowledge and to specify the ultimate purpose to which the desired new knowledge is to be put and the learner's level of desired expertise. With this information the system produces a series of tutorials and lessons customized to the current learning needs of the system user.

government or government services. Nevertheless, the 80/20 logic still holds true in many areas of government service that are discretionary (e.g., participation in recreation, wellness and social service programs, service on boards and advisory groups, use of economic development offerings, etc.). Also, it is frequently noticed that a small percentage of the citizenry account for the vast majority of complaints about services or decisions. However, these vocal complainers are likely to contribute to a more general level of dissatisfaction among the citizenry. As such, better management of and attention to these more sensitive citizens could pay off in terms of higher levels of satisfaction with government and greater support for new governmental initiatives. Similar processes could assist with management of consultants and government partners.

KNOWLEDGE MANAGEMENT AND CORE TECHNOLOGIES: DATA WAREHOUSING AND METADATA

Data Warehousing in Knowledge Management

Knowledge management and data warehousing are related in the sense that data warehousing or the use of IT systems to bridge or coalesce data from dispersed and possibly incompatible systems will typically enable managers to put in place more powerful knowledge management applications.

Data warehousing is typically described as having three components: (1) an input component to acquire data from legacy systems and outside sources. This component identifies, copies and formats data for loading into the warehouse; (2) a storage component that is typically centered around a large relational database addressed through computers that use multiple processors to speed input, querying and output; and (3) an access component that allows different end-users (e.g., PCs, terminals, workstations, etc.) to draw data from the warehouse in ways that are most helpful to the particular users of the system. The more sophisticated the design of the access component— that is, the more this component includes data mining and analysis applications such as data discovery, statistical, and data visualization tools—the more data warehousing approaches the implementation of a knowledge management support system.

Ultimately, however, what distinguishes knowledge management from a well-developed data warehousing operation is the focus of knowledge management on generating new work routines. That is, in a knowledge management effort the tasks of data formatting, input, storage, extraction and interpretation are developed with the idea of refining how workers go about their jobs. Obviously, data warehousing can be an important tool in a knowledge management effort. One can establish a data warehouse for the more limited purpose of simply improving one's ability to access information quickly and effectively. If this is the case, then integrating the data warehouse operation with efforts to change organizational practices may not be needed. However, if one does want to more tightly integrate information, knowledge and practice, the effort will likely take on an entirely different character. These issues will be explored more fully in later chapters.

Metadata in Knowledge Management

Earlier in this chapter, I identified some technologies (e.g., Web search engines) for the finding, capturing and retrieving phases of the knowledge management process. Despite the increases in the power of today's search engines, these technologies still tend to provide a high level of unsatisfactory results. The situations in which unsatisfactory results are most likely to occur are those where little is known about the data being searched. Knowing something about the data being searched makes them easier to find. When information about data is systematized and appropriately stored for retrieval, it is called metadata. What makes metadata so important is that they allow us to find information more quickly and with fewer false turns. They provide labels (e.g., subject headings, name of authors, date of origin, category of information) or key information that will enable more efficient searching. Metadata are essentially an electronic version of the old library card catalog. Metadata typically extend to issues that are beyond the scope of the ordinary library card and may include such information related to the origin, location, scope, scale and focus of the data as well as the number, type and content of records and fields, and the available data formats or conversion utilities. A database of metadata would facilitate searching documents by key concepts (e.g., crime data), function or data domain (e.g., payroll, budget, personnel, inventory, insurance, etc.) or document type (e.g., an e-mail, a data file, a word processing file, an image or an audio file). By knowing these facts about the data, one can narrow one's search and can also better understand the meaning of the data once they are retrieved or check for potential data anomalies. For example, if the metadata told the value ranges for particular data fields, the manager would be more likely to know whether the data were realistic or not. If the metadata indicated that values of the numbers in the public employee salary field ranged from $10,000 to $1 million, a public manager would certainly want to take a second look at the data quality. However, were the same metadata indicated for a database of budget figures, there would be few obvious reasons to question the accuracy of the data. Metadata can convey the context for a piece of information. This is particularly useful in geographic information system files, where the scope and projection of a map as well as the objects it contains are often as important as the area that the file covers.

As the variety of file types and application types has increased, metadata have become more important to managers. Data about information are needed in order to manage the information. One must be able to know, for example, that a word processing file is a WordPerfect file in order to be able to get to the information in the file. Similar data about data are needed for voice mail and e-mail systems, image and picture files, GIS files, CD-ROMs, books and paper files, movies, and Web pages. In each case, different data may be needed. For example, you may need to know when and where a photograph was shot and the subject of the photo, but the photo's delivery date may not be important. In contrast, with an e-mail, data about the time of delivery can be very important. Public managers who oversee Web publishing operations may be particularly concerned with data about copyright and fair use of an image or document, while a public manager in a GIS department may be most interested in whether the scale of a GIS map tile will match the scale needed to successfully merge existing data with the base map.

Providing metadata can promote more effective sharing of information and thereby prevent public managers from having to reinvent a product or service that has already been developed elsewhere. However, creating metadata has its own costs. These costs can be particularly steep if the organization has many noncataloged information products. Hence, managers need to identify the potential return on investment of particular metadata projects. Metadata projects that are related to information about images or maps have been particularly cost-effective because the alternative is to have individual human beings view thousands of photos or watch hundreds or thousands of videos to find the small number of items that might fit the search criteria. The time spent in these manual searches can easily be cost prohibitive. Metadata projects related to cataloging text-based documents may be less cost-effective because of the ability of search engines to find desired documents based on keywords, word patterns or even whole concepts. The cost of developing metadata for text-based documents must be weighed against the expected future costs of conducting information searches without the benefit of metadata.[4]

Metadata management has its own technology tools and organizational imperatives. Foremost among the tools are metadata registers, data dictionaries, organized or hierarchical directories, locators and search engines. Table 4.3 shows a sample line from a data dictionary created by the U.S. Office of Personnel Management.

Organizationally, metadata management should be handled by the unit in charge of information management. When such a unit does not exist, or when the actual work of information management is being done elsewhere in the organization, metadata management should be handled where the actual work is being done because it is often important that the people registering the metadata are knowledgeable about the content of the data being cataloged.

Public managers who create metadata systems may forget that even as metadata make it easier to find needed information, they can also help critics to find information that may reflect poorly on the government. Public managers who would like to avoid helping their critics, however, will have little legal recourse because the same state and federal freedom of information laws that open basic information or records to the public also open metadata files. In many cases the courts are requiring that public managers

Table 4.3
Sample Data Dictionary Record

Data Element Number	Data Element Name	Data Element Description	Shortname	Format
7	Absence_ Continuous_No	"No" check box indicator that the employee had a continuous absence of at least 3 weeks on account of sickness or injury	Absence_Cont _N	1X (a single character field)

Source: Official Personnel Folder Data Dictionary. (1998). Washington, DC: Human Resources Technology Council, U.S. Office of Personnel Management, December, p. 7.

treat metadata in the same way as the information being described. That is, they need to be stored with the same security and corruption precautions and must be made available as evidence for disputants in court cases (CIO Council 1999).

THE FUTURE OF KNOWLEDGE MANAGEMENT

As part of a business consultant product line, knowledge management may go the way of other business consulting fads (Business: Fading fads 2000). Moreover, a good argument can be made that knowledge management is not for all organizations, and that it represents a level of system and organizational development that must be founded on having achieved earlier development goals (e.g., related to data processing, business process redesign, etc.). However, as more organizations become proficient in the basics of information systems, technologies and organizational development for their implementation, knowledge management—whether it is still called by the same name or not—will take on increasing importance. Nevertheless, for knowledge management to progress as a management function, we will need to fill some of the gaps in our understanding of it. For example, Alter (2000) has identified three such gaps:

1. A gap between what knowledge management practitioners and researchers say about assessing the value of knowledge. Practitioners tend to be pessimistic about such measurement because of the intangible nature of the units of knowledge. Researchers, on the other hand, suggest that executive managers and financial officers will not take knowledge management seriously until such measures become available and usable.

2. A gap between practitioners who identify successful knowledge management projects as those that have narrow, precise goals and IT consulting firms that want

organizations to build very large and comprehensive (ERP-like) systems for gathering and storing knowledge and retrieving information.

3. A gap between what IT staff think of as the core of knowledge management (i.e., computers) and what visionary thinkers like Xerox Parc's chief, John Seely Brown, see as the core and appropriate focus of knowledge management (i.e., how people interact with and use information).

Overcoming these gaps will likely demand more collaborative research among practitioners, academic researchers and business consultants.

NOTES

1. This list was adapted from several chapters in Duffin 1988.

2. Conversation with Edward Stern, OSHA manager in charge of expert systems development, July 12, 2000.

3. A pivot table is an interactive table that summarizes and analyzes data from existing lists and tables.

4. California Governor Gray Davis and New York Governor George Pataki, "Internet Voting: Possibilities and Challenges," *San Diego Union-Tribune*, January 18, 2000.

REFERENCES

Alter, A. E. (2000). Knowledge management's "theory-doing gap." *Computerworld* 34 (15): 33.

Armour, P. G. (2000). The case for a new business model. *Communications of the ACM*, 43 (8): 19–23.

Bittner, J., C. DuBois, and J. O'Looney. (1998). *Wiser Purchasing: Improved Results for Georgia's Children and Families*. Athens, GA: Carl Vinson Institute of Government.

Brown, J. S., and P. Duguid. (2000). Balancing act: How to capture knowledge without killing it. *Harvard Business Review* 78 (3): 73–82.

Business: Fading fads. (2000). *The Economist*, 355 (8167): 60–62.

CIO Council. (1999). What every CIO needs to know about metadata. February. Found at http://www.cio.gov/docs/metadata.htm.

Cohen, S., and J. Moore. (2000). Today's buzzword: CRM (customer relationship management). *PM* 82 (4): 10–13.

Davenport, T. (2000). Power to the people. *CIO Magazine*, June 1. http://www.cio.com.

Duffin, P. H., ed. (1988). *Knowledge Based Systems: Applications in Administrative Government*. Central Computer and Telecommunications Agency. London: Ellis Harwood Ltd.

Electronic College of Process Innovation. (1995). *Acquisition Best Practices: Section 1: Summary of Acquisition Reform Benchmark Cases*. Washington, DC: Electronic College of Process Innovation.

Emerson, T. (1999). What comes after knowledge management? Wearable computers, smart rooms, and virtual humans. *Information Outlook* 3 (4): 13–14.

Erwin, W. B. (1995). *Acquisition Best Practices: Section 11: U.S. Patent and Trademark Office*. Washington, DC: Electronic College of Process Innovation.

Hargadon, A., and R. I. Sutton. (2000). Building an innovation factory. *Harvard Business Review* 78 (3): 157–169.

Kidd, R. C., and R. J. Carlson. (1992). A truly magic solution. In *Innovative Applications of Artificial Intelligence* 4, ed. Carlisle Scott and Phil Klahr. Menlo Park, CA: AAAI Press, 237–47.

Laurent, A. (2000). Results rule. *Government Executive* 32 (1): 11–14.

Liebowitz, J. (1997). *The Handbook on Expert Systems*. Boca Raton, FL: CRC Press.

Maeil Business Newspaper. (1998). Knowledge management, knowledge organizations and knowledge workers: A view from the front lines. Dr. Yogesh Malhotra's interview with *Maeil Business Newspaper*. *Maeil Business Newspaper*, February 19.

National Center for Simulation. http://simulationinformation.com/index2.html.

Nelson, S. (2000). Gartner Interactive: Past Questions and Answers. Found at http://www.gartner.com/public/static/crm/crm_qa.html.

O'Looney, J. (1997). *Beyond Maps: GIS and Decision Making in Local Government*. Washington, DC: International City/County Management Association.

Postel, V. (1998). The freedom of order. *Forbes*, ASAP Supplement 106, August 24.

Ross, J. W. (1999). Clueless execs still keep ERP from delivering value. *Computerworld* 33 (38): 30.

Shaw, M. R. (1988). Applying expert systems to environmental management and control problems. In *Knowledge Based Systems: Applications in Administrative Government*, ed. P. H. Duffin. Central Computer and Telecommunications Agency. London: Ellis Harwood Ltd.

Soh, C. (2000). Cultural fits and misfits: Is ERP a universal solution? *Communications of the ACM* 43 (4): 47–52.

Stedman C. (1999). Failed ERP gamble haunts Hershey. *Computerworld* 33 (44): 89.

Taylor, V. (1999). Technology innovation and processing information: Content and context. *Vital Speeches of the Day* 65 (7): 201–4.

Van Buren, M. E. (1999). A yardstick for knowledge management. *Training and Development* 53 (5): 71–78.

Willcocks, L. P., and R. Stykes. (2000). The role of the CIO and IT function in ERP. *Communications of the ACM* 43 (4): 32–39.

Young, D. (2000). An audit tale. *CIO Magazine*, May 1 (http://www.cio.com).

5

The Dark Side of Digital Government and Knowledge Management

In the discussion so far, the emergence of wired government has been viewed as a positive development—though one that presents plenty of challenges to public managers. In this chapter, we explore aspects of digital or wired government that more deeply challenge traditional public management values, practices, ethics and customs. The term "dark side" is not meant to have bad or sinister connotations, however. Rather, it is used here to indicate that we can only "see darkly" the impact of particular new technologies, trends and practices that have arisen as part of the e-government revolution. This lack of complete understanding is particularly evident in terms of possible impacts on democratic governance and the legitimacy of public management.

PROFILING AND PRIVACY IN THE PUBLIC SECTOR

Two potential problems with knowledge management approaches have been identified. First, it may be inappropriate for governments to attempt to improve their image and service delivery evaluations through processes that involve cross-referencing of information, creation of citizen profiles, and the personalizing of levels and types of services and information based on a citizen's profile. For example, to what degree is it appropriate to treat a frequent service user (or frequent voter) who expresses a concern about service quality differently than a person who only infrequently interacts with government on any level? What about a citizen who has several children involved in a government program? Is it appropriate to send the frequent service user to one's most experienced or skillful staff while sending the infrequent user to a novice staff member? Is it appropriate to spend more time with one citizen than another? If so, how much more? Should systems be designed to accurately inform staff about the frequency of complaints made by individual citizens? What about the frequency of compliments or commendations?

HEARING, UNDERSTANDING AND RESPONDING TO THE PUBLIC VOICE

Becoming a wired organization will depend heavily on policies that prevent governments from suffering a loss of legitimacy due to an inability to respond to citizens in expected, traditional ways. In particular, policy makers will have to decide how to handle the additional information citizens can generate and transmit to government using electronic networks. There is increasing evidence that the availability of electronic communication networks has substantially changed the operations environment for governments. For example, when the U.S. Department of Agriculture allowed public comments via e-mail on a proposed rule, the number of responses increased from an expected 4,000 (based on experiences with written communications) to over 275,000.[1] Similarly, at the local government level, staff who work with citizen advisory boards are finding that board members who once might have written an occasional short letter on an issue are now sending several e-mails a week.[2]

Ideally, using knowledge management tools would allow these communications to be better aggregated, understood and responded to and appropriately incorporated into government decision making. Unfortunately, the ideal applications of knowledge management may not yet be possible. Without ideal knowledge management tools, governments must develop policies and standards that use knowledge management principles, but imperfectly. For example, given an overload of requests for government information, public managers will likely be forced to develop standards for the timely and appropriate response to receipt of e-mail requests. Given the availability of citizen profile information (through knowledge management systems that cross-reference and compile information from disparate sources), it is probable that we will see the development of standards for response times and completeness of responses that may differ depending on such things as the status of the person making the request, the number of previous requests, the number of requests made within a particular time period, the time and expense demands on staff in completing the response, and the topical area of the inquiry. While circumstances (e.g., the need to protect staff from communications overload) may force managers to create standards that determine who will receive more immediate or more thorough responses from government, some managers may be tempted to avoid developing explicit policies regarding priority responses, as these could appear to involve their making a "political" choice about the worthiness of certain issue areas or certain citizen groups. In such instances, public managers may prefer that these priorities be left unstated. Public managers who take this position, however, are essentially leaving an important public policy area in the hands of employees. While trusted employees may use their discretion in exemplary ways, other employees may use their discretion in ways that can undermine the efficiency or credibility of the government. In addition, avoiding standard-creation does not mean that "preferential" treatment does not occur; rather, it means that the preferential treatment that does occur will not be visible to managers, making it less likely that they will be able to minimize the political fallout of a staff member using his or her discretion inappropriately. Finally, avoiding the development of standards for citizen (or stakeholder) response can also mean that the government will not be able to use knowledge management tools (e.g., tools that assign a priority weight to a citizen query) to help improve their overall responsiveness to citizens.

Obviously, public managers are also responsible for notifying policy makers that the communications workload has increased and that new resources may be needed to maintain appropriate dialog with citizens, advisory bodies and interest groups. Although policy makers may never provide sufficient resources to fully create the desired citizen response system, public managers are not thereby exempted from the duty to develop the best response system possible within budget limitations.

Technology and Mediating Communications Among Governments and Their Constituents

Finally, public managers need to look toward the future and develop policy for implementing technology that acts as a mediating mechanism with respect to communication between (or among) governments, citizens, contractors, interest groups and advisory groups. Mediating mechanisms are technical or social practices that act to channel, sort and filter information in ways that make it more understandable as a whole in a more timely manner. Examples of such mechanisms to decrease the burden of administrative rule making include the following:

- The use of artificial intelligence to summarize the natural language inputs of citizens.
- Providing a public forum Internet space for citizen discussion, and charging the volunteer participants in this discussion with producing a majority (and possibly a minority) report.
- Government organization (or citizen self-organization) of an issue into subtopics to be processed in Internet discussion spaces (with the subgroup responsible for a committee report).
- Having to pass a "basic knowledge test" prior to providing online input that will be guaranteed a hearing by a public official (content for the test would be provided by a frequently asked questions briefing).

- Government promotion of speech norms that discourage the repetition of ideas already posted.
- The requirement that a citizen get another citizen to validate that an opinion was original and worthy of consideration.
- Requiring citizens to provide basic identifying information.
- The use of a one-click "ditto" option that would allow a citizen to indicate agreement with an already posted comment without having to repeat it.
- Charging citizens a nominal fee (e.g., 25 cents to deliver an e-mail to a government office holding online public input on a policy issue) to cut down on duplicative messages or e-mails that are forwarded versions of the same message.

Some of these mechanisms rely on technology (e.g., artificial intelligence) to fix a problem that was created by a defining feature of another technology (e.g., the ease of dashing off an e-mail), while other mechanisms (e.g., requiring a posting fee or validation of one's communication by a fellow citizen) attempt to put in place a process that helps to reestablish the earlier, pre-Internet relationship between government and its correspondents. Obviously, many of these mechanisms are not desirable—except in light of potentially even more undesirable alternatives such as the inability to establish and implement a policy agenda in a timely fashion.

PREMATURE CODIFICATION OF BEST PRACTICES

A third potential problem with knowledge management is that it may lead to a premature codification of knowledge and enforced best practices, rather than to more innovative and effective decisions and services.

Writing in *Fortune*, Michael Schrage (1999) paints the following picture of a knowledge management–oriented organization:

At world-class organizations like General Electric and Asea Brown Boveri, intranets that once carried urgent e-mail and turgid PowerPoint presentations now store databases enumerating the performance standards and process practices deemed "best." In theory, such immaculately networked cultures are supposed to "empower" people to be better employees. In practice, these knowledge-management networks and "best practice" databases create brave new infrastructures that effectively enforce employee compliance with organizational norms. (p. 198)

In some ways the problem Schrage identifies is based on a straw-man version of knowledge management. However, every management technique, implemented without subtlety, can become a straitjacket for organizational development. Theoretically speaking, once a practice is codified into new procedural rules and processes, it should cease to be understood as part of knowledge management. Rather, codification of best practices is really work reengineering. When work is reengineered, the role of knowledge management then becomes to identify the new informal practices that are used by employees either to make the procedures work or to get around procedures that present barriers to the mission of the government. Real knowledge management is about creating the conditions for ongoing applied research in an organization. Nevertheless, it is the nature of all new management practices to ossify into something much less liberating than was originally intended.

THE MALLEABILITY OF GOVERNANCE IN CYBERSPACE

The fourth potential dark area in the establishment of digital government concerns the creation of new channels and routines for decision making. The channels, which will combine new virtual public spaces and the management of knowledge and communications within those spaces, will have the greatest impact as they begin to replace the key ways in which democratic governments have made decisions—via open meetings and administrative rule making. While it is understood that knowledge management impacts the administration of government, when new channels for decision making are created, the impact will be much more profound. Within this general area of the malleability of governance procedures, two subtopics are addressed below: (1) electronic policy and rule making and (2) electronic meetings.

Electronic Policy and Rule Making

Citizens have numerous avenues by which to influence government behavior, for example, through electoral politics, service on boards and advisory groups, petitions, lobbying, and attendance at public hearings and forums. One of the most effective ways to influence government behavior, however, is through participation in rule making. Rule making occurs whenever an executive department is charged with deciding how to implement a policy developed by the legislative branch. Policy is often strategic in nature, outlining the general goal or legislative intent. Rules, on the other hand, represent the "details." These details often make the difference between an effective and a gutted policy or law.

Whereas elected officials are the key players in strategic policy making, public managers are the key public sector players in rule making. However, rule making does not take place in a vacuum any more than policy making does. Traditionally, however, citizen and interest group participation in rule making has been limited to policy insiders and groups with a strong interest in a policy area. Obviously a citizen or business leader's desire to participate in rule making will be limited to those cases where they have a strong material or political interest in the issues or programs being defined by the proposed rule. However, even among interested citizens participation is often circumscribed by logistical difficulties inherent in the rule-making process. In particular, citizen participation has often been constrained by individual citizens' lack of resources or lack of access to high-quality information. Progressive public managers can and likely will employ Internet services and other electronic communications technologies to address this situation. However, in doing so, these public managers need to be careful about how the choice of technologies will impact governance in the long term.

Before identifying IT developments impacting administrative rule making, it is important for the reader to have some understanding of the law underlying the rule-making process. The federal government and most state governments have administrative procedure acts that define the exact steps for rule making within the respective jurisdiction. For our purposes, these procedures can be categorized into four types: (1) notification, (2) format, (3) consideration, and (4) reporting.

Notification

Notification is generally the stage at which resource-poor citizens are most disadvantaged by the traditional rule-making process. Governments typically provide for at least thirty day's notice of a proposed rule-making decision. Many governments also mandate that a short summary of the rule be created so that citizens do not have to read a long, complex notification document to determine a possible interest. Where the system tends to break down is in the notification publication and distribution. At the federal level, notification through the primary publication sources (chiefly the *Federal Register* and *Commerce Business Daily*) is often unsuccessful because the chosen notification outlets are so voluminous as to essentially hide the desired "twig" of information within a forest of other notices, pronouncements and offerings. These primary notification outlets are in many cases too broad in the scope of information they provide to be useful to the average citizen. To keep track of proposed new rules within a single bureau of a U.S. government department, a citizen must obtain daily access to these publications and must review at least the table of contents, and sometimes more than that. Administrative procedures acts will often provide citizens or interest groups with more time-husbanding information services—if the citizen is willing to pay. For example, Georgia's act reads as follows:

The notice shall be mailed to all persons who have requested in writing that they be placed upon a mailing list which shall be maintained by the agency for advance notice of its rule-making proceedings and who have tendered the actual cost of such mailing as from time to time estimated by the agency.

While this service is indeed preferable to being kept in the dark, it will likely be superseded by intelligent notification services for proposed rule making. Such a service is already being developed for the state of Alaska (see http://notes.state.ak.us/pn/pubnotic.nsf/). This Online Public Notice Web site provides comprehensive listings of proposed rule changes as well as meeting and contract opportunity notices. The listings are searchable and are organized by category, department, location and publication date. Unfortunately, users of the service must still drill down through varied departmental information to be able to identify the rule or notice of interest. However, once the site is further developed, it should be able to manage an e-mail list of persons who wish to be informed on particular topic areas. Based on an interview with an employee of Radian, Inc., located in Northern Virginia, there are definitely plans at this firm to create a sophisticated notification system for federal government rule making.

Format

The format of citizen participation is also frequently specified in the government's administrative procedures act. In Georgia, for example, the agency proposing a rule or rule change must "afford to all interested persons reasonable opportunity to submit data, views, or arguments, orally or in writing."

There are additional rules specifying when the government must afford opportunities for oral or written presentations. What is interesting is that procedural rules like Georgia's can, unbeknownst to the rules' authors, be biased against electronic transmission of views or arguments. This is the case because it is possible for courts to interpret electronic transmissions as not being writing. Such a situation occurred in Georgia a few years ago when an office of the Department of Transportation refused to consider a document submitted by fax as being "writing," the format for submittal specified by law. This confusion has since been rectified by new legislation, but the problem with public managers wanting to open up rule making to electronic delivery may not always be a trivial one. For example, Keith Johnson, the U.S. Department of Agriculture manager who first experimented with electronic rule making at the federal level, had to first get the approval of the general counsel before initiating the project.

Johnson's experience with electronic rule making suggests the following lessons regarding the format for soliciting citizen input:

- If one is interested only in quantity and ease of commenting, e-mail is the best vehicle for channeling comments. However, use of e-mail is more likely to reduce the overall quality of the comments and suggestions.
- Using a Web form for comment solicitation presents a number of advantages, including:
  - The ability to capture name, address and legislative district information that can then be used to develop customized reports for legislators.
  - The ability to structure information in ways that facilitate the understanding and organization of the information by department representatives.

- The ability automatically to store the information in databases for analysis.
- The ability to provide real-time listing of comments by responders. This posting of comments, in turn, leads to:
  - more dialog, feedback and responses among the citizens making comments; and
  - reduction in the "wait till the last moment to submit one's comments so that no one has time to respond to one's points" syndrome that Johnson had observed in the typical written comment process.

Attempts to have users identify the specific rule section on which they are commenting will often fail. Users will typically choose the "All Sections" default choice even when they are commenting on a specific section. Users are not willing to work to make the lives of bureaucrats easier. As such, the intelligence for organizing the comments will likely need to be transparent to users. One possible method would be to have links for comment forms/ e-mail boxes built into a Web version of the document. A citizen could, for example, click on a link that brought up a form for commenting on that particular section or point. The link itself would contain information about the section, so the user could simply make a statement such as "I don't agree with this" without having to cite the section itself. On the receiving end, the public manager would read something like "Jane Jones does not agree with the part of the proposed rule (Section 10-b) that calls for limiting the use of pesticides on soils containing more than 20% residuals."

Consideration

Consideration concerns the level of attention that a public employee is required to give to a citizen's views or comments. In the Federal Administrative Procedures Act, the standard for consideration is "fully and completely assess." The parallel act in Georgia simply asks that the agency "consider fully all written and oral submissions." What this means in practical terms, however, is not always clear. A brief review of cases involving alleged violations of the Administrative Procedures Act indicates that agency actions are likely to be set aside only where the agency has entirely failed to consider an important aspect of the problem or has offered an explanation for its decision that runs counter to the evidence before the agency. (See *Motor Vehicle Mfr. Ass'n* v. *State Farm Mutual Auto. Ins.*, 463 U.S. 29, 43 [1983].)

While agencies are unlikely to be reversed by the courts for minor violations of the mandate to "fully and completely assess" citizen comments, agency legal counsels are very likely to rule against the use of new technologies that could suggest an attempt to avoid this mandate. Yet, as agencies open up their rule making to easier participation by citizens, there may be a need to use automated content processing and analysis technologies to effectively provide full and complete assessment without having to hire dozens of new employees just to read the mail. The problem of giving consideration to each and every citizen comment came to the fore during the first use of electronic rule making at the Department of Agriculture. Keith Johnson reported that his office received 275,000 public comments related to proposed rules on organic produce. This was many hundreds of times the number of comments normally received through the mail. When Johnson's staff had completed assessment of the comments, they calculated that approximately 160,000, or about 58 percent, were comprised of cut-and-paste or forwarded form letters that had been sponsored by interest groups. However, a "full and complete assessment" of these copied letters requires as thorough a reading as one would conduct were the comments original. This is the case because without a full reading one cannot be sure that someone's comments do not diverge from the form letter contents halfway through the text. As a consequence, government offices that take the initiative to encourage citizen participation by bringing rule making online are essentially punished for their effort, condemned to read the same text over and over again.

Obviously what is needed to address the problem of having to consider too much material is the use of technology or the implementation of new procedures for online commenting on proposed rules. A listing of potential reforms for easing the burden of consideration would contain many of the ideas presented earlier in the section on technology and mediating communications among governments and their constituents.

While each of these methods takes a different approach to the problem, the use of artificial intelligence/natural language processing (NLP) may present the greatest promise in the long run, since this method would create little or no change in citizen behavior. However, employment of natural language processing does involve citizens being willing to trust that the technology will lead to a level of consideration equivalent to that provided for in current practice. Should we trust such a technology? Unfortunately, unlike database applications or applications for data analysis (e.g., SAS or SPSS) or even qualitative data analysis (e.g., Nudist), there are no truly off-the-shelf natural language processing programs that offer citizens assurance of an adequate level of consideration. Moreover, the applications citizens use that involve this technology (e.g., natural language search engines such as Ask Jeeves) have not exactly inspired confidence. The reason for this is that NLP programs are only as good as the underlying knowledge base. A knowledge base outlines the contexts and relationships among concepts, objects, actions, modifiers and qualifiers within a knowledge domain. For an NLP application to be able to simulate (e.g., through accurate summarizing of thousands of documents) the kind of consideration that human bureaucrats can give to a citizen's comments, the knowledge base must first be sufficiently developed. A few efforts of this type are currently being supported by government agencies such as the National Science Foundation. Additionally, a number of private firms (e.g., Brightware) are working with government and other organizations to develop practical uses of knowledge ware. Unfortunately, it is too soon to know whether an agency that invests in the development of a knowledge base for one rule-making procedure will then have a sufficiently rich and easily modified template so as to enable inexpensive and effective use of this technology in numerous rule-making tasks. However, even if the expense and effort involved in developing elaborate knowledge bases delay the full-fledged employment of NLP in rule making, simpler versions of these NLP technologies could be put to work in the near future. Drawing on the experience of the Department of Agriculture with electronic rule making, it is evident that the department could have benefited from a relatively simple NLP tool. Specifically, if it had an application that could identify and count all the form letters of a particular type, government staff would be freed from this onerous task.

Reporting

Administrative procedure acts also tend to specify the reporting on the adoption of a rule. In Georgia, for example, an agency, if requested to do so, must issue a concise statement of the principal reasons for and against its adoption and the reasons for giving consideration to a specific course of action.

At this stage in the process, the effective employment of information technology is much more contingent on the nature of the rule in question. While some analytical tools can support decision making by agency administrators, rules are only occasionally susceptible to definitive analysis. For example, a rule that implements a new land use policy may be analyzable within a geographic information system in terms of how the rule will impact such factors as transportation time, storm water runoff, and the need for new school buildings. In contrast, a rule that, for example, defines the term "organic" in terms of material inputs into farmed vegetables may not allow an analyst to measure the impact on existing organic farmers due to a lack of data about existing farming practices.

When there are opportunities for data analysis, a likely scenario is one where competing analyses are presented to the agency. In such cases, public managers can help support the values of an open society by offering to put entire analyses and research reports on the Internet. While it is unlikely that such data will be examined by a large number of citizens, the symbolic value of having complete access to the information used by decision makers is probably worth the small cost of electronic publishing.

Electronic policy making is still in the infant stages of development. However, much more will be learned about this process as public managers explore the various combinations of network protocol, data structuring and automated information processing. Before wholesale adoption of any one electronic policy-making process, it would be worthwhile to sponsor studies. One interesting study would be to have two parts of the same agency conduct rule making in both the traditional and in the most technologically enhanced manner, and then compare the two.

Electronic Communications and Open Meetings

While public managers will play the dominant role in developing IT support for administrative rule making, they are also likely to be substantially involved in decisions about developing the rules and architecture for public electronic meetings and other communications among citizens, public managers and policy makers. This section looks at administrative, legal, social and technological design issues involved in building electronic systems to support official public deliberation of policy issues.

Internet communications can now connect government officials—including elected officials—to each other in a dizzying variety of ways. While individual-to-individual e-mail is the most frequently used Internet communications method, governments can also sponsor or employ group or broadcast e-mail, chat, threaded discussion forums and listservs. One of the uncharted implications of these new communications methods is the degree to which a succession of electronic messages can simulate the dynamics of a meeting. The creation of meeting-like communications through electronic mediums represents one of the hidden benefits of the Internet. The federal government was the first to explicitly use the Internet for sponsorship of national electronic open meetings. As this benefit of cyberspace has become more salient, public officials are increasingly eager to use Internet communications tools to conduct the public's business. However, in some cases the ability to use this medium in a new manner represents a challenge to traditional legal conceptions and cultural understandings of "open public meetings." Given our desire for convenient and ubiquitous electronic communications and the flexibility of digital applications, it is likely that some form of electronic meetings will fulfill open meetings requirements. In the long run, however, overcoming legal barriers to electronic meetings will be less of a hurdle than our particular choice among the thousands of possibilities for virtual public meeting architectures. This choice will likely lay the groundwork for the future of democratic deliberations. In the following sections, I examine the current ways in which governments define open meetings and the required characteristics of these meetings. Then I outline some of the ways in which states have attempted to incorporate telecommunication opportunities into open meetings regulations. Finally, I identify eight key issues that need to be resolved before electronic public meetings can be effectively and appropriately incorporated into public deliberations.

The Basics of Open Meetings Laws

Most states' open meetings laws were obviously based on the understanding that public meetings will take place in a physical space and time. As the Texas Governmental Code states, "A governmental body shall give written notice of the date, hour, place, and subject of each meeting held by the governmental body" (Sec. 551.041). The typical open meetings law also requires that public officials announce the place and time of a meeting a certain number of hours in advance of the actual meeting.

Because of the underlying assumption that meetings will have a defined place, the time frame for such meetings is typically limited in that people will only be able to gather in a place for a relatively short span of time. As such, even though a council or commission may have a number of items on an agenda, citizens can usually participate in the part of the meeting in which they are interested without having to wait for unreasonable periods of time while other issues are discussed.

Although states differ somewhat in their definition of public meetings, the trend is definitely toward more openness. This trend is occurring along two dimensions. The first dimension is related to the characteristics of a discussion among public officials that would lead it to be subject to an open meetings requirement. On this dimension, for example, Texas law defines a deliberation that is potentially subject to open meetings regulations as "a verbal exchange . . . concerning an issue within the jurisdiction of the governmental body or any public business." While Texas law goes on to allow an exception to this definition in cases where the members of the governmental body are attending a convention, conference or workshop, Georgia recently amended its law so that a wider range of events are now subject to open meetings regulations, that is, those at which any public matter is to be discussed or presented. Because no exceptions (other than the typical exceptions for real estate and personnel matters) were identified, the effective meaning of a "meeting" in this case could include such events as press conferences or conventions, or participation in an electronic forum.

The second dimension on which open meetings law is becoming more strict concerns the number of people who need to be involved before open meetings requirements are invoked. Typically, open meetings laws will state that a meeting occurs when a quorum (usually defined as a majority of the members of the governmental body) is present. Again, the underlying assumption is that physical presence is an element of the process. Recently, the Georgia Attorney General's Office was asked to review a potential open meetings violation case involving a series of conversations among members of a local school board. In this case, no meeting in the classical sense of the term was alleged to have occurred. Rather, it was alleged that the series of one-on-one conversations constituted a meeting over a period of time. Although in this particular case the Attorney General's Office ruled that there was no violation of the open meetings act, the fact that the attorney general agreed to investigate suggests that this area of the law is still under development and that the emergence of electronic communications among public officials will present additional challenges to this development.

In addition to requiring that the public be given notice and that meetings be open, many states' open meetings laws also require that "the public be given a reasonable opportunity to comment on matters considered by the board."[3] Electronically based or enhanced citizen involvement in public meetings presents all of the challenges addressed above with respect to electronic rule making, plus some additional challenges identified below.

Open Meetings and Telecommunications

Even though current law is based on the assumption that public meetings are a space-time rather than a cyberspace event, some states already allow for limited electronic expansion of meeting participation via electronic networks. In Georgia, for example, some state agencies allow their public officials to participate via a teleconferencing network. In Texas, a meeting by telephone conference call can be held only if it is a specially called meeting, if immediate action is required, and if it is difficult or impossible for a quorum of the governing board to convene at one location. States that allow such expansion of physical space sometimes mandate that the linkup among participants meet specific criteria. For example, in Georgia, if a state public body is allowed to include a distant participant in a public meeting, the attorney general has stated that "the telecommunications equipment being utilized should permit the members not present in the room to hear all matters being discussed, and to allow them to participate with all other members in discussions. Accordingly all participants in the meeting, and members of the public in attendance, must be able to collectively hear and speak with each other." Similarly, California allows some agencies to use teleconferencing under certain conditions. The Commission on State Mandates, for example, can use teleconferencing given that (1) each teleconference location is identified in the notice of the meeting and is accessible to the public; (2) the portion of the teleconference meeting that is required to be open to the public is audible to the public at the location specified in the notice of the meeting; and (3) all votes taken during a teleconference meeting are by roll call. In Texas, teleconferenced meetings must be tape-recorded. A liberal interpretation of Texas law would suggest that it would be possible, assuming that the immediate action requirement is met, for all the persons of the public body to meet via a teleconference link. However, the law still requires that the meeting "be audible to the public at the location specified in the notice of the meeting as the location of the meeting" (Sec. 551.125).

In addition to setting out basic rules for allowing teleconferencing or video conferencing, states will typically define the degree to which a linked member can be considered part of the quorum. For example, in Texas, video conferencing can expand the number of participating officials, but only in cases where a quorum already exists at the called meeting. In contrast, Georgia law makes it possible (in cases where teleconferencing is permitted) to establish a quorum based on a telecommunications link.

Meetings in Cyberspace

Although to my knowledge no state specifically allows for a cyberspace meeting alone to fulfill the requirements of an official public meeting, it is already the case that many states are supplementing physical meetings or hearings with electronic communications. In addition, some states have passed legislation that allows governmental bodies to meet the notification provisions of open meetings acts by delivering meeting notices by electronic means in lieu of, or in addition to, U.S. mail. In Virginia, unless the requester objects to electronic notification, a public body may notify the requester by posting the notice on its Web site, sending e-mail, or utilizing a list service.[4]

This usage of the Internet for meeting notices and for supplemental meetings or hearings is likely to expand dramatically in the coming decade, particularly as rates of e-mail penetration among registered voters go above 80 or 90 percent. The potential is great for using electronic meetings or hearings to cut back on costly physical meetings with their associated travel time and space issues. This is a particularly attractive option considering the ability of electronic communications channels to increase both the amount of deliberation by public officials and the amount of dialog between these officials and the general public.

Assuming that the use of electronic meetings as supplements to physical meetings does not violate the letter of relevant open meetings laws, the question remains whether such a practice violates the spirit of these laws. If we assume, for example, that some issues may be raised in an electronic forum that may not also be raised in a physical meeting setting, should we conclude that supplemental electronic meetings or hearings should be prohibited since some citizens will not have easy access to the electronic forum or media? Would access to the electronic meeting via a public library computer link meet the requirement for access, or is another standard needed to ensure that citizens on the other side of the digital divide have an equal chance to influence public policy?

Although the use of electronic media as a supplemental forum for discussion is likely to occur in a fairly visible manner, an equally important or more important trend in the use of computer-mediated communications is taking place informally. That is, some public officials may already be using electronic media in a manner that approximates the key elements of a public meeting. Having three or four public officials gather informally at a local restaurant to talk shop and having the same officials sending out group e-mail, employing a series of sequential e-mail communications, or participating in chat or discussion forums may be a distinction without a difference. That is, where once the difference between correspondence and meetings was a distinct one, with the short distribution and turnaround time of electronic correspondence, this may no longer be the case. In states like Georgia and Florida that have strong and broad open meetings statutes, elected officials who send or use e-mail to discuss public matters may already be violating the spirit if not the letter of the law.

Unfortunately, legislation in the area of open meetings has not kept up with technology. Some states have clarified the status of electronic records, making them equal to written records in the transactions of state and private business, but the meaning of this legislation for electronic meetings is usually not clear. For example, in a state that allows electronic records to be valid copies of written records, can the storage of an electronic version of meeting minutes be sufficient to meet the mandate of "keeping a record of the minutes of the meeting" without also having to create a paper record?

More critical than the issue of electronic archiving is the need to identify and assess the appropriateness of the options for structuring electronic meetings in the future. A key feature of electronic communications is the wide range of ways in which dialog can be shaped or mediated by the code, architecture or user interface of the application being used. Physical meetings generally share common standards for communication and interaction. For example, in physical space we can typically see the faces of the citizen members of the audience. We can also signal our agreement with a speaker by any number of signs such as a smile, a clap, a wink or a cheer.

In contrast to the underlying similarity of physical meetings, the formats of cyberspace meetings can be incredibly diverse. Using application code it becomes possible to amplify, mute, censor, extinguish or add aspects of meetings that we have taken for granted in physical meeting space. For example, in cyberspace, applications could be developed that would allow (even without all participants having a video camera turned on them) participants to communicate via a set of signals similar to those available to participants in physical space meeting. For instance, participants could view icons of different facial expressions based on individual or aggregated signals sent by other participants. Alternatively, however, new signals and capabilities could be added. For example, a participant in an electronic meeting might be able to

- sort and analyze the reaction signals of the different participants based on participant characteristics.
- identify key characteristics (race, religion, age, etc.) of opponents and proponents of particular policies.
- poll the other participants and announce the results of the poll in real time, thereby potentially affecting the outcome of the deliberations as they occur.

On the other hand, one could also code out or limit the capabilities of the citizen audience to communicate with each other or with officials in specific ways. For example, public officials might demand that a "foul language elimination filter" be used, particularly during a very controversial discussion.

Another key factor that can be controlled in electronic meetings but not in physical settings is identity. Should some parts of a public meeting be structured to allow for anonymous communications by citizens or even among the public officials? Sometimes a citizen's or a public official's comments are not given even minimal consideration because of the speaker's personality, politics or history of conflicts with other officials. Being able to communicate anonymously could improve public decision making in these instances. However, in other cases, it is important to identify a speaker, particularly if that person is in a position to vote or to heavily influence a discussion based on identification factors (e.g., living next door to property that is being considered for rezoning). We will need careful study and thought to determine which deliberations should proceed with some level of anonymity and which should not.

Given the complexity and sensitivity of human decision making, public managers will need to ensure more congruence between the kinds of issues being addressed and the nature of meeting structures and formats that will be used to discuss the issue at hand. Thus, a more contingent set of rules for electronic public meetings is desirable. In developing such a contingent set of rules, public officials will want to examine policy options in the following areas:

• Public Access: Under what conditions, if any, could a public agency hold a virtual or all-electronic meeting? Would providing Internet access in a single meeting room or at public libraries be sufficient?

• Authorization and Notice of a Meeting: Currently, members of a public decision-making group are unlikely to show up for a meeting without a call from an authorized member. However, if an electronic forum exists for the discussion of a public issue, the potential for decision makers to gather to discuss the public's business is greatly increased. If the electronic discussion forum allows for anonymity, it may even be the case that decision makers are not aware that a quorum has been established.

• Synchronicity and Time Frame: Electronic meetings can potentially be asynchronous. That is, they could take place over a long period of time with substantial pauses between speakers and responders. In theory, such extended meetings could enhance attendance and participation, but they could also diffuse potential grouping of citizens (because a critical mass of citizens is never present at any one point in time). Some basic questions include: Do electronic discussion forums that are used over a long period of time by decision makers (and the public) constitute a public meeting? Does electronic mail that is sent among a quorum-sized group of decision makers constitute a meeting? If the mail is sent to a smaller group, but subsequently forwarded to other decision makers, has a meeting occurred?

- Citizens' Capacity to Provide Feedback: Under current public meeting guidelines, public viewpoints are generally limited to a particular part of the meeting and to a certain length of time. Similar structures could be established for electronic meetings. The reality of controversial nonelectronic public meetings is one that includes "groans and cheers" from the public. These expressions often act as informal polling processes. Should electronic meetings guarantee a similar capability on the part of citizens to provide a spontaneous reaction? If so, in what form would this capability be established? By vocalization? By text/chat? By responses to preset polling questions?

- Inter-Citizen Communications: The thrust of open meetings law is to ensure that citizens can monitor and influence public decisions, but in physical space the effect of the law is to ensure that groups of citizens with an interest in a policy issue also have a chance to communicate with each other. If we move toward electronic meetings, will we ensure that the same opportunities for citizen-to-citizen discussion take place?

- Public Officials' Obligation to Digest Information: While no public official can be compelled to listen to and digest information, the existence of a meeting in physical space makes it difficult for a public official to be completely inattentive without risking public disapprobation. A meeting held via video-conferencing technology would afford the same level of citizen review of a public official's intake of presented information. Should all electronic meetings be required to use video? In what circumstances is this level of citizen review unnecessary? Are there other, perhaps more effective, means of ensuring that public officials are really listening?

- Anonymity and Identity: Under what conditions could citizens speak anonymously? Could citizens be both anonymous and yet identified as belonging to a certain group (e.g., as residents of a certain jurisdiction)?

- Standards for Establishing or Certifying Identity: When, if ever, would citizens be required to provide a digital certificate or possibly a biometric mark to establish their identity?

As this list of issues suggests, governments will be making a number of strategic choices about the nature of public meetings in cyberspace. Unfortunately, there is very little research to guide them in their choices. Because of the experimental nature of federalism it is likely that some state will take the lead in moving toward a future where electronic meetings will be the norm for deliberation and voting on certain issues. Before this occurs, however, we may see electronic meetings used to supplement or even supplant corporate governance. George Kobler, writing in the *Alabama Law Review* (1998), has argued that allowing shareholder voting over the Internet would lead to a large increase in shareholder participation. Considering that the low level of citizen participation in democratic governance is at least as critical as the low level of shareholder participation in corporate governance, we will want to watch developments in this area closely.

Internet Voting

In addition to being asked to provide advice on and to administer versions of electronic rule making and electronic meetings, public managers will also likely be asked to help devise methods and ensure security for Internet voting. In the most visible voting situations—primary and general elections—Internet voting is likely to be an issue involving intense policy discussion and cautious action. However, it is also likely that more and more groups will ask to use Internet voting technology to indicate their opinion or vote in numerous circumstances, including but not limited to online initiative, referendum and recall petitions; campaigns to get a candidate or an issue on an election ballot; certified government-sponsored surveys; remote voting by elected representatives; and certification that a single person or group is not attempting to make their opinion in an electronic rule-making process look more popular than it actually is. Public managers will have the most influence on the less visible, but still very important, opinion surveying procedures. While public managers will not directly decide on implementation of Internet voting systems for general elections, many of the issues associated with Internet voting for general elections will parallel issues that managers will deal with in implementing less visible forms of remote voting.

The California Internet Voting Task Force (2000) has given considerable thought to the issues involved in Internet voting and associated procedures. While the task force is not pessimistic about the potential for Internet voting, it does recommend a high level of caution in moving toward use of these new voting technologies. Specifically, the task force has noted that technological threats to the security, integrity and secrecy of Internet ballots are very real. In particular, the task force suggests that denial of service attacks, submission of electronically altered ballots, and hacking into Internet voting Web servers are significant threats, but they are also preventable ones. Preventing all the possible threats will involve gaining experience and testing the technology in a step-by-step process. One of the problems in this regard is that the e-commerce technologies that are sometimes touted as possible solutions to Internet voting problems actually ensure integrity by trading privacy for security. That is, one's credit card number is designed to tie one's purchase (or dollar vote) to one's identity through a bank that has assured itself of your identity. In contrast, in a voting situation, the key goal is to separate one's identity from one's vote so as to have a secret ballot (Gerck 2000). Technologies that strip one's identity from one's vote and that provide for multiple authority tabulations are being developed, but have not yet been tested across the full spectrum of possible situations. In addition to the need for caution in developing technology to address security issues, the California Internet Voting Task Force also identified the expense of developing the Internet voting infrastructure and the continued existence of a digital divide as hurdles to the implementation of full-fledged Internet voting. Specifically, the task force and others have called for a four stage implementation of Internet voting:

Stage 1. Internet voting at existing polling places. This stage would help introduce the technology to the citizenry and educate them about it as well as allow for testing of the basic technology.

Stage 2. Internet voting at other public places. This stage would involve citizens voting at public libraries, courthouses and community centers, thereby expanding access and convenience. However, the voting computers and network connections would still be under the control of election officials.

Stage 3. Remote Internet voting at sponsored places for special populations. At this stage groups such as military personnel, residents in nursing or retirement homes, and absentee voters would be allowed to vote remotely through Internet computers owned or operated by a responsible organization. Voters would essentially follow the same procedure for authentication that is used today for absentee ballots (e.g., they would have to request a ballot in advance and provide proof of identity to election officials).

Stage 4. Remote Internet voting from any Internet-connected computer. At this stage voters would be asked to use a password or personal identification number (PIN) in combination with a digital or biometric signature provided by either a government agency or a government-approved certification authority.

As with most computer systems, increased security and higher levels of privacy can be provided by increasing the complexity of the system and the burden on the user. The success or failure of Internet voting in the near term may well depend on the ability of computer programmers and election officials to design a system where the burden of the additional duties placed on voters does not outweigh the benefits derived from the increased flexibility provided by the Internet voting system.

The Arizona Democratic Party's recent experience with Internet voting in the 2000 Democratic presidential primary marks the beginning of a likely wave of controversial experiments with electronic voting. Even before the votes had been tabulated, the results of the Arizona experience were being hotly debated. The facts are these: Of the over 80,000 citizens voting, approximately half voted online. This 80,000 represented approximately 10 percent of the registered Democratic voters and a large gain in the number and proportion of citizens voting in comparison to the previous presidential primary. Most of the Internet voting appeared to take place from home or business locations rather than from public access sites. Internet voters were able to vote over a period of days rather than on a single day, as was required of non-Internet voters, and some limited and flawed telephone assistance was provided for Internet voters. A private firm provided the Internet voting system employed in Arizona.

The debate over the meaning of these facts has been particularly intense with regard to a couple of points. First, because the 2000 election was contested (compared with the 1996 uncontested Democratic primary), because the private company spent considerable resources marketing the Internet voting option, and because Internet voters had a longer period of time to exercise their vote, opinions of observers have differed on whether the Internet voting option by itself would lead to higher voting participation rates. More controversial still has been the debate over whether Internet voting is appropriate when a digital divide exists. The argument here is that if the affluent, who are more likely to own an Internet-connected computer, are the ones to receive the largest share of the benefits of Internet voting, then it is also likely that the voting rate among affluent citizens will increase relative to that among less affluent groups. This argument is voiced both by representatives of minority groups and by public interest groups whose chief concern is with the integrity of the voting process. One of these groups, the Voting Integrity Project (VIP), filed a voting rights lawsuit challenging the Arizona Democratic Party's plan to conduct their presidential primary utilizing remote online Internet voting. Citing Commerce Department statistics that African American and Hispanic households are only 40 percent as likely as white households to have home Internet access, VIP's lawsuit alleged that the Internet voting system used in the Arizona Democratic presidential primary would have the effect of maximizing affluent white participation relative to nonwhites, in violation of the Voting Rights Act of 1965.

While progressive political observers would probably not dispute the potential for Internet voting to provide a temporary advantage to certain technology-rich groups, some of these observers have nevertheless questioned the motives of the Voting Integrity Project. These observers argue that the VIP, which is led by Deborah M. Phillips, a former chairwoman of the Republican Party of Arlington County, may be motivated as much by political advantage as by concerns for voter integrity. Ironically, the VIP's white paper, "Are We Ready for Internet Voting?," argues that Internet voting is likely to have an impact just the opposite of that claimed by VIP in its Arizona lawsuit. Specifically, in the paper, the VIP argues that voting convenience may actually reduce voter participation. VIP compares Internet voting to other policies (e.g., the relaxed absentee ballot and early voting) that make voting more convenient. While we do not know the precise impact of Internet voting on voter turnout, research suggests that no-fault absentee balloting and early voting, where tried, have had a negative impact on voter turnout. That is, the more convenient the voting, the lower the turnout. The VIP quotes from a study of no-fault absentee and early voting policies conducted by the Center for the Study of the American Electorate (CSAE) to suggest that states that adopt other policies that are likely to have the same convenience-boosting effect (e.g., Internet voting) are no more likely to experience increased turnout. To explain this paradoxical impact, VIP argues that "that which is too easy is often forgotten." This conclusion is drawn from calls to the VIP hotline following Oregon's first mail-only ballot program. "Voters stated that a ballot mailed days or weeks in advance of an election was too easily set aside for later execution and then forgotten."[5] The implication here is that Internet voting, which currently depends on voters being sent a PIN number through the mail, will similarly be forgotten by busy voters.

While the VIP's positions (if not all of its arguments) are currently in line with the historic interests of the Republican Party, it is unlikely that either of the major political parties will choose to be anti–Internet voting in the long run. In fact, it is no fluke that Internet voting came first to a primary election rather than to a general election. The party seen to be the most innovative in terms of Internet voting will likely gain a first-adopter advantage among educated but disaffected citizens. The Internet "bandwagon effect" can clearly be seen in a joint editorial in the San Diego *Union-Tribune* (2000) by Governor George Pataki of New York, a Republican, and Governor Gray Davis of California, a Democrat. While this editorial was far from being a ringing endorsement of Internet voting, it suggested that neither the Democrats nor the Republicans wanted to be seen as out of touch with the call for Internet convenience.

Currently, bills to study Internet voting, such as one introduced by Rep. Jesse L. Jackson, Jr. (D.-Illinois) on November 5, 1999, are slated to be examined later in 2001. Jackson's bill directs the President to study the most frequently cited issues related to the use of Internet technologies in voting—security, the standardization of systems, effects on participation rates, system accessibility, and the potential to advantage particular groups. While these are important issues, the current trends in improved computer security and in improved access to the Internet by minority groups suggest that they relate to concerns that are likely to be short-lived.

The deeper discussion of Internet voting is likely to concern a different set of issues—three in particular. First, as the VIP and others have pointed out, there are no guarantees that voters will not share their passwords with other people. By allowing Internet voting, are we not also essentially giving our approval to proxy voting? This is not necessarily a criticism of proxy voting in certain circumstances. I am not adverse, for example, to the kind of informal proxy voting that would result in a wife voting for a husband or close friends voting for each other as the need arises. Such familial proxy voting would not substantially change our political culture. However, the same process that allows this type of proxy voting would also allow more wholesale efforts to garner proxies. It does not take much imagination, for instance, to visualize a situation where a political activist comes to your door to solicit your vote—only now the activist has a hand-held wireless computer connected to the Internet. In this case, a simple nod in agreement to political persuasion can easily be transformed into a completed vote. Alternatively, unless restrictions are put on the number of proxies that any one person or group could gather, the activist could simply ask for the voter's PIN or for an imprint of a biometric signature that would then be used at a later time to complete the vote. In either case, the situation represents a substantial change in our political culture.

Second, people who object to Internet voting frequently cite the potential for coercion of voters. This coercion could take place in a work setting or as part of a civic or social group such as a neighborhood association. While one could imagine such scenarios, one can also imagine that the institution of strong laws when combined with existing social taboos against such behavior could prevent any substantial threat to voting integrity from this direction. Legal regulations of this type would also reduce aggressive tactics by political activists as described in the previous paragraph.

Third, Internet voting may undermine a long-standing civil ritual. This concern is one that is difficult to fix or to legislate away. At a time when the amount of public space has dwindled due to the "malling" of America, the expansion of private education, and the growth in gated communities, it may be imprudent to add on-site voting to the list of diminished civic spaces and rituals. Unfortunately, in recent times most polling places have lost (or never had) many of the features that facilitate meaningful public dialog. The key feature that comes to mind in this regard is waiting. While having to wait is generally seen as a negative feature that reduces voter turnout, the positive aspect of waiting is that it encourages citizens to talk about the candidates and issues with their neighbors. With more efficient polling places and automated voting booths, the wait at polling sites has been considerably reduced in recent decades. Unfortunately, it is probable that prevoting discussions have experienced a similar decline. Obviously, waiting could be made more comfortable and inviting (e.g., take a number and go to a room where you and your neighbors can talk over coffee and donuts) while retaining the pro-dialog feature of this inconvenience. Moreover, this waiting room could be equipped with Internet hookups where citizens can do last-minute research.

Given that most polling places do not possess or even strive to possess this kind of positive, comfortable and dialog-initiating combination of conveniences and inconveniences, I cannot argue with conviction that much would be lost by moving to Internet voting. However, I can argue that Internet voting should attempt to emulate the best features of public space. For example, perhaps some of the time saved by getting to vote on the Internet should be "lost" through a series of online invitations to visit informative Web sites and to enter public dialogs about the candidates and the issues. We might even emulate the fortuitous inconvenience of a queue that has been the hallmark of traditional voting and of serendipitous conversations among citizens. There is no telling what a three-minute delay from log-on to vote could produce. I know in my own voting experience that it has resulted in my voting on issues and candidates that otherwise would have been bypassed due to my failure to become sufficiently informed.

NOTES

1. Personal communication with Keith Thurston of the General Services Administration, January 2000.
2. Personal communication with Julie Morgan, City Planner, Athens-Clarke County, Georgia, August 1999.
3. This notice is provided by the Vermont Secretary of State publication: *A Pocket Guide to Open Meeting Law* (1999), Vermont Secretary of State, 1 V.S.A. § 310 et seq.
4. Senate Bill 806, Va. Gen. Assembly, Regular Session, 1999.
5. Voting Integrity Project 2000, *Voting Technology* (Arlington, VA), found at http://www.voting-integrity.org/projects/votingtechnology/internetvoting/ivp_9_turningout.shtm.

REFERENCES

California Code, Title 2. Administration, Division 2, Financial Operations, Chapter 2.5, Commission on State Mandates, Article 2, Commission Meetings §1182.5.
California Internet Voting Task Force. (2000). *A Report on the Feasibility of Internet Voting*. Sacramento: California Secretary of State Bill Jones, January.
Democracies Online. http//www.e-democracy.org/do/.
Gerck, E. (2000). Would you vote naked? *The Bell* 1(2): 1–2.
Kantor, J. (2000). Arizonans vote in their pajamas. *Slate*. Posted March 14, at http://slate.msn.com/netelection/entries/00-03-14_77288.asp.
Kobler, George Ponds. (1998). Shareholder voting over the Internet: A proposal for increasing shareholder participation in corporate governance. 49 *Alabama Law Review* 673 (Winter).
Ledbetter, J. (2000). "Virtual voting" faces real-world concerns. *Slate*. Posted March 16 at http://slate.msn.com/netelection/entries/00-03-16_77458.asp.
Lessig, L. (1999). *Code and Other Laws of Cyberspace*. New York: Basic Books
Schrage, M. (1999). When best practices meet the Intranet, innovation takes a holiday. *Fortune* 139(6): 198.
Some Assembly Required: Building a Digital Government for the 21st Century. (1999). Albany, NY: Center for Technology in Government, March.
State of Georgia, Department of Law. (1994). Official Opinion 94-11, March 16.
Texas Government Code. Title 5, Subtitle A, Chapter 551.

PART III
MANAGING THE TRANSFORMATION

6
Staffing and Design of Wired Organizations

ARE WIRED ORGANIZATIONS STILL BUREAUCRACIES?

When Max Weber first outlined the characteristics of a bureaucracy, his model was influenced by the new industrial bureaucracies that grew out of successful efforts to mass produce standardized products. Simplifying somewhat, a bureaucracy is designed to mass produce a standardized service. As such, bureaucracies have followed a mass production model. The elements of this model include hierarchy of authorities, the codification of processes and routines, the division of authority by jurisdiction or function, and the specialization of skills and standardization of qualifications. Being wired need not change these basic elements of a bureaucracy, but it can.

Traditional bureaucracies in an unwired organization are able to maintain their boundaries through simple inertia. Essentially, people will remain in their roles and routines because they do not have sufficient contact with persons outside (or inside) the bureaucracy, or because the information and examples needed to foster change are unavailable. Even when such contacts, information and examples are available, the transaction costs of getting help with a change effort and the uncertainty of change are typically too high to support an organizational transformation. An organization that is wired, however, is in a different position. Here managers and staff can communicate internally and externally without time delays, across functional areas, and across hierarchical levels, using data mining, e-mail, listservs, and chat rooms—asking all the essential follow-up questions that must be answered before there is a willingness to go forward—all without the customary high costs of technology transfer. In this sense, a wired organization is potentially more open to change. (See Table 6.1.)

Table 6.1
Traditional Bureaucracy and Wired Organization Compared

Traditional Bureaucracy	Wired Organization Makes Possible or Demands
A hierarchy of authorities	Ad hocracies, fluid project teams, matrix organization
The codification of processes and routines	Allowance for new processes and routines to be discovered through improved heuristics and knowledge management
Division of authority by jurisdiction	Cross-jurisdictional collaboration and alliances
Division of authority by expertise	Multiple, cross-functional sources of authority
Specialization of skills and delineated role	More enriched jobs, more integrated work and more fluid roles
Standardization of qualifications	More general ability to integrate information and manage cases across specialty areas

Moreover, although information technology can and has been used to reinforce command and control working environments, many of the emerging technologies in the private sector are being designed to enable empowered work teams to focus on serving customer requirements. Such teams depend upon a free flow of information across business processes and increased accountability and decision-making authority. If the flow of technology continues along its recent historical path from the private sector to the public, there is likely to be a great deal of confusion and dissatisfaction in cases where a public sector command-and-control-oriented organization adopts technologies that were originally developed to support an entirely different type of organization. At a minimum, such public sector organizations are unlikely to obtain the optimal impact, and in some cases the net impact will be negative. This could occur, for example, as a result of public sector employees using the technology as it was intended by its designers to be used, but for purposes or in ways not desired by public managers. The resulting disturbance is likely to lead to change—probably unplanned change.

Because the wiring of governments will occur as the result of both externally and internally defined technologies and developmental paths, there is a great deal of uncertainty about how governments are likely to be transformed in the process. While public managers have little control over the development of technology in the private sector, they do have some ability to impact the organizational conditions for adopting, customizing and using new technologies. In this chapter, we will examine how human resource development and organizational development are critical to implementing a more wired approach to the delivery of governmental services.

Before addressing how governments can marshal their human and organizational capacities to effectively use new technologies, it is important to recognize that only some governments currently engage in a substantial use of these capacities as part of efforts to effectively employ new technologies. Rather, as Fletcher et al. (1992) have shown, many governments focus on using technology as part of a repair or cutback effort rather than as part of a transformational effort. In the former case, little attention is given to engaging organizational capacities in a substantial way because the technology plays only a minor role in the organizational culture and routines. Specifically, Fletcher et al. offer case studies of how county governments organize and reform their information management systems and departments. These case studies suggest that there are five ways in which governments address the need for reform in these systems and departments:

1. The strategic restructuring response. This response is generally equivalent to a serious reengineering effort that involves a reorganization of functions and personnel (e.g., setting up cross-functional teams and new cross-function work processes).

2. The work process design response. This response is equivalent to a less in-depth change that may only involve a reworking of a single business process.

3. The steady state response. Technology is used to maintain the status quo.

4. The cutback management approach. Technology is focused on maintaining an ability to keep up with information demands within a set budget.

5. The downsizing strategy. Technology is developed to fill in gaps created by the laying off of employees.

At the time of Fletcher et al.'s study, knowledge management was not a well recognized IT development strategy. Therefore, this list probably omits some reform approaches that would be included were a similar study of governments conducted today. However, keep in mind that many different forces or motivations are driving the development of new technology in government organizations. The following ideas for reforming human resource and organizational systems are based on the assumption that the prime motivation for reform of information management systems is to enhance total effectiveness and efficiency within an environment where continuous improvement in both human and technical systems is a primary goal.

HUMAN RESOURCE DEVELOPMENT

Human resource development for a wired organization involves a wide variety of tasks and activities. (See Table 6.2.) In addition to the traditional

Table 6.2
Human Resource Factors in Traditional and Wired Organizations

	Traditional	Wired Organization Makes Possible
Design of Work	Work involves a single task within one functional area.	Work is redesigned to unite many if not all of the tasks and functions in a single process (e.g., needs assessment, purchasing, payments, accounting, receiving, inventorying, etc.). Through expert systems and knowledge management, an individual worker can take on a broader array of tasks and responsibilities. Generic case managers with minimal subject matter expertise can use information technologies to process the vast majority of routine cases (Hammer 1990).
Design of Careers	Career path within one department.	Career path includes stints at a number of related departments (e.g., those who serve a similar customer). For example, a person might work in building inspections, planning and public works—generally serving the same customer group in different but related roles.
Classification Systems	Job classifications tend to remain behind the technology.	New job classifications are adopted simultaneously with the adoption or development of new technologies. For example, with new imaging technologies, a new job category may need to be created so that one can pay a salary that is more than an information clerk but less than a systems analyst (Fletcher et. al. 1992).
Reward System	Salary based on seniority or performance. Focus is on past or current performance.	Salary based on knowledge and skills. Knowledge and skills are seen as important for the future performance of the government.

Table 6.2 (continued)

	Traditional	Wired Organization Makes Possible
Accountability System	The —— department becomes a scapegoat for late products or services because of poor planning upstream and the lack of adequate time-tracking tools.	Tools that track real activities across processes help to identify (and eventually break down) the points of delay or barriers in work flow (e.g., the walls between engineering, accounting and distribution) (Willets 1996).
Career Ladder	From line to middle-management to senior staff to executive.	Flattened supervisory career ladder holds few opportunities for advancement. New opportunities for advancement are based on knowledge ladder that will include ability to incorporate new technologies.
Training	Limited training due to both the high cost of training and the low utility of non-on-the-job training.	Realization of the greater value of training to the organization's performance. Expanded opportunities for training due to access to low-cost on-line training and education.
IT Training	IT training is haphazard and is generally conducted through expensive, but unaccounted for, executive time spent with support staff on "futzing around with the computer."	IT training is rigorous, systematic and conducted for staff at all levels. Minimum proficiency is set for all job categories.
IT Support	Generally considered non-mission critical, and is therefore often provided through on-call specialists or an understaffed IT department.	Considered central to the organization's capability and is therefore conducted in-house.

Table 6.2 (continued)
Human Resource Factors in Traditional and Wired Organizations

	Traditional	Wired Organization Makes Possible
IT Leadership Training	Leadership receives minimal IT training through public administration preparation courses.	Leadership training is ongoing and special provisions are made to insure that leaders are well oriented to IT issues (e.g., they may be trained first; they may be sent to a high status training institute; they may be trained one-on-one or in exclusive groups so as to avoid their having to expose their ignorance) (Heeks 1999).
Performance Appraisals	Used as a weapon for the old-line manager.	Used as a means to collect previously agreed-upon data from individuals, team members and customers.

areas of recruitment, training, leadership, and motivation, human resource development also can involve issues of organizational culture and attitudinal responses to technology. These issues are addressed separately in Chapter 7.

Studies of information technology costs and productivity have suggested that the major cost of implementing new technologies in organizations is that of developing the human capacity to take advantage of the new computing power that has become available. Much of this cost, however, is hidden. As pointed out in a *Scientific American* review of the productivity performance of computers in American business, much of the purported benefit of computers is frequently eaten up by managers and staff "futzing around" or setting up or troubleshooting computers and software applications. This process is particularly costly when the time spent futzing around is high-cost managerial or executive time (Gibbs 1997). The tendency for public sector organizations to skimp on dedicated resources for information technology training can be seen in a study of county government information management processes. This 1991 study found that less than 1 percent of information management positions in the counties reporting data were dedicated to training. Although these data may disguise the existence of outsourced training, they are still telling in that they indicate a low level of in-house capacity. In addition, the study findings suggest that training was often the first area to be cut in county budgets and that 24 percent of all county training positions were vacant, a further indication of the lack of emphasis on IT training. The authors of the study argue that training should be a higher priority and should be implemented as a continuous process rather than a one-time event. Without increased attention to training, they suggest that the return on investment in information technology is likely to be disappointing (Fletcher et al. 1992).

Obviously, most organizations cannot be characterized as having either a fully traditional or a fully wired set of human resource management practices. Table 6.2 compares and contrasts traditional human resource factors with factors that make it possible or more probable that an organization will become wired for success. In this regard, Table 6.2 can provide a manager with a checklist of sorts for identifying areas in which there may be cause for concern or improvement. In addition, in any effort to improve the human resource capacities in the organization, the individual items on the list should probably not be viewed in isolation. Rather, organizational improvement efforts in one itemized area are likely to be much more effective if coordinated with other efforts. For example, an effort to foster IT leadership through the training of public managers in information technology and technology implementation will probably have a much larger impact if followed by work redesign efforts or efforts to extend IT training to the rest of the staff.

The human resource action areas in this table suggest that public managers can potentially do a great deal to improve the wiredness of the organization even without having substantial resources. That is, public managers often have some leeway to make adjustments in career ladders, reward structures, accountability and performance appraisal systems, and the like without having to dedicate substantial amounts of new resources in the effort.

ORGANIZATIONAL DEVELOPMENT

As with choices about human resource development, public managers also make choices, consciously or not, about the organizational shape and structure of the administrative part of the government. These choices, in turn, impact the overall capacity of the organization to adopt and integrate technology and to generally operate in a wired fashion. As with the preceding table on human resources, Table 6.3 compares the orientation and characteristics of a traditional government with that of a wired one.

The list of organizational features that distinguish traditional from wired organizations is large, suggesting a number of potential developmental paths toward a more wired organization. As with the list of human resource development ideas, public managers may benefit from charting out complementary sets of organizational change activities. For example, changing from a program level to a more enterprise level of budgeting for information technology needs could be coordinated with the increased involvement of

Table 6.3
Organizational Factors in Traditional and Wired Organizations

	Traditional	Wired Organization Makes Possible or Demands
Completion of Repetitive Tasks and Choice of Labor or Capital	Performed by low-cost, low-skilled labor.	Performed by automated machine-based processes. Machine processing is preferred even when it might be cheaper to use labor. This is due to a desire to go down a learning curve more rapidly.
Leadership	Leaders have IT specialists who make IT decisions and have administrative assistants who operate personal computers for routine executive communications.	Leaders continually update their knowledge about how information technologies and communications are impacting work routines. They become directly involved in IT projects, particularly in setting guiding principles (Strassmann 1995), and use computer applications as part of their daily routine.
Place of IT in the Organizational Structure	IT has little prestige and visibility (Lucas 1984); used primarily for automating a few high-volume, routine operations such as water bills; IT may be centralized or decentralized.	IT used as a major means of computer-mediated/enhanced communications, budget preparation and decision support (Rocheleau 1999). IT exists to support a more centralized "data warehouse" approach to information management.
Organization of IT Projects	IT is seen as primarily a technology problem. Projects are placed in the IT department with input from program managers.	IT projects are viewed as change-management projects. General managers and politically savvy leaders are put in charge of cross-departmental teams.
Role of Artificial Intelligence	To replace decision makers.	To aid decision makers and provide improved access to knowledge on which decisions are based.
Architecture of Information Technology	Haphazard.	Centralized with input from program managers.

Table 6.3 (continued)

	Traditional	Wired Organization Makes Possible or Demands
Decision Making Process & Information Flow and Control	Generally top-down. However, top-down decision making and control are limited by the inability to transfer and aggregate information through layers of middle management. As such, traditional organizations provide street-level bureaucrats with a certain degree of discretion by default.	All methods of decision making can be more effectively implemented in the wired organization. That is, an organization can be wired for more effective collaborative, bottom-up or top-down decision making. For example, a wired organization can strategically allow for anonymity in certain discussions, thereby reducing the impact of organizational status on decision making. Alternatively, a communication system could be designed to provide graphic cues as to a person's place in the organizational hierarchy.
Control of & Sharing of Data	Data are controlled by single departments or units (Rocheleau 1999).	Data are centrally controlled. Central information office identifies and addresses discrepancies in overlapping data or in data quality problems that prevent sharing and integration.
Design Authority	IT unit designs the applications.	Unit using the information designs the application.
Standards for Hardware and Off-the-Shelf Applications	Mixed and highly dependent on departmental prerogatives and the particular desires of individual public managers.	Standards created and enforced with an eye toward enterprise-wide sharing and integration of data and files.
Level of Design and Financing of IT	IT projects are generally designed and financed at the program level. Financing is based on the expected return within the program function and relies heavily on tax-levy budget.	IT projects are generally designed and financed at the strategic level. Financing is based on the expected return across multiple program functions. Assessment of return on investment also includes the impacts on customer service and the ability to enhance governmental capability in other programs or in the future.

	Traditional	Wired Organization Makes Possible or Demands
		Multiple financing opportunities are explored and exploited, including having users of services pay when they are the ones that benefit, and implementing budget reforms that emphasize multiyear, cross-department, and cross-jurisdiction service integration innovations, use of capital funds, revolving funds, shared-risk investments with the private sector, etc.
Role of Elected Policy-Making Officials	Minimal. Due to lack of expertise, elected officials tend to defer to IT professionals.	With near universal computing and expanded use of personal computers, more elected officials will be or will see themselves as contributing to IT decisions (Pevtzow 1989).
Management Focus	On price and purchase of equipment (Kraemer & King 1976).	On how applications fit together and fit the redesign of work and the aggregation of knowledge.
Role of Information in Decision Making	Information breadth and access are restricted. Information for decision making is drawn from a single analysis model that is controlled by executive-level staff (or managers).	A broad array of linkable information is available to most stakeholders. Multiple analysis models are created and their results are compared (O'Looney 1997; Dutton and Kraemer 1985).
Role of R&D	Occasional employment of personnel with R&D skills.	Creation of centers of innovation that examine practices and technologies from a cross-functional perspective. Complex technologies are created by self-organizing networks that behave as learning organizations for success in innovation (Rycroft & Kash 1999).
Place of Work	Office, factory, warehouse or store.	Anywhere. Telecommuting and mobile offices.

Table 6.3 (continued)

	Traditional	Wired Organization Makes Possible or Demands
Time of Work	Daytime.	Anytime.
Location of Information	In on-site databases.	In networked databases or data warehouses, enhanced by knowledge management applications.
Learning and Innovation Networks	Limited to single location, on-site, within field learning.	Learning networks that serve multiple training sites/locations and multiple functional areas.[1]
Scope of IT Work Across the Spectrum of Tasks and Processes	IT work is primarily back-office work (e.g., Fletcher et al. 1992 found that most county information systems departments keep to the traditional view of their role with respect to interactions with citizens. That is, they were not very interested in implementing technologies to support government-citizen interaction).	Management of relationships with citizens is viewed as a major area in which information technology can be applied (see discussion of customer relationship management or CRM in Chapter 4).
Integration of IT and Communication	Public sector IT departments focus primarily on traditional office functions and have not integrated communication functions (e.g., satellite transmissions, radio communications, videoconferences, and teleconferences) into their role.	Communications and IT are fully integrated, and a single department has primary responsibility for both.

1. While the organization of training in a wired government is likely to have an advantage in terms of overall cost-effectiveness, the wired approach to training, which incorporates distance learning technologies, is not without a particular weakness. That is, online training is generally less effective in developing tacit know-how and skills, and in easily integrating the talents and expertise of individuals into work groups and teams. Collaboration software can help with this weakness, but other "high touch" resources are needed. On the positive side of the tacit-knowledge problem, wired organizations can be more effective (e.g., through improved communications) in supporting a "regional innovation system." Such regional institutions and associations are believed to help develop a healthy combination of codified and tacit knowledge (Bellandi 1999).

elected policy makers in IT strategic planning so that as these policy makers see the need for a more strategic approach, they will support the complementary changes in budgeting approaches. Similarly, efforts to allow the time and place of work to be more flexible may need to be coordinated with the development of online databases and data warehouse operations to support anywhere/anytime work.

Some organizational changes such as support for more automated and fewer labor-intensive investments may need to be coordinated with human resource development strategies that would, for example, allow the government to continue to hire at the same rate from disadvantaged groups.

The reader may have also noticed that the list of comparative organizational features does not support a simplistic dichotomy between wired organizations (as centralized or decentralized) and traditional organizations (as the opposite). Rather, the list suggests that becoming wired does not favor any single change in the direction of information flows. Rather, it is most likely that a wired government will be one where, all else being equal, the total flow of information is likely to increase in all directions.

The list of organizational changes in Table 6.3 also suggests that the role and place of the information technology or information systems department are often key factors in how information systems develop or fail to develop. Case studies of information management in U.S. counties in the early 1990s indicate that at this level of government the central Information Systems Department (ISD) tended to dominate the IT implementation process. However, these case studies suggest that as the use of the microcomputer within individual departments spread, the relationship between the central ISD and the more program-oriented departments has become more tense. In particular, these other departments will often view the ISD as acting dictatorially or as providing only slow or poor service. In such situations, program-oriented departments will likely complain that ISD employees have only a narrow view of the technology and do not really understand the business that the department is trying to conduct (Fletcher et al. 1992). Unfortunately, there is no single or fully adequate solution to this tension. However, practices such as the following could help:

- Hire IT specialists who have had some program experience.
- Provide IT specialists with substantial orientation to the program areas they will be supporting.
- Recruit program staff as potential candidates for IT jobs.
- Develop joint IT-program staff teams.
- Experiment with different IT work-order arrangements and involve program staff in the design and testing of these arrangements.

OVERCOMING BARRIERS TO BECOMING A WIRED ORGANIZATION, OR WHY WIRED ORGANIZATIONS DON'T JUST HAPPEN WITH THE AVAILABILITY OF NEW IT

New information technology can be successfully introduced within the context of many different types of organizational structures and regimes. Similarly, it is possible for the same organizational structure to be associated with unsuccessful technology implementations. Sometimes a technology implementation will fail because of the fiscal context of the implementation (e.g., the budget does not allow for sufficient training in the use of the new technology, or the introduction occurs in conjunction with the laying off of key personnel). More commonly, specific causes for failure are difficult to trace. In these cases, if one digs deep enough, it is often possible to identify resistance on the part of managers and staff. This resistance will typically take the form of side-stepping, undermining or simply ignoring the new technology entirely. Resistance can have a number of different causes, from loss of prestige to staff simply not being willing to give the extra time or effort it takes to learn the new technology (see Table 6.4 for specific examples).

Obviously, strategies for overcoming resistance will demand the generation of broad support for the proposed change. Moreover, in generating such support, public managers will likely find it necessary to meet the needs of multiple stakeholders. The effort needed to meet these diverse needs may take the form of wide-ranging negotiations among the stakeholders. These negotiations, furthermore, could involve the coordination of trade-offs among the impacted parties. For example, if the introduction of the technology is likely to lead to a lighter workload for Department A but a heavier workload for Department B, some transfer of resources from A to B may be in order. However, as any manager who has tried to transfer resources from one unit to another knows, such changes are not readily accepted by the division that is losing resources. In such cases, further negotiations may be needed (e.g., as to how costs and benefits are to be measured) before Department A agrees to relinquish its resistance to the new technology.

Because the possibility of substantial resistance is real, public managers need to inventory their technology implementation situation. At a minimum, public managers considering an IT-based reform effort need to be able to provide answers to all the who, what, when, where and why questions regarding the proposed change. In addition, they should be able to answer the following questions in the affirmative:

• Is the executive-level leadership in the government prepared to lead the change effort?
• Have government employees and oversight bodies been prepared for the change?

Table 6.4
Barriers to Successful Adoption of New Information Technology and Possible Solutions

Barriers	Possible Solutions
Dictatorial or Narrow Orientation of the IT or IS Department: Information technology specialists do not serve or understand the business goals of the program-oriented departments and therefore tend to provide poorer than desired assistance or consulting.	Clearly identify the IT or IS department's role as a supportive one. Develop a plan for the IT specialists to provide needed training that will be evaluated by the other departments. Create a service satisfaction evaluation/feedback system and base future raises on satisfactory performance. Develop a technology mentoring program with some specific goals (e.g., that at least one person in each department will be able to provide first-level troubleshooting help to others in the department).
Skill Base and Technical Orientation: Basic skills of the workforce do not allow for easy implementation of a new technology. Workers who lack skills may tend to be overly technophobic, making it difficult to implement even simple technologies.	Provide good basic technology orientation and skills training. Support workers who go back to school in technical areas. Continually increase the minimum technical skills required for entry-level positions. Advertise that these skills are desired.
Transaction Costs: The cost of executing a transaction under an existing technology or standard seems to be much lower than doing so under a new innovation. (See Sussman 1999.) Although substantial long-run savings for using the new technology may exist, they are not apparent to staff and managers.	Raise the cost of using the old system. Provide additional resources to units that agree to adopt the new technology exclusively, thereby lowering the effective cost of using the new system. Create an "early adoption race" or contests and incentive programs that give rewards to persons or units that have more thoroughly adopted the new technology. Remove the "old technology" alternative.
Learning Curves: The cost of learning the new system makes it difficult to get the job done, so workers continue to use the old system without informing the technology team.	Identify a "lead worker" in every unit who is most likely to be a good mentor for the others in the unit. Provide lead workers with extensive training in the new technology and reward them for training others in the unit. Create certain times of the day when the new system will be used in a test mode. Allow people to experiment with the system and to make mistakes. Move to the new system only when the level of mistakes falls to the same as in the old system.

Table 6.4 (continued)

Barriers	Possible Solutions
Political Position: Established groups that have benefited from existing technologies and organizational patterns may lose out by the introduction of new technologies. Marginal groups, on the other hand, have fewer costs associated with deviating from the existing configuration of technology and organization (Clemens & Cook 1999).	Provide established groups with assurances that their status will not be harmed and may in fact be improved through the introduction of the desired technology. Create teams comprised of established and marginal groups to jointly lead the adoption process. Within the team, the marginal groups' enthusiasm can counter the established groups' resistance. Encourage entrepreneurial activity on the part of marginal groups to lead the adoption process. Foster healthy competition between established and marginal groups with the goal of being the group that most rapidly implements the needed technology and organizational changes.
Dangers of Sharing Information: Managers who share information may fear that the reason for their unit's existence may come into question or that the unit's weak performance may become more evident (Davenport et al. 1994).	Managers and staff may need to be assured, at a minimum, of job security if efforts toward data sharing are to move forward without resistance. In organizations where fluid teams are not the norm, data sharing that threatens unit integrity could be stymied even though basic job security exists. If a manager is not willing to ensure full unit integrity in exchange for enhanced cooperation around data sharing, it may still be possible to ward off resistance by allowing the development of cross-unit teams that still involve a large measure of "old-tie" relationships among unit members.
Position of Knowledge-Bearing Elites and R&D Staff: Knowledge-bearing elites who have an interest in experimentation and the introduction of new technologies have a weak role in the organization. R&D units are not considered part of the core of the organization. (See Ziegler 1997.)	Create a high-status knowledge or R&D unit. Establish competition to be a member of the unit. Provide the unit with appropriate perks such as enhanced training opportunities, access to better equipment and staff support, and so on. Have this unit regularly brief senior staff regarding technology trends.

Table 6.4 (continued)
Barriers to Successful Adoption of New Information Technology and Possible Solutions

Barriers	Possible Solutions
Effect on Discretion/Position of Staff: The willingness of public employees to implement a new technology is often related to the extent to which that technology impairs or enhances their discretion. Technology that impairs discretion is less likely to be accepted (Culpan 1995). Exercise of discretion can give public employees a sense of power and pleasure. When processes are automated or reengineered, it is sometimes the case, for example, that workers who had been able to expedite a process for valued customers can no longer do so due to "fairness" rules that have been designed into the system. Washburn (1998) describes this problem in a building inspection office setting where new information technology ensured that inspection reviews took place in the order in which they were received. This built-in fairness worked against the status of the office expediters who formerly had been able to earn thanks from important or repeat customers by speeding up the review of their proposed building plans. Expediters and their privileged clients are thought to have spread false reports about the success of the new system, thereby impeding its chances for success.	Because of the malleability in the design of most information technologies, it is not necessary that a system be used to change the discretionary authority of expediters. If a feature of the technology is designed to undermine existing practices and norms, public managers need to understand that and make a choice as to whether the technology design feature is valuable enough to risk the failure of the implementation of the technology. If it meets this standard of value, managers who introduce technology that conflicts with the dominant culture will need to use a number of strategies for changing the culture (see Chapter 7) and will likely need to increase the time that is planned for live testing of the system.
Recruitment and Training Programs: The organization may fail to recruit or train staff capable of introducing a new technology (Windrum 1999). In the early phase of Internet development, for example, few local governments recruited or trained staff in the key Internet technologies.	Provide for regular briefings on technology trends by outside consultants. Create an in-house "future technology" position that is responsible for identifying emerging and critical technologies and related organizational innovations.

Table 6.4 (continued)

Barriers	Possible Solutions
Personnel Rule Barriers: Moving to a wired government may make the skills of current employees obsolete, and hiring rules may not allow for the retraining of these employees in lieu of recruiting new employees who already have the needed skills. Kost (1996) reported that such a situation occurred when the Michigan Department of Transportation chose to move from mainframe to client/server technology.	The best solution to this problem is preventive. That is, government technology training programs should base their training expectations on what new technologies are likely to become necessary for the government in the next two to three years. Combined with this more expansive technology planning time frame, public managers can lobby for more technology generalist job categories that are less likely to have to be eliminated in a shift to newer technologies.
Path Dependence: An organization may never seek to introduce a new technology if the organization's awareness is constrained by a specific technological trajectory or development path (Dosi 1982). Since mainframe (as opposed to client-server) technology was the dominant computer technology adopted by local governments in the 1970s, 1980s and early 1990s, the path for adopting Internet technologies (which are built on a client-server architecture) in the mid-1990s was not adequately developed.	Hold regular brainstorming sessions among technical and nontechnical staff and managers for the purpose of identifying possible path dependencies and path alternatives. Create technology plans that allow the organization to retain a capacity for possible alternative technologies. For example, a local government may adopt a Windows standard for desktop technology, while allowing a technical staff person to continue to use, test and explore the capacities of Linux-based workstations.
Leadership Gap: Leaders who view technology as a separate and subapplication rather than as a vehicle for organizational change will tend not to give new information technology the broad organizational support needed for successful implementation.	In this case, the advice given to leaders in *Eight Imperatives for Leadership in a Networked World* is apt: "Learn how digital processing and communications are revolutionizing the work-place and the nature of work, ideally through becoming directly involved in IT projects and working with computer applications as part of your personal routine. (Using a laptop, personal digital assistant, e-mail, and/or the Web is a good way to get started.) Focus in particular on the strategic triad of: a) developing the organizational infrastructure and capacities you will need to function; b) adding value through network-enabled public services and regulations; and c) building support within your oversight community and the general public" (Mechling and Fletcher 2000, p. 6).

Table 6.4 (continued)
Barriers to Successful Adoption of New Information Technology and Possible Solutions

Barriers	Possible Solutions
Motivation and Reward Structures: Reward structures will always play a role in successful technology implementations. For example, private firms with rewards programs that effectively encourage creativity and innovation were identified to be more than twice as likely as other companies to report excellent financial performance in 1998/99. Rewards can be effectively expressed in monetary terms, and such rewards may prevent dissatisfaction. However, rewards, by themselves, rarely create motivation. Rather, motivation is fostered by a good mixture of internal interest and social support. In some organizations the persons interested in technology are identified as nerds rather than heroes.	Do not deviate too far from the market compensation rates for technical professionals. Compensation rates that fall below 90 percent of the average for the occupational grade will likely result in constant turnover. However, once compensation rates are deemed acceptable, leaders should focus on informal rewards, which are cited as success factors just as frequently as formal compensation. One famous example of an informal reward system that has benefited both technical professionals and the organization is the permission given to 3M researchers to take a certain amount of company time to work on projects that they personally believe in—whether or not such projects are part of the firm's R&D plans. Similarly, technically oriented staff are often motivated by intrinsic and job-related rewards such as • flexibility in hours and work tasks • being given a development challenge such as being asked to build an application that could be outsourced but that is within the capability of the staff • time and support for advanced training or to attend conferences and seminars • being able to work in different functional areas to provide technical support

- Can the organizational structure be adapted to support the change?
- Do management and staff have the right mix of skills to facilitate the change?
- Can one reasonably expect success, or is the goal too ambitious?
- Are mid-level managers properly committed to the change?
- Are sufficient resources available to support the effort?

Action to support change needs to be based on an understanding of the unique characteristics of a specific organization. Questions that public managers can ask to evaluate the change potential in an organization include:

- What is it in the situation (i.e., the process or practice that is the object of a change effort) that leads one to think that an organizational change is also needed?
- What are the components of the situation (i.e., the who, what, when, where and why of it)?
- Who wants or does not want the change to occur? Why? What motivates them?
- Are these motives consistent with the dominant organizational culture, or are they unique?
- Who can be counted on to support the change or the IT implementation? Why and how will they support it?
- Who will probably resist the change effort, and what will be their basis for resistance?
- What kinds of resources, incentives and mandates are executive-level managers willing to employ in the change/IT implementation effort? Where would these resources have the greatest impact?

While some public managers will have an innate sense of how to answer these questions, managers of large organizations may need to think through exactly how a major IT/change project will impact the various stakeholders in the environment. The Department of Defense (1994) suggests that managers involved in a process improvement or reengineering effort ask questions about the potential impact of the change, including the following:

- What individuals and groups (functional units) will be affected?
- How severe will this impact be?
- How will impacted individuals be involved in the change (labor hours, costs, disruption, etc.)?
- How will these individuals/groups benefit from the change, and will this be an immediate or long-term benefit?
- Will significant costs be incurred in the short term for a benefit that will not be realized in the current budget cycle?
- Who will ultimately gain or lose resources?
- Who will gain or lose power, positions, prestige, work, customers or suppliers?
- What trade-offs or benefits can be used to compensate for losses?

The change manager's role will obviously involve some degree of effort in trying to minimize losses as well as compensating those whose losses are most likely to be severe.

Finally, public managers should be prepared to address any or all of the barriers to successful adoption of IT-based change identified in Table 6.4.

LEARNING AND ACCEPTANCE CURVES

People find it difficult to accept what they do not understand, but they also avoid understanding what they do not accept. This suggests that in addition to overcoming specific barriers to the acceptance of new information technology and related systems, public managers will need to be sensitive to the timing of their activities in support of an implementation effort. Ideally, public managers will move staff down both the learning and the acceptance curves in a coordinated or parallel fashion. If they do not, they are likely to encounter people who do not accept the technology but have now learned enough about it to marshal more effective arguments and activities against its implementation. Or they may encounter people whose initial acceptance is so unquestioning that they fail to work aggressively to improve the technology in the design and testing phases of implementation. Their failure in this regard would be due to their not knowing enough about the technology to understand how it might be improved.

TRUST AND KNOWLEDGE MANAGEMENT

Knowledge is a unique resource in the sense that, unlike land, labor or capital, its availability cannot be guaranteed ahead of time through purchasing or forcing people to do one's will. Coaxing people to draw on their knowledge and creativity is the ultimate test of a manager's skill. Research by Kim and Mauborgne (1997) suggests that a key to managing knowledge is building trust. The puzzle that these researchers have tried to solve is why some managers of local units fail to share their knowledge or crucial information with headquarters executives, while others do so even when the rewards for doing so are not apparent. For Kim and Mauborgne the explanatory factor is the fairness of the decision-making process. Executives who are seen as being fair are much more likely to be trusted with important information from subordinates than those who are seen as less fair. Fairness, say Kim and Mauborgne, involves three behaviors. First, the fair executives tend to involve people in decisions that directly affect them. Second, they work hard to explain why decisions are made in a particular way, and third, they are very clear about what will be expected after the changes are made. While a fair process cannot make up for the lack of internal motivation and skill, it does appear to be a necessary condition for engaging workers' cooperation and creativity.

INVESTING IN KNOWLEDGE PRODUCTION

Because knowledge production and creativity cannot be compelled, there are a limited number of ways to invest in these important functions. In addition to investing in a fair decision-making process, organizations can attempt to boost the sources of knowledge and creativity. These include skill and expertise, flexibility and playfulness of mind, and motivation. While all three are often necessary, they tend to involve different cost curves. For example, it can often take several years of college to achieve a particular level of skill or expertise, or several months of mental exercises to increase a person's ability to think outside of conventional frameworks. In contrast, increasing the field of action for people who are already intrinsically motivated can represent a relatively smaller investment. According to Amabile (1998), managers can increase the level of activated motivation by making adjustments in

1. the amount of challenge they give employees,
2. the degree of freedom they grant around processes,
3. the way they design work groups,
4. the level of encouragement they give, and
5. the nature of organizational support.

Amabile suggests that managers can influence motivation by, for example, matching tasks to people in ways that present employees with a challenge that is feasible (i.e., not too easy, but also not too difficult). Similarly, they can give basically motivated workers the ability to decide not the goal but how they will go about achieving the goal. This increased freedom can even include decisions regarding membership on different work teams.

REFERENCES

Amabile, T. M. (1998). How to kill creativity. *Harvard Business Review* 76 (5): 76–88.
Bellandi, M. (1999). The associational economy: Firms, regions, and innovation. *Regional Studies* 33(3): 290–91.
Clemens, E. S., and J. M. Cook. (1999). Politics and institutionalism: Explaining durability and change. *Annual Review of Sociology* 25: 441–46.
Culpan, O. (1995). Attitudes of end users toward information technology in manufacturing and service industries. *Information and Management* 28(3): 167–76.
Davenport, T. H., and D. B. Stoddard. (1994). Reengineering: Business change of mythic proportions? *MIS Quarterly* 18: 121–27.
Department of Defense. (1994). *Framework for Managing Process Improvement*. Washington, DC: Electronic College of Process Innovation, December 15.
Dosi, Giovanni. (1982). Technological paradigms and technological trajectories: A

suggested interpretation of the determinants and directions of technical change. *Research Policy* 11 (3): 147–63.

Dutton, W. H., and K. L. Kraemer. (1985). *Modeling as Negotiation: The Political Dynamics of Computer Models in the Policy Process.* Norwood, NJ: Ablex Publishing.

Fletcher, P., S. I. Bretschneider and D. A. Marchand. (1992). *Managing Information Technology: Transforming County Government in the 1990s.* Syracuse: Syracuse University, School of Information Studies, August.

Gibbs, W. W. (1997). Taking computers to task. *Scientific American* 277(1): 82–90.

Hammer, M. (1990). Reengineering work. *Harvard Business Review* 90(4): 105–114.

Heeks, R. (1999). *Reinventing Government in the Information Age: International Practice in IT-Enabled Public Sector Reform.* London: Routledge.

Kim, W. C., and R. A. Mauborgne. (1997). Fair process: Managing in the knowledge economy. *Harvard Business Review* 75 (4): 65–76.

Kost, J. M. (1996). *New Approaches to Public Management: The Case of Michigan.* Washington, DC: Brookings Institution, Center for Public Management.

Kraemer, K. L., and J. L. King. (1976). *Computers, Power and Urban Management: What Every Local Executive Should Know.* Beverly Hills, CA: Sage Publications.

Lucas, H. C. (1984). Organization power and the information services department. *Communications of the ACM* 127: 58–65.

Mechling, J., and T. M. Fletcher. (2000). *Eight Imperatives for Leaders in a Networked World: Guidelines for 2000 Election and Beyond.* Cambridge, MA: Harvard Policy Group on Networked Services and Government, March.

O'Looney, J. (1997). *Beyond Maps: Geographic Information Systems and Local Government Decision Making.* Washington, DC: International City/County Management Association.

Pevtzow, L. (1989). Bitterly divided Naperville leaders decide computer strategy. *Chicago Tribune*, August 17, pp. 1, 12.

Rocheleau, B. (1999). The political dimensions of information systems in public administration. In *Information Technology and Computer Applications in Public Administration: Issues and Trends*, ed. David Garson. Hershey, PA: Idea Group Publishing.

Rycroft, R. W., and D. E. Kash. (1999). Innovation policy for complex technologies. *Issues in Science and Technology* 16(1): 73–79.

Strassmann, P. A. (1995). *The Politics of Information Management.* New Canaan, CT: Information Economics Press.

Sussman, O. (1999). Economic growth with standardized contracts. *European Economic Review* 43(9): 1797–1818.

Varden, E. (2000). Human error. *CIO Magazine*, May 15. Found at http://www.cio.com/archive/051500_people.html.

Washburn, G. (1998). Building-permit delays spur city shakeup. *Chicago Tribune*, May 10, pp. 1, 10.

Willets, L. (1996). Human resources: First stop for reengineers. *Enterprise Reengineering*, July. Found at http://www.reengineering.com.

Windrum, P. (1999). Simulation models of technological innovation. *American Behavioral Scientist* 42(10): 1531–50.

Ziegler, J. N. (1997). *Governing Ideas: Strategies for Innovation in France and Germany.* Ithaca, NY: Cornell University Press.

7
Wired Governments and Wired Cultures

While the structural and human resource supports for innovation in a wired organization are fairly well established in the literature, cultural support for a wired organization, though recognized as important, is more difficult to pin down. Obviously, existing attitudes toward technology are important. Here, the social environment has a major role to play. Public managers who believe that the use of rational management techniques, such as those described in the previous chapter, can by themselves overcome cultural barriers to change are probably mistaken. As one study of the implementation of geographic information systems in local governments concluded, public managers who want to obtain substantial returns on their investments in technology need to devise approaches congruent with the social and political realities of their government departments (see Campbell & Masser 1996).

Similarly, MIT professor Wanda Orlikowski's 1993 study of the use of Lotus Notes' file sharing and e-mail system in a major U.S.-based consulting firm suggests that new technologies by themselves are unable to overcome traditional ways of working. Even though the consulting firm's chief information officer was very supportive of these new technologies for sharing ideas, he greatly overestimated the degree to which the professionals in the firm would actually invest their time in learning about and using Notes. The reason why few consultants were interested in learning Notes or in using it was not related to the design of the software; rather, it was due to the consultants' beliefs that the company's reward system did not support their spending time to learn new software and share their expertise. In short, the firm did not have a knowledge culture.

If managers are not to be fatalistic, at some level they must view culture as less than an immovable force. Culture talk should not be an excuse for failure to achieve performance goals or for failing to even try. Rather, an understanding of culture should help managers become aware that some vectors for changing organizations are compatible with the dominant culture, while others are not. While organizational culture is a composite of the norms, practices, beliefs and attitudes of all the members of an organization, it would be foolish to suggest that public managers—at least those who survive for more than a six-month stint—do not in some measure embody the culture they are charged with changing.

The importance of culture can be identified in areas of the historical development of IT systems. For example, even though new concepts of information technology (e.g., for decision support, for work redesign, and for knowledge management) have been developed since the introduction of computers for data processing, many of the custodians of information systems still share a culture that is oriented almost exclusively toward the technology (Alavi, Wheeler & Valacich 1995). That is, the culture of IT specialists has not changed as fast as the theory of information system development. Since IT specialists typically act as teachers of information systems to program managers and staff, there may be a tendency on the part of all concerned to underestimate or misunderstand the potential for information systems to support comprehensive organizational reform (Khosrowpour 1988). In a worst case scenario, technologists will encourage the adoption of the most technically desirable systems, and when these systems fail to provide the touted level of benefits, the nontechnologists become even more suspicious of technology in general.

CULTURE AS SOCIAL DESIGN

Whether consciously or not, organizations will make *social choices* about the sociotechnical configurations of their information systems (Jewett & Kling 1994). "Social design" refers to the design of both the technological characteristics of an information system and the social arrangements under which it will be used.

Social design includes many of the elements of organizational structure and human resource development addressed in the previous chapter. In addition, however, social design has to do with issues such as

- how technology projects are selected for consideration
- how criteria for technology selection or evaluation are developed
- how access to machines and data is managed or controlled
- who decides on the design of a system or what system elements will be standardized or independent
- the availability of additional or complementary resources such as space, storage media, backup provisions, and so on.
- the level of monitoring of use or productivity

How these broad elements of policy and social practice are organized or made routine will create or restrain opportunities for ownership and "belief" in the system. These "social choices" are the hidden dimension of computerization in large part because they are often not formally decided on or entirely within the control of any single manager. When these social choices are ignored (e.g., because the new system is not much different than the old one), managers may live to regret their lack of awareness. In such cases, the unwitting choices made by system developers, rather than by operations managers, often lead to systems that are less successful than they would have been were explicit social choices made.

Social choices about technology can occur even when new technologies are not part of the implementation. Kling (1992) describes a situation in which a university chancellor called for all university system memos to be sent electronically. While this directive is likely to save printing and distribution costs, implementing it in the context of multiple network and e-mail systems placed an unspoken demand on the various university departments and their staffs. Departments would need to dedicate new resources to ensure that staff would have the skills to negotiate the different networks involved in an electronic distribution of a memo. Similarly, Bullen and Bemmett's (1991) study of how people actually use groupware applications suggests that many groups may not be socially ready to take advantage of the features embedded in commercial groupware products. In some cases, moreover, adopting the practices that make the technology effective may lead to a redistribution of productivity rather than a net gain. For example, if one hundred professionals who normally keep convenient wallet calendars are also required to enter their calendar events into a groupware calendar, the result may be an increase in the productivity of an administrative secretary but a net decrease in the productive use of professional time.

A number of information system researchers suggest that social design should be the primary focus in a business process redesign effort. This approach, which is sometimes called sociotechnical systems design, puts people and their relationships with each other and with the work to be done—as opposed to a rational analysis of ideal workflows—at the center of reforms that involve information technology (Zuboff 1988). A sociotechnical systems approach looks for ways to empower workers and to enrich their jobs. IT is used to support these more humanistic goals rather than to support a straight-line productivity improvement effort. Jewett and Kling (1990), for example, describe an effort in a pharmaceutical firm to transform sales clerk jobs into more active and responsible positions. In this case, new information systems were designed to support the broader social design that included a reconceptualization of sales clerk and other key jobs. Hence, the information systems needed to be designed so as to support completion of tasks (e.g., identifying product features, availability, shipping times, expected price changes, etc.) and a level of authority (e.g., to complete orders) that are not typical for the positions.

Similarly, Zuboff (1988, 1991) has suggested that managers learn to distinguish between systems that automate or replace human activity and those that "informate" or make visible to workers processes, objects and behaviors that would otherwise remain hidden. The process of informating is in some ways the reverse of automating. That is, in many cases informating acts to translate automated activtives into data and to display those data. Rather than replacing human activity, informating enables workers to obtain more control over their own activities and those of the machines they use. Zuboff describes an informating example in which workers in a paper plant are provided continuous feedback about the costs of making paper from an information system that has been grafted onto existing paper making equipment. Based on the feedback provided by the system, workers are able to test various equipment settings to identify those that are least costly given the current conditions. One can imagine the use of similar informating technologies in government settings that might provide workers and citizens with real-time cost data for the provision of particular services. For example, workers in a building inspection office (and contractors) could be provided with real-time cost data on each job. These data could be used to move to a real-cost pricing of the building inspection work as well as to the design of different price offerings for inspections. For example, the data may reveal that were the department able to group inspections in a particular area, the average cost of inspections would be reduced by half. Grouping inspections, by necessity, dictates a longer response time on the part of inspectors. However, it may be the case that many of the inspection department customers would be more than willing to trade a slower inspection process for a less expensive one. In addition to identifying new possibilities for service arrangements, informing technologies may also provide managers with ideas for changing the social design of the work. Extending the building inspections scenario, one could also imagine how informating technologies might allow inspectors with a specialty in one area (e.g., heating and air systems) to also conduct basic-level inspections in other areas with the aid of an information system that would identify features of the building site that might call for a more specialized inspection.

Informating technologies obviously have a great deal to offer. Moreover, the principle of informating suggests a path for technology development that should be (and is often not) seriously considered by organizations that are using technology to redesign or reengineer business processes. Informating technologies conceptually fall very much within the family of knowledge management technologies. Nevertheless, informating should probably not be taken as an imperative, particularly in cases where automation would provide substantially greater productivity returns or where it would free up workers to do other more enriched jobs.

When automation does hold a potential for downsizing or elimination of certain job categories, sociotechnical design principles suggest that the people whose jobs will be impacted are unlikely to be enthusiastic about the work and are unlikely to share their ideas for system development with the application designers (Jewett & Kling 1994). Similarly, these principles suggest that there is often a trade-off between systems capabilities and the need for social and training support. That is, the more capable the system in terms of features, customization and flexibility, the greater the need for support and training. Hence, the most flexible applications tend to be the most open to programming by users, but also the ones that are often most difficult to get up and running.

Technology Impacts on Culture

In addition to the impact of social and cultural norms on the success of technology, public managers also need to consider the impact of technology on social relations. Unfortunately, it is sometimes difficult to unravel the nexus of technology and social relationships, since each impacts the other. For example, there is research that suggests that electronic mail and other forms of computer-mediated communication can result in certain behaviors or results (e.g., less inhibited communications, more informal verbalizing, longer times for reaching consensus, more shifts in decisions or choices, and more equal participation) (Kiesler, Siegel & McGuire 1984). Nevertheless, a good case can be made that these findings are organizationally specific. Less inhibited verbalizing and informal attitudes toward communication, for example, are found in some bulletin board or newsgroup settings but not others (Lea et al. 1992). Similarly, Zuboff (1988) observed that in one firm that used electronic mail, the nonmanagerial recipients of the e-mail tended to treat the messages as formal policy statements rather than as informal decisions or observations. The managerial lesson from these studies is that one must proceed carefully with the introduction of new technologies, basing decisions as much on the perceptions and attitudes of stakeholders as on a rational understanding of how the technology may encode certain social capabilities.

In addition to managing social attitudes, public managers should also be aware of the need to manage the choice and use of computer-mediated interaction media according to particular needs. For example, if accomplishing the task requires straight-line rationality or if it could be derailed by personality factors, technologies that filter out nonverbal social cues may be appropriate. However, if the task is one that requires adept reading of nonverbal social cues or the processing of ambiguous information, the use of technologies such as e-mail or online polling that filter out these cues may be less appropriate than technologies that have fewer filtering impacts, such as online video conferencing. Moreover, if the task demands substantial recall capabilities, face-to-face information processing may be the better choice. (For example, Ohaeri [1999] found that participants who had been in face-to-face groups recalled more items alone later than those who had been in electronic groups.) Because of findings like these, the emerging norm for many group tasks appears to be a front-loading of face-to-face meetings followed by greater use of computer-mediated communications. Recent research suggests that it can take a period of weeks for users of computer-mediated communication to acquire the level of social cues that is evident up front in face-to-face meetings (Walther 1993).

Electronic Work Groups

A key aspect of organizational culture is the nature of work groups. With respect to information technology, electronic work groups provide an alternative to face-to-face work groups. While electronic work groups have some clear-cut advantages in situations where the alternative is no work group at all, in many situations public managers will need to decide the appropriate combination of electronic and face-to-face communications. In addition, managers will face choices among many different types of electronic communications media (e.g., text only, online polling, collaborative white boards, threaded discussions, audio conferencing, audio-video conferencing, etc.). These choices will filter to different extents the nonverbal cues and social signals that are available, for good and ill, in face-to-face interactions. As such, public managers will need to create greater congruence between the task and the communications technology being used by the work group. For example, there is some evidence that electronic work groups may be better able to generate new or creative ideas than face-to-face ones. Siau (1995), for example, found that electronic brainstorming can help overcome the problems of free riding, evaluation comprehension and production blocking—problems that tend to occur more frequently in face-to-face verbal exchanges. Moreover, Dennis and Valacich (1993) found that electronic groups were even more creative than nonelectronic nominal groups (i.e., groups where individual contributions are pooled). Similarly, certain types of electronic group work may overcome conflicts that are based on status or role factors that tend to support unequal discussion time and "groupthink" in face-to-face settings (Barnes & Greller 1994). Other research suggests that electronic group work support systems tend to increase decision quality, increase time to reach decisions, increase equality of participation, and increase the degree of task focus, while these systems decrease consensus and satisfaction (McLeod 1992). The beneficial impact of these systems on the quality of decision making has not been a consistent finding (see Kiesler & Sproull 1992). What is less disputed is the general beneficial impact of appropriately designed electronic communication systems on the ability of persons with disabilities to participate in electronic work groups (Marlett 1988).

In addition to findings related to the costs and benefits of electronic communications, communications experts have identified some key dimensions related to the successful development of electronic work groups, including size, place (or the ability to supplement electronic work with face-to-face meetings), openness of participation, and linkage to market forces. Unfortunately, existing research does not allow one to advise public managers as to ideal configurations of these factors with respect to building successful electronic work groups. The size factor is one that appears to have provided the greatest amount of useful research findings. For instance, successful electronic work groups appear to meet a certain critical size or proportion of the whole reference group (Markus 1987). That is, the group must be large enough to maintain a conversation over time. On the other hand, for groups that are naturally large or that involve a high level of interest or required participation, size can inhibit successful communication. The problem of very large-scale conversations is likely to occur in instances where a government or government agency sponsors a public forum on a controversial issue. For example, the U.S. Department of Agriculture's sponsorship of electronic rule making related to definitions of organic foods generated over 275,000 responses from the public. Sack (2000) has suggested that the problem posed by very large-scale conversations on the Internet will ultimately lead to the development of new navigational systems. In particular, Sack states that these systems should combine social navigation (where people help people find information they are interested in), semantic navigation (where computer-based language processing helps us find information) and spatial navigation (where information relationships such as among concepts A, B and C are mapped onto a two- or three-dimensional image or space). To date, Sack has developed a tool that allows one to map conversations that occur over a network. His Conversation Map System takes a body of thousands of messages and analyzes them using a set of computational and linguistic techniques. The product is a summary of the messages including who is talking with whom, the important themes of the discussion, and some of the emergent definitions and metaphors. In addition, system users receive a diagram of the social networks that have been created during the conversations. As public managers begin to experiment with electronic rule making and other forms of online citizen and staff participation, tools like the Conversation Map System offer important aids in understanding key ideas and relationships in the larger community of online participants.

Studies of the use of electronic communications in different scientific fields suggest that geographical factors (e.g., the distance among communicators) and coupling factors (i.e., the degree to which work in one area is linked to or dependent on work in another area) will tend to impact the use of electronic communications. Specifically, Walsh and Bayma (1997) found that fields such as particle physics, which are characterized by tightly coupled work among geographically dispersed groups, use electronic communication more heavily than those (e.g., experimental biology) where work is generally completed independently of other groups. Additionally, Walsh and Bayma identified fields such as mathematics that are more removed from market forces as more prone to use informal electronic communication when compared to practitioners in fields that are more tightly linked to commercial markets (e.g., chemistry). Although there is no parallel research related to public sector communications, it is likely that similar tendencies exist. For example, electronic communications may be used more to maintain regional or national relationships than local ones. Similarly, we would expect planning departments to have more substantial communications with public works than might a leisure services department, since planning is more tightly coupled with public works than are leisure services. However, with respect to market impact on communication style, in the public sector, communication style is more likely to be impacted by such factors as closeness to a publicly visible person or process (e.g., public information office for an elected official) or by professional norms (e.g., norms held by public sector attorneys). It is probably the case that electronic communications with these more visible public offices will be more formal than other interpublic communications.

CULTURE AS THE VISION OF LEADERS: TECHNOLOGY THROUGH THE EYES OF THE PROGRAM MANAGER

How public sector program managers look at technology often will set the defining tone for efforts to transform the government into a wired organization. Heeks (1999) studied the views of government program managers on technology-based reform and arrived at what he terms a "four-eyes" model for categorizing four different approaches to reform:[1]

1. *Ignore.* Program managers, being ignorant about information technology and related systems, are unable to consider using such technologies and systems in their plans for reform. IT expenditures are small, and few professional IT managers are appointed to positions of responsibility.

2. *Isolate.* Program managers are still personally computer illiterate and lack understanding of the role of knowledge of information in their organizations, but they are aware of the potential for IT impacts. As such, they invest in technology but see it as the responsibility of "IT professionals." Implementation of IT projects tends to remain at the level associated with data processing. Some managers will simply include the purchase of IT equipment because everyone is expected to have a computer—even if no use for the computer has been identified. IT managers get sufficient funding and sufficient freedom, but little backing from executive-level management.

3. *Idolize.* Program managers are somewhat technically literate. They use computers and are aware of their potential, but not of their limitations. They believe that IT by itself can transform governmental operations and are eager to initiate IT

projects and place these projects at the heart of the reform effort. IT managers are well paid, IT projects are well financed, and credit for successful projects is sought as a major prize.

4. *Integrate.* Program managers focus on the meaning of information within and beyond individual business processes. IT is viewed as one of a number of means of achieving better information and information flow. The reengineering of work processes, knowledge management, and supporting technologies are now integrated into the process of organizational reform and transformation. The IT manager role is redefined as that of an information or information systems manager.

While it is possible to see these four views as developmental in nature, Heeks indicates that this is not always the case. For example, he suggests that public managers in India appear to be moving directly from the ignore approach to the idolize approach.

In examining reform efforts undertaken during different phases of the "four-eyes" model, one is least likely to discover failures at the integration phase. However, it should be recognized that failure is much less likely to occur in the ignore phase than in the isolate or idolize ones. In these latter phases, governments are more likely to start expensive projects that are doomed to fail because they have not identified and worked on the necessary complementary reforms to standard procedures, rules, human resources and organizational systems.

Sometimes during an idolization phase, forceful public managers will have the strength to make the technology work. However, in many cases this success is based on the presence and continued support of one or two idolizing managers. Bhatnagar (1997) and Rocheleau (1999) suggest that efforts of this type are not likely to be sustainable or replicable. Rather, when a public manager who has acted as the project champion leaves, the project itself loses its force and gets watered down or collapses entirely.

Also, an understanding of the organizational culture may at some point lead a manager to acknowledge that more long-term cultural change is needed if key goals are to be achieved. The following discussion is organized around two responses: using (or flowing with) the culture and changing the culture. Using the culture is a necessary tactic whenever a manager is tasked with implementing new technologies in a short time frame. Changing the culture represents a longer-term and deeper strategy that is built around the idea of creating organic congruence between the culture and the approach to the adoption and infusion of technology.

USING THE EXISTING CULTURE TO FACILITATE TECHNOLOGY ADOPTION

While no hard and fast rules have been thoroughly validated through research for achieving such congruence, there is a body of anecdotal advice that can help public managers think through this problem. In particular, keen observers of the introduction of new IT systems have suggested a number of approaches that will facilitate the acceptance of the IT project by the existing organizational culture.[2] (See below.)

Advice on Integrating IT Projects with the Existing Culture

- Include the end-user in the design of the IT applications.
- Identify as the setting for early adoption the department or unit that is most likely to accept the new technology.
- Provide early and frequent orientation to technology changes.
- Create and support informal user groups that are interested in information technology.
- Make user-friendliness a key factor in selection of hardware and software.
- Identify and implement as a priority the aspects of the technology that will provide some personal benefit to the user.
- Provide easy access to help desks and technology consultants.
- Develop or secure good and easy-to-use documentation and train staff in its use.
- Survey staff to identify perceptions about technology and related organizational change and directly address possible "myths" about these.
- Don't outsource new information technologies unless the benefits of doing so (or the costs of not doing so) are high. Keeping technology in-house helps create a culture of innovation and signals that this is an important core capability of the government.

Enhancing the Value of Information Through Social Validation

As the world becomes more wired together, the key problem with respect to the management of knowledge is not a lack of content, but rather an overload of content such that people are forced to wade through lots of irrelevant information before coming to what they need. Unfortunately, technical solutions to this problem (e.g., sophisticated search engines and filtering software) are not yet up to the job of distilling information from data. A less technical approach involves the social validation of information or a process whereby knowledgeable people filter out irrelevant information and bring to the fore what is likely to be the most important information of that remaining. Among the various Web search engines, for example, Yahoo uses human beings to index Web sites according to a human understanding of what these sites contain as well as to highlight what the Yahoo raters believe are the most useful or interesting sites.[3]

Social validation of knowledge is likely to be as important and as valuable in a specific organization as it is on the World Wide Web. The knowledge management system created to support the work of Xerox customer service representatives (or reps) provides a good example of how organization-focused information validation can work. This system employs a human-centered approach to building (and controlling the quality of) the knowledge base. Brown and Duguid (2000) describe this approach as follows: "Reps, not the organization, supply the tips [for fixing Xerox machines]. But reps also vet the tips. A rep submits a suggestion first to a local expert. Together, they refine the tip. It's then submitted to a centralized review process. . . . Here reps and engineers again vet the tips, accepting some, rejecting others, eliminating duplicates, and calling in experts on the particular product line to resolve doubts and disputes" (p. 80). Obviously, a tip that survives this process will tend to be reliable.

The social validation of information, Brown and Duguid suggest, needs to be part of a larger culture of knowledge. At Xerox, for example, the company was prepared to pay the reps for their tips. The committee working on the system, however, decided against this plan because they felt that it would lead to a focus on quantity rather than quality. Instead of a monetary reward, the committee chose to attach the name of the tip's author to the tip record. This system, Brown and Duguid explain, provides tip authors with social status or social capital in the same way that scientists earn status among their peers for their scientific articles. Authors of high-quality tips are reported to have received spontaneous standing ovations at meetings of their peers.

BUILDING A WIRED CULTURE

Unfortunately, even if public managers were to implement all the specific suggestions for creating a wired culture outlined above, they might not see a wired culture develop in their organization. This is the case because at a deeper level wired cultures exist only within organizations that encourage exploration and responsibility. In short, these cultures are self-governing communities very similar to the original model of the knowledge community—the university. The culture of the university has a number of key components that are beginning to be developed in organizations that are known for innovation. These cultural components include:

- A recruitment system that focuses on strong interests in knowledge acquisition and creation. University professors have typically spent years in school, conducting research and writing reports, before they are recruited for a position. This emphasis on recruitment has been identified as one of the key activities of innovative companies such as W. L. Gore (the maker of Goretex). Gore conducts extensive research on applicants because the company has discovered that people who want to just come to work and do the same job do not last long in an environment where the needs of the business change rapidly. Gore's background research focuses on identifying people who want to continually learn and increase their skills.
- Hiring for commitment, not for the job. University faculty are expected to be committed to a field of study that they will also help direct and change. Innovative

organizations build on this same type of commitment to outcomes rather than to specific tasks.

- A means of honoring those who are good at creating knowledge. In universities honor is bestowed through promotion to higher professorial ranks, and also through endowed chairs and membership in groups such as the National Academy of Science. A similar approach to encouraging knowledge creation is now being taken in some high-tech industries. For example, Sun Microsystems has created a community of distinguished engineers. To be a member of this community one has to be elected by existing members—a process that mirrors the National Academy's process for selecting new members.

- Support for encouraging, helping and allowing other associates to grow in knowledge, skill and scope of responsibility. The obligation to spend time in peer review sessions is a vital one in universities. While on the surface these reviews appear critical in nature, they in fact represent a large commitment of intellectual resources to helping new associates improve their skills. Also, one of the key impacts of the tenure system is that it allows university faculty to hire new faculty who are more skilled than themselves without being concerned that the new faculty will replace them. While peer review and tenure systems provide structural mechanisms for supporting growth in knowledge, more informal means such as mentoring or sponsoring programs can be used for a similar effect. In the Gore Corporation, for example, new employee sponsors act as advocates for their charges, and they collect information and feedback on personal development from peers and leaders. That information is then shared with a compensation committee.

- Opportunities to volunteer. In universities faculty are expected to provide service in addition to teaching and research. However, the exact nature of the service is generally left up to the individual faculty. The rationale is that people will take greater ownership of a volunteer opportunity if they themselves chose it.

- Expectations of an open culture. In such a culture information sharing is expected and withholding information is punished. Here the culture of science provides a good model. In this culture one gains fame and glory from publishing the results of one's investigations. If one delays publication or fails to share one's findings, it is likely that someone else will get credit for the discovery.

- Expectations that everyone will be involved in managing knowledge so as to create more and better choices for decision makers. Here the expectation placed on college faculty that they participate in conferences and other joint knowledge sharing activities provides an example of this cultural component.

- Trusting relationships. People learn all the time, but only share what they learn under certain circumstances. Historical studies of innovative organizations suggest that this sharing is more likely to occur when people care about and trust each other. Hence, small, family-like research and development businesses have often been better at innovating than larger, impersonal ones. As Margaret Wheatley has written, "What's been missing in this pursuit of knowledge management is what's missing in most of our thinking in management and leadership: We're missing. All of the things that are missing are what make us human: emotion, passion, spiritual quest, family concerns, a desire to contribute" (1999, p. 87). Although universities may not have reached the ideal in terms of the development of trusting relationships, the promise of job security in the form of tenure does provide a strong institutional basis for trusting relationships to form and be maintained. That is, job security removes one of the key barriers to organizational trust—the threat of a discontinuance of employment. While such a policy is not sufficient to instill trust, the lack of a similar degree of job security can undermine the potential for trust, particularly between management and staff.

A wired organization is one where a knowledge culture is evident and creativity is valued. The culture at a wired organization is designed to overcome the tendency to hoard knowledge. Because knowledge is a type of power, in societies that are capitalist or based on private property, the culture of self-interest works against the sharing of knowledge. Despite the general enthusiasm for collaboration found in the literature on organizations, actual collaboration among employees or across agencies tends to go against the grain. Knowledge management can facilitate an existing desire to collaborate, but it cannot by itself overcome a reluctance to share that is more ingrained in the organizational culture or society at large.

NOTES

1. Definitions of the approaches adapted from those provided in Heeks (1999).
2. Zorica Budic's article, "Implementation and management effectiveness in adoption of GIS technology in local government," *Computers, Environment, and Urban Systems* (May 1994), provides some excellent case studies of IT implementation.
3. Most of the other search engines use computers to process the pattern of language that is found on each site. The results of this machine language process are often flawed due to the inability of current systems to understand and interpret words in relation to implied contexts that human beings take for granted but that must be supplied to machines.

REFERENCES

Alavi, M., B. Wheeler, and J. Valacich. (1995). Using IT to reengineer business education: An exploratory investigation of collaborative telelearning. *MIS Quarterly* 19(3): 293–310.
Barnes, S., and L. M. Greller. (1994). Computer-mediated communication in the organization. *Communication Education* 43(2): 129–42.
Bhatnagar, S. C. (1997). Information technology-enabled public sector reforms: Myth or reality? Paper presented at Conference on Public Sector Management in the Next Century, University of Manchester, Manchester, UK, June 29–July 2.
Brown, J. S., and P. Duguid. (2000). Balancing act: How to capture knowledge without killing it. *Harvard Business Review* 78(3): 73–82.
Bullen, C., and J. Bemmett. (1991). Groupware in practice: An interpretation of work experience. In *Computerization and Controversy: Value Conflicts and Social Choices*, ed. Charles Dunlop and Rob Kling. San Diego: Academic Press.

Campbell, H., and I. Masser. (1996). A social interactionist perspective on computer implementation. *Journal of the American Planning Association* 62(1).

Dennis, A. R., and J. S. Valacich. (1993). Computer brainstorms: More heads are better than one. *Journal of Applied Psychology* 78(4): 531–37.

Heeks, R. (1999). *Reinventing Government in the Information Age: International Practice in IT-Enabled Public Sector Reform*. London: Routledge.

Jewett, T., and R. Kling. (1990). The work group manager's role in developing computing infrastructure. *Proceedings of the ACM Conference on Office Information Systems*. Boston: Association for Computing Machinery.

———. (1994). The social design of worklife with computers and networks: An open natural systems perspective. In *Advances in Computers* 39, ed. Marshall Yovits. Orlando, FL: Academic Press, 239–93.

Khosrowpour, M. (1988). A comparison between MIS education and business expectations. *Journal of Computer Information Systems* 28(4): 24–27.

Kiesler, S., J. Siegel, and T. W. McGuire. (1984). Social aspects of computer-mediated communication. *American Psychologist* 39(10): 1123–34.

Kiesler, S., and L. Sproull. (1992). Group decision making and communication technology. *Organizational Behavior and Human Decision Processes* 52(1): 96–123.

Kling, R. (1992). Behind the terminal: The critical role of computing infrastructure in effective information systems' development and use. In *Challenges and Strategies for Research in Systems Development*, ed. W. Cotterman and J. Senn. New York: John Wiley, 153–201.

Lea, M., T. O'Shea, P. Fung, and Russell Spears. (1992). "Flaming" in computer-mediated communication. In *Contexts of Computer-Mediated Communication*, ed. Martin Lea. New York: Harvester Wheatsheaf.

Markus, M. L. (1987). Toward a "critical mass" theory of interactive media. *Communication Research* 14(5): 491–509.

Marlett, N. (1988). Empowerment through computer telecommunications. In *Information Technology and the Human Services*, ed. B. Glastonbury and W. LaMendola. Chichester: John Wiley and Sons, 244–64.

McLeod, P. L. (1992). An assessment of the experimental literature on electronic support of group work: Results of a meta-analysis. *Human-Computer Interaction* 7(3): 257–80.

Ohaeri, J. O. (1999). Group processes and the collaborative remembering of stories. *Dissertation Abstracts International: Section B: The Sciences and Engineering* 59(12-B):6502.

Orlikowski, W. J. (1993). Learning from Notes: Organizational issues in groupware implementation. *The Information Society* 9(3): 237–50.

Rocheleau, B. (1999). The political dimensions of information systems in public administration. In *Information Technology and Computer Applications in Public Administration: Issues and Trends*, ed. David Garson. Hershey, PA: Idea Group Publishing.

Sack, W. (2000). Navigating very large-scale conversations. *DIAC 2000: Shaping the Network Society*. Seattle: Annual Conference of Computer Professionals for Social Responsibility, May 20–23, 73–81.

Siau, K. L. (1995). Group creativity and technology. *Journal of Creative Behavior* 29(3): 201–16.

Walsh, J. P., and T. Bayma. (1997). Computer networks and scientific work. In *Culture of the Internet*, ed. S. Kiesler. Mahwah, NJ: Lawrence Erlbaum Associates, 385–406.

Walther, J. B. (1993). Impression development in computer-mediated interaction. *Western Journal of Communication* 57(4): 381–98.

Wheatley, M. (1999). Knowledge tapper. *Government Executive* 31(9): 87.

Zuboff, S. (1988). *In the Age of the Smart Machine: The Future of Work and Power.* New York: Basic Books.

———. 1991. Informate the Enterprise. National Forum (Summer): 3–7.

8

Managing the Trade-off between Ease of IT Implementation and Performance Benefits

A fairly large proportion of public sector IT projects is believed to have experienced either partial or complete failure (Willcocks 1994). While failure is undesirable, it is arguable as to whether public sector organizations would be better off were they to put in place mechanisms for avoiding all failure. To understand this point of view, we first need to understand the roots of IT project failure. As the preceding discussion has suggested, successful IT projects tend to be implemented in supportive organizational, human resource and cultural environments. Unfortunately, managers cannot always wait until the environment is good, nor will they necessarily have the time and resources to change that environment. At some point managers must attempt to reduce the gap between an ideal conception (of a business process or service delivery operation) and the structural, human resource and cultural realities of the organization as it is. Information technology projects are often employed as part of a larger strategy to move an organization toward the ideal or to decrease the gap between the ideal and current practice. When the gap between the ideal conception and the reality is large, the opportunities for improvement are substantial, but so is the challenge. Unfortunately, the existence of such a large gap, while making a technology project more attractive, will also mean that the project will have a higher probability of failure (Heeks 1999). This trade-off between risk and reward may help explain two simultaneous and seemingly incongruent reports about reengineering efforts: (1) that they produced tremendous gains in efficiency and effectiveness, and (2) that a high proportion of reengineering efforts failed (Strassmann 1994).

The public manager's role in implementing IT projects is particularly difficult because public sector organizations provide fewer levers for introducing linear or rational processing. At the same time, public sector organizations tend to have more channels for political influence (e.g., through elected officials, advisory boards, or citizen participation, etc.) and for idiosyncratic cultural development (e.g., based on the triangles of interest groups, agency personnel, and subject-matter specific legislative committees). The features that distinguish public sector organizations from private sector ones also tend to make the use of IT projects as a centerpiece for reform efforts more risky in the public sector. Commonly recognized public sector organizational features include multiple and conflicting goals; multiple types of legal and political accountability and performance measures (rather than the single profit measure used in the private sector); a larger role played by professional associations and interest groups; the existence of hard-to-change statutory restrictions on organizational structures, budgets and routines; and a higher level of access to organizational information and routines by external stakeholders. These features generally produce public sector processes with outcomes that are less standard and less rational. Management-oriented IT, however, assumes that processes will, for the most part, be rational.

Obviously, certain routine data processing functions such as billing can be automated as easily within a single unit of government as they are in the private sector. However, as functions become less routine and as public managers attempt IT projects that span categorical programs and jurisdictional divides, the public sector's disadvantages are more likely to come into play. As such, technologies such as decision support, expert systems or enterprise-wide management information systems that may be implemented with ease in the private sector can present numerous difficulties in the public sector. The more that an IT system assumes objectivity and accuracy in the available data, the existence of a formal process in the organization, the presence of high skills, and a supporting culture, the more likely the system is to fail.

THE ASSUMPTION OF ORGANIZATIONAL RATIONALITY AND THE CONTINUUM OF SYSTEM CHOICES

Fortunately for managers who are faced with decisions about how to use IT successfully to move the organization from its current state to an improved state, there are a range of information technologies from which to choose. These are presented in Table 8.1. The appropriate choice of technology will depend first on how much of the gap between the ideal or rational conception and the unordered organizational reality a manager is attempting to bridge. A manager who can fully control the operational environment and who can assume a high degree of rationality in the operation itself will get the most bang for the buck out of fully automated systems or expert systems. The fallacy of early attempts to create and implement such systems outside of the domain of routine operations lay not in the

Table 8.1

Continuum of Systems Used to Support Completion of a Complex Task or Function

Range of Environmental Rationality	System Type Used to Support Completion of a Complex Task or Function	Development Cost	Use Cost	Benefit
High Assumption of Environmental Rationality	Automated Processing: All steps in the process are based on preset rules that define all the possible actions.	Moderate	Low	Very High
	Expert System: Worker is advised as to expert thinking in similar situations based on probability patterns that cover the vast majority of cases. System cannot be used for cases that are outside the range of its expertise (e.g., to query for new information).	Moderate	Moderate	High
	Decision Support/Management Information System: Worker is provided with: —preset summary information; —reports of situations outside of the system norm; —background information that is probably relevant to the case; and —general rules of thumb for handling cases that are outside the norm.	Moderate	Moderate	Moderate to High
	Structured Database with Data Validation and Output Control: Workers can only enter or receive data or conduct analyses within certain categories. Queries within those preset categories can be wide ranging.	Moderate	Moderate	Moderate
	Free-Form Database: Rules for entering information and for querying the data are few, but data is still structured into preset fields and sets of fields or records.	Moderate	High	Moderate

Table 8.1 (continued)
Continuum of Systems Used to Support Completion of a Complex Task or Function

Range of Environmental Rationality	System Type Used to Support Completion of a Complex Task or Function	Development Cost	Use Cost	Benefit
	Structured Natural Language Input Forms and Queries: Users input natural language data via moderately structured forms. The system uses a knowledge base and qualitative analysis tools to aggregate data across inputs.	High	Low	Moderate to High
	Free-Form Natural Language Input Forms and Queries: Users input natural language data via unstructured forms. The system uses a knowledge base and qualitative analysis tools to aggregate data across free-form inputs.	Very High	Low	Moderate to High
Low Assumption of Environmental Rationality	Free-Form Communications: No restrictions on user input and no attempt to use IT to summarize.	Low	Very High	Moderate to Low

systems themselves but in the incongruent graft between the system and the organizational culture or accepted practices.

Within the range of IT system-type choices, there are different development costs, use costs and potential benefit levels. Fully automated systems that are seen as successful will tend to have a high net benefit in three respects. First, development costs will be in the low to moderate range. Essentially, these systems will tend to require hiring an engineer only one time to codify a straightforward set of rules for the system. Second, the ongoing use costs (e.g., to train people to use the system) are low because the system has essentially replaced human judgment in the operation. As such, lower-skilled workers can perform the tasks using the system. Finally, the benefits are very high because the system performs most if not all of the work, eliminating the need for high-skilled, high-cost labor. At the other end of the spectrum are free-form communication technologies such as e-mail. For the purpose of general communications these systems are tremendously valuable, and they are also low cost. However, without a very high level of training in the use of these systems, staff are unlikely to use them efficiently and appropriately in situations where the task is complex. That is, these systems do very little to make up for staff who are unskilled or unknowledgeable, or who cannot communicate clearly about the task. Because the level of training needed to make these systems useful is both high and ongoing, the net benefit of such systems is rarely substantial or sustainable beyond the initial burst of productivity that occurs due to more efficient communication.

Database applications have traditionally been the technology of choice for managers who want to introduce new information technologies that stand somewhere in between strictly defined automated systems and more free-form communications technologies. For managers wanting a greater challenge, a management information system could be included as part of the development of a database application. The more structured the database on both the input and the output side, the lower would be the ongoing costs for training staff to use the system. At the same time, however, the system would have less power to incorporate new concepts and to identify and communicate new ideas. More free-form databases do a better job of incorporating new ideas and allowing a wider range of inquiry by the users, but the costs of training staff to use advanced querying and modeling capabilities is substantial.

Natural language systems represent the new alternative for managers who want to achieve operational improvements but need to do so within environments whose rationality is less than desirable. These systems represent the most sophisticated level of knowledge management systems available. They cost a great deal to develop both because they are new technologies and because available software must often be customized to meet the needs of a specific knowledge domain. These systems essentially act like expert systems but without users having to answer numerous preset questions, follow a single path to a solution, or conform their understanding to the system's logic. Instead, users interact with the system in a more conversational format. Moreover, the "conversation" can produce a valid solution based on any number of paths taken. In addition, the most sophisticated of these systems are designed to be self-correcting. By analyzing and incorporating new queries and new data about the results of the "advice" given by the system, the advice can potentially be improved upon as the system learns from its mistakes. These features tend to make the systems more effective over time. A second benefit is related to the low cost of use. Because users do not have to conform their understanding of the situation to a very limited set of machine logic or a user interface that only allows one to use the machine in one correct manner, training costs are potentially much lower than in most systems.

CONFLICTING AND COMPLEMENTARY TECHNOLOGIES IN LARGE, MULTIFUNCTIONAL GOVERNMENTS

Public managers will typically not be able to choose the type of system they want to implement within a "blank slate" technology environment. Instead, implementation will likely take place in an environment where some technologies have already proven their worth and others have been rejected. Managers should obviously inspect the array of current technologies as well as those that have been rejected. In this regard, they should ask themselves a number of questions, including the following:

- Where along the continuum of rationality expectations do or did these systems lie?
- What features of the system appear to have created success or failure?
- How would the proposed new system build on, conflict with, or complement existing systems?
- Is there a trend in user expectations regarding system design or features? (E.g., many users may be more likely to accept an intranet system, one that has an Internet browser interface.)

In addition, public managers need to be aware that new IT systems designed to improve organizational control over complex processes and tasks are likely to conflict with other new technologies. The existence of e-mail throughout the organization, for example, can act to create new pockets of political and cultural power, along with "super-empowered" individuals. If these new individuals and groups are set against the implementation of more management-oriented technologies, a public manager may find that being wired in terms of e-mail capability may actually work against becoming wired with regard to better organization of resources around a complex task. Large, multipurpose public sector organizations that contain conflicting professional views are most likely to experience this problem.

MATCHING TECHNOLOGY ROLES AND STYLES TO ORGANIZATIONAL CULTURE

Information technology systems are tremendously malleable. As such, public managers who are able to make choices about the design of new systems should consider how design elements might facilitate or undermine the desired role of the system and the desired style of interaction between the system and the user. Systems that are built within the same functional domain can, depending on the design, play or emphasize any one or all of the following roles:

- assumption of routine work processes
- guidance in making work consistent

- the application of knowledge to a wider range of cases
- the archiving and sharing of information across areas
- the structuring of cases and knowledge into groups
- the training of new staff

The appropriate role for technology will often depend on the particular circumstances, challenges and goals of the government organization. Depending on the role that is desired, public managers may want to work with the program or application designers to have the system facilitate a particular style of interaction. The interaction style embedded in the applications' routines should probably mirror the role that the system plays in the business process. For example, if the system is assuming a particular work routine and is going to complete the work autonomously, the style of interaction is likely to be one where the system provides only periodic diagnostic information as to maintenance needs or performance measures. However, if the system is designed to be a co-producer or a component of a process, it may need to provide more detailed information about its production function. For example, if the system is designed to provide part of an eligibility assessment, it might be programmed to provide information about the probability of a particular eligibility determination being accurate. The user can then take this information and combine it with his or her own findings and tacit knowledge to decide whether further screening is needed before making a referral.

Systems can also be built that have a consultation style that works at every stage of a process to provide the user with a steady stream of advice or encouragement, or a watchdog style that intervenes in a process only when there is a danger of error. Alternatively, the system can be developed to allow users to make choices as to what parts of a job will be assumed by the application and what parts the user will assume (Warden 1988). Obviously, designing a system in a style that is congruent with the organizational culture will help ease implementation and potentially increase performance.

REFERENCES

Allerton, H. E. (1998). The Disney approach to managing for creativity and innovation. *Training and Development* 52(7): 25.

Anfuso, D. (1999). Core values shape W. L. Gore's innovative culture. *Workforce* 78(3): 48–53.

Bhatnagar, S. C. (1997). Information technology-enabled public sector reforms: Myth or reality? Paper presented at Conference on Public Sector Management in the Next Century, University of Manchester, Manchester, UK, June 29–July 2.

Campbell, H., and I. Masser. (1996). A social interactionist perspective on computer implementation. *Journal of the American Planning Association* 62(1): 99–108.

Ferris, N. (1999). Knowledge is power, really. *Government Executive* 31(6): 63–64.

Heeks, R. (1999). *Reinventing Government in the Information Age: International Practice in IT-Enabled Public Sector Reform*. London: Routledge.

Strassmann, P. A. (1994). The hocus-pocus of reengineering. *Across the Board*. Electronic College of Process Innovation, http://www.c3i.osd.mil/bpr/bprcd/5535.htm.

Verespej, M. (1999). Knowledge management: System or culture? *Industry Week* 248(15): 20.

Warden, R. (1988). Integrating KBS into information systems—the challenge ahead. In *Knowledge Based Systems: Applications in Administrative Government*, ed. P. H. Duffin. London: Ellis Horwood Ltd.

Wheatley, M. (1999). Knowledge tapper. *Government Executive* 31(9): 87.

Willcocks, L. (1994). Managing information systems in UK public administration: Issues and prospects. *Public Administration* 72(1): 13–32.

9

Management-Level Policy Development for Wired Governments

Chapter 4 outlined some of the challenges for managers related to the cycle of creating, capturing, storing, analyzing, representing, codifying, transmitting, interpreting, using, and recreating data, information and knowledge. While some of these challenges were well within the scope of the role of public executives or program managers, others, I suggested, were more properly in the domain of policy makers. For example, managers with technical backgrounds can probably be trusted to make good choices about the formatting and storage of information, while decisions about what information will be regularly reported and how this information will be analyzed, represented or displayed are ones that could potentially have important policy implications. As our governments become more wired, the potential for wiring in good or bad analytical or reporting routines, formats or information displays is great. In particular, elected policy makers need to be involved in decisions about these routines, as they are likely to heavily impact policy makers' agenda setting. If what we attend to is what we act on, the importance of this effort cannot be overstated. At a minimum, policy makers should be substantially involved whenever a decision is made to introduce new technologies that will significantly change a long-standing analytical or information reporting routine.

Similarly, elected policy makers need to attend to the foundation issues of privacy, information filtering for decision making, and the design of new virtual public spaces. At the level of organizing for service delivery, however, public managers will still decide plenty of policy issues by themselves or have substantial input into the decisions made by elected officials. Among these policy areas are:

- Regulating and documenting the flow of electronic information
- Copyright
- Policies for Web publishing and forums
- Open source software
- Government ownership of intellectual property
- Public-private partnerships for technology development
- Digital signatures and electronic records
- Public access
- Policies for staff use of public and private networks
- Reliability of business operations and communications
- Telecommuting
- Privacy
- Personalization of services and information

REGULATING AND DOCUMENTING THE FLOW OF ELECTRONIC INFORMATION

As governments become more wired, public managers will have a major role in shaping the communications channels. These channels will involve both communications between citizens and government and those among government employees. A recent survey of American households highlights one of the problems related to citizen-government communications channels. Of the 1,016 people surveyed, 12 percent reported sending e-mail to a government official, but only 5 percent received a response to their e-mailed message (Keegan 2000). This finding suggests that one possible priority for public managers is the establishment of policies and practices to ensure that electronic communications with the public receive the appropriate level of attention.

A second area of concern centers on the potential for electronic communication channels to become much less defined or ordered. This tendency can be the result of the technology itself (see Chapter 11 for a discussion of electronic communications research findings), but is more likely to be the result of officials making specific social choices within the context of the existing organizational culture. An example of possible consequences can be seen in what happened when Stephen Goldsmith, the mayor of Indianapolis, encouraged public employees at all levels to e-mail him directly on any issues of concern. Goldsmith reported that he began to receive and read 400 e-mail messages a day (Rocheleau 1999). While public managers can do little to change the communications patterns that elected officials attempt to create, they have some control over the flow of electronic information within the government administration. Executive-level public managers in particular will have a number of choices to make with respect to encouraging or discouraging the use of electronic means of communication by public employees and citizens. At the most permissive end, a manager may encourage open communication in all directions without any regard for organizational hierarchy, command channels, or even the need to identify oneself. On the other end of the spectrum, public managers may discourage the use of e-mail for any purpose that needs bureaucratic documentation, while also requiring specific indications of identity on each document, such as signed memos. In between, managers may rule that employees should use written paper formats for particular types of communication (e.g., personnel or budget matters) while using e-mail for others. Managers will also need to decide whether electronic communications will have to follow the same rules as other written communications (e.g., you must make a copy for your boss) or those for the less demanding practices of telephone communications that are not typically recorded and copied.

Public managers may also dictate the design of more complex communication systems that allow for greater (or less) management control and meta-information. For example, the city of Boston's Web site allows for citizen feedback to be both routed to multiple persons (e.g., the city manager, elected officials, the appropriate department head, and technical staff person) and tracked according to category. With such a system, a manager can track the number of complaints received by each department and identify trends over time.

Information and the documentation of information flow represent forms of power. Managers will need to think carefully about how the operational rules and technical architecture of information flows in their organization will affect their own power and that of their trusted staff and colleagues. Instituting rules and technologies that help maintain one's power can be an important strategic concern, but decisions of this type need to take into account other factors as well. That is, managers should also be concerned about the congruence of mandated rules and channels for information flow, on the one hand, and their "advertised" management style and the key challenges facing the organization on the other.

COPYRIGHT

Knowledge management involves both a broader search for information as part of a continual environmental scan and a broader broadcasting of this information throughout the network (e.g., via an intranet or the Internet). As digital documents and products become easier to copy, governments have an interest both in keeping employees from violating the copyrights of private citizens or corporations and in protecting whatever copyrights they have established as part of the knowledge creation process. Although copyright procedures in networked settings are not more exacting than in print-oriented settings, in the latter, professional staff have typically been trained in copyright law. In wired governments, however, many more people will be creating, borrowing and transferring intellectual property. As such, policies and procedures that once applied only to small groups will need to be expanded to larger groups of government employees. That is, at a minimum it may be necessary to familiarize all potential users of a knowledge management system with copyright law (O'Looney 2000a).

Also, particular attention will need to be given to the new media forms of intellectual property (e.g., computer animated graphics, virtual worlds, and audiovisual media) that are more difficult to incorporate into a knowledge base without explicit permission of the owner. This difficulty stems from the fact that while these digital media have become as easy to copy (e.g., off the Internet) as it is to copy text, managing the "fair use" of these media is much more difficult. This is the case because the value of many of these media tends to be holistic. That is, it is difficult to make fair use of a picture or video when one would have to incorporate the entire picture or video for the media to make sense. In these instances, a fair use that was less than total use would be of no value.

Finally, public managers should request the public attorney to keep abreast of emerging cyberlaw issues. An issue that is still being sorted out by the courts, for example, is whether Web site owners who knowingly link their sites to those that publish material in violation of copyright law are themselves subject to liability for contributing to the infringement of a copyright. Other copyright-related issues that manager and attorney should attend to include the following:[1]

- Use of "deep links" into a nongovernment Web site that bypass the site's intended homepage or site navigational structure.
- Use of browser frames that incorporate the content of another's Web site or knowledge base into the structure of the local government's knowledge management system or Web site.
- "In-lining" or drawing an image or content from another's server into a government knowledge base.

POLICIES FOR WEB PUBLISHING

Identifying What Must Be Published

For citizens to be able to rely on Internet-based information about a local government's activities, governments will likely need to establish policies for ensuring that certain information is published on the Internet and that the publication is timely. Such policies may also need to identify a standard for accuracy and freshness of information. The list of "must-publish" information could be limited to those items that are most relevant to democratic

Table 9.1
Rules for Public Forums

Government Web sites need to follow constitutional principles related to public forums. If a government chooses to offer an open public forum:

- it may not regulate the content of speech in a public forum unless the regulation is needed to serve a compelling state interest, and

- it must use the most narrowly drawn regulations to achieve the state interest being protected.

In most cases these guidelines mean that governments must allow unlimited free speech with the usual exceptions related to imminent danger and obscenity. However, governments can also sponsor issue-specific forums. In these forums, governments may regulate the content of speech as long as the regulation is reasonable and not an effort to suppress any speaker's view. Hence, if a government sponsored a forum on a proposed new pollution regulation, it could not filter out points of view that it disagreed with, but it could reasonably filter out irrelevant or repeated ideas if the purpose of the forum was to generate new policy ideas. However, if the purpose of the forum was to gauge support for different ideas, such filtering would be suspect. The key consideration with regard to the sponsorship of forums is truth in advertising. If a government wants "credit" for being open, it needs to really be open. If it wants credit for organizing discussion on a particular issue, it has to be clear about its purposes in this regard and then regulate speech only in ways that are least restrictive given the stated purposes of the forum.

---

decision making. However, as the Web becomes the primary way to deliver services, the must-publish list could easily extend to a more comprehensive compendium of information related to services both in and outside of government.

Identifying What Can (and Cannot) Be Published and by Whom

At one extreme, some governments will not allow any material to be published without the approval of a public information officer or other executive-level manager. At the other extreme, there are governments that provide a large spectrum of staff who publish to the Internet at will and even support free-form discussion areas for citizens to publish their views. In between these extremes are governments that allow a certain amount of departmental latitude to publish their own materials without central office approval.

While some decisions, such as whether or not to allow citizens' views to be published on a government Web site, will probably be made by elected policy makers, public managers will need to advise these policy makers regarding the legal rules for the operation of public forums. (See Table 9.1.)

Furthermore, public managers will probably have a great deal of discretion when it comes to deciding what can and cannot be published and by whom in the agencies or units that they manage.

With regard to the appropriate use of this discretion, public managers will need to assess their own management style and situation to determine the best course of action. However, they should understand that many of the traditional control mechanisms for government publication have arisen as much out of a desire to limit the costs of publishing as out of other control needs. To the degree that this is true, public managers may want to reconsider (in light of the new economics of electronic publishing) publication policies that have been based on the economics of paper publication.

Given the low cost of Web publishing, there is no budgetary reason that governments cannot publish more widely and under more categories related to levels of "officialness," reliability, accuracy and objectiveness. For example, governments could create some Web site areas that are tightly controlled and only include accurate, official proclamations by policy makers. At the same time, governments could create other areas that are not so controlled and that include opinions, ideas and data that may be useful in deliberations about issues but that do not represent an official position of the government and have not been entirely fact-checked. Each area would need separate policies for publication and standards for reliability, accuracy and identification of speakers or authors.

OPEN SOURCE SOFTWARE

The debate over open source code is one of the most interesting and divisive in the information technology community. Open source code or software is a mixture of a philosophy, an infrastructure, a culture and the practice of thousands of volunteers. The product of this culture is free software or software whose underlying source code is transparent to anyone with the skills needed to understand it. In addition, anyone is free to take and use this code (e.g., by adding to it or incorporating it into their own products), provided that they make the resulting improvement open to the public as well, that is, make their source code visible. The open source model is essentially the model of scientific development. With programmers worldwide working to improve software, innovations will occur more quickly and there will be less duplication of effort, since new discoveries will quickly be known and be able to be incorporated by others. Also, with free or nearly free software, computerization would be cost-effective across a wider range of uses.[2]

While the open source approach and culture are clearly congruent with the development of wired governments using knowledge management strategies, the difficulty lies in getting to the promised land. As the development of the Microsoft monopoly demonstrated, there are substantial network economies to be achieved through interacting organizations adopting the same software. These same economies could obviously be achieved, all else being equal, through the wholesale adoption by governments and businesses of open source code alternatives to Microsoft. Unfortunately, the costs to the first movers in this adoption of open source may be substantial in that the works they create may not be transferable (or at least not easily transferable) to others who are still using the standard or monopoly software. The obvious solution would be for a number of large governments (e.g., the federal government or a number of large state governments) to adopt open source standards. In the meantime individual public managers are unlikely to attempt to work outside the standard. However, this does not relieve public managers of the responsibility to both advise policy makers about the potential of open source code and to use their professional organizations to help lay the foundation for collaborative action. It should also be recognized that collaborative action cannot end with government adoption of open source software. This is the case because the open source movement exists because of a substantial foundation of skilled and altruistic software developers. Many of these developers, however, are able to be altruistic in some measure because they have been able to earn a good living from developing non–open source software for purchase. Hence, if governments attempt to lead our society in the direction of a more open source approach to development of key software components, they will also need to develop the means of support for software developers who devote substantial amounts of time or skill to the open source effort.

At the level of national policy, there are many reasons why government should favor open source code as well as some reasons for not favoring it (e.g., it could undermine American leadership in the proprietary software business). In addition, the impact of open source code depends on the domain in which it is used. For example, government action to ensure that the Internet remains an environment where the source code of the network itself is open is (at least in the current technological environment) substantially different than an effort to ensure that all departments adopt a particular word processing package. For public managers at the state and local levels, however, the decision about whether to adopt open source software may be preempted by an inability to change existing standards without substantial costs and disruption. In such cases, it may nevertheless be possible to follow a strategy that allows the government to use open source software in some systems (e.g., to run file and Web servers) while keeping the official or standard software on the desktops of users. In this way, governments can help maintain the needed technical capacity to prepare for a day when open source software is broadly used while not incurring the short-term costs of being one of only a few governments to adopt open source systems exclusively.

Government Ownership of Intellectual Property

The direct opposite of the open source philosophy, which involves the government as the promoter of knowledge sharing, is the idea of government as entrepreneur. If public management is about consistency, it may be difficult, if not impossible, to make a case that governments should promote both open source software and an underlying culture of knowledge creation and transfer, while at the same time arguing for protecting its right to sell to commercial firms software (or other intellectual property) that it has developed. However, one could imagine a case where a government spent substantial amounts of public funds to develop software that had an internal governmental use as well as being potentially valuable to a narrow group of commercial software developers. Assuming that this software would not be of more general interest to the software development industry or to open source programmers, a government that had adopted an open source approach to software might nevertheless be justified in attempting to regain some of the development costs of its application. Whether or not this would be desirable and consistent with the open source goals would involve a judgment call on the part of a public administrator.

Moreover, public managers in these circumstances would need to be sure that any software sales were in accordance with state law. That is, in some states the software code produced for the manipulation of governmental records is itself considered a record and thereby is subject to open records statutes. Fortunately, many states have generic government work product laws that should prevent people from being able to use this source code for their own gain or to create a public loss. Other states such as Washington have developed specific legislation designed to address this issue. Washington allows municipalities to protect source or object code from disclosure but limits the protection to cases where the code is less than five years old and the disclosure would produce private gain and public loss. Nevertheless, some states may not have provided themselves with sufficient protection in this regard.

Ownership rights need not be an either-or issue. Governments can make distinctions between citizen use and commercial use of published data and can define who has rights to further distribute or reuse data and under what circumstances. Also, governments may need to define the circumstances, if any, under which government Web space is to be made available for use by nonprofit organizations or commercial entities. Potential uses of network capacity by nongovernmental bodies might include notification, advertising, or joint coordination of community resources such as meeting rooms controlled by both government and the private sector.

PUBLIC-PRIVATE PARTNERSHIPS FOR TECHNOLOGY DEVELOPMENT

Although elected policy makers will likely have an interest in some aspects of public-private partnerships for development of information technology, the details of these partnerships will often be left up to public managers. Elsewhere (O'Looney 2000b), I have examined in greater depth a number of different models for such partnerships, including forming promotional and purchasing alliances, extracting value from contractual arrangements, and obtaining ownership and development rights.

Forming Promotional and Purchasing Alliances

These alliances tend to be organized for the purpose of increasing the supply and quality of local network technologies while also aggregating the purchasing power of the alliance members. As these are voluntary membership organizations that charge nominal fees, are not exclusive, and have educational as well as business goals, public managers can safely join without too much worry about maintaining policy-level political support for the partnership. While the objectives of these groups tend to be consumer focused, they will also often include service providers, which may tend to reduce the political fallout of the government joining a consumer union–type organization.

Extracting Value from Contractual Arrangements

Governments that have something valuable to sell to network building companies (i.e., rights of way or existing conduits or poles) can often negotiate with these firms so as to produce win-win partnership terms. For example, as part of a contract for wiring municipal office facilities, cities have been able to extract agreements that include such benefits as providing a technology center for low-income citizens, setting aside a certain percentage of the gross revenues for technology training for employees or citizens, or providing an enhanced level of service (e.g., broadband services for basic cable TV subscribers) or lowering prices to consumers. The city of Anaheim's agreement with FirstWorld, for example, created two development funds from the partnership fees. One fund is used to support Internet access by low-income residents, while the other is used to promote information technology activities that will result in further economic development for the community.

Obtaining Ownership and Development Rights

While most public-private partnerships involve the private sector retaining the ability to reap substantial profits for innovative investments, in a few cases governments have begun to identify opportunities for profit (or tax refunds) that also help the government meet particular objectives. At the national level one can point to the much publicized organization by the Central Intelligence Agency of a public corporation that will act as a venture capital firm for high-technology start-ups. The firm, called In-Q-It, is charged with investing in high-tech firms, sharing information with universities, and forming joint ventures to work on problems of network security and information gathering and filtering techniques. At the local level, an agreement between the city of LaGrange, Georgia, and the local cable TV franchise has given the city and the cable company joint development rights in the unused portion of the broadband. Either party can develop ideas for the use of this bandwidth. The remaining partner can decide whether or not to join in the proposed use.

Partnerships for Regulating the Private Use of Public Information or Transactions

A number of state and local governments have been able to jump-start their plans to develop electronic commerce applications for government (i.e., applications that would enable citizens to pay a tax or a ticket, register and pay for a recreational program, or purchase nonpublic information) by allowing a private IT firm to build the e-commerce or e-government application in return for the right to charge a transaction fee for the service. Because of the potentially expanding and changing nature of these contractual agreements, some governments have purposely set up public-private boards or authorities to oversee and refine the terms of the agreements. CivicNet Indianapolis is an example of such a board. While the concept of a public-private oversight role can be a good one, public managers need to ensure that representation on these boards is broad and that the board is not captured by the same private interests that the board is designed to regulate.

Exclusive Versus Multiple Partner Models

In developing IT partnerships with the private sector, public managers may need to choose between partnering with a single company or with multiple companies. Typically, the former type of partnership will occur when the task of the private sector partner is to build or maintain a network or system, while the latter model is more likely to be appropriate in situations where the government has built a network with excess capacity that it can then lease to one or more private firms for retail marketing.

DIGITAL SIGNATURES AND ELECTRONIC RECORDS

Policies for the use of digital signatures will likely be set by state or federal statute. The current trend is toward fairly liberal policies that essentially put digital signatures on the same footing as written signatures. Such policies give legal backing to any type or level of electronic signature (from a simple unsecured e-mail to a high-level public key-encrypted digital certificate backed by a government acting as a certificate authority) as long as the parties to the transaction have agreed to use that level of electronic signature. (See Appendix A for a short primer on digital signatures.) Although the larger policy for the use of digital signatures will be set through legislation, public managers will still need to take the following steps:

- Identify areas of potential use for digital signatures.
- Identify the levels of security, authenticity and guarantees against tampering that are needed for the completion of different transactions and agreements. For example, a transaction with an outside vendor or contractor may need a higher level of all three of these qualities than would be needed for an employee in completing a travel voucher or by a citizen in applying for a hunting license or a building permit. Also, for some transactions (e.g., personnel actions), security against unwarranted viewing will be the key quality, while for others (e.g., the publication of a controversial policy statement), guarantees against tampering will be the key desired characteristic of the electronic record or file.
- Identify the technologies that will meet the identified needs for various degrees of security, authenticity and guarantees against tampering.
- Advise policy makers at the program level about the need for and benefits and costs of the government acting as an issuer of digital certificates or as a certificate authority.

The benefits of digital signatures have yet to be fully realized for a couple of reasons. First, most public managers have not come close to implementing the less difficult technologies that will allow citizens, employees and government contractors to do business electronically without the use of digital signatures. In Georgia, for example, the Department of Banking and Finance discovered, after it had worked on a digital signature pilot project, that it did not necessarily need a digital signature to conduct some of the transactions that it wanted to complete electronically. Second, in states where the use of certain technologies for electronic signatures and records is prescribed, the level of technology mandated is fairly high. As such, this level of technological capability must be spread to the key user groups before any implementation can take place. In states that are more permissive about what technologies will be used and what levels of security, authenticity and guarantees against tampering are needed, the technological barriers to implementing electronic transactions are fewer, but the policy and administration of the system tend to be more complex because all the parties involved have many more choices available.

PUBLIC ACCESS

While every state's public access laws will differ, courts and state legislatures are likely to affirm that the right of public access should evolve with changes in the way public records are created and stored. Thus, as governments adopt computers and networks as their means of keeping records, the public's right to access public records will probably expand to include access to computerized record formats. In Ohio, for example, local governments must give citizens access to electronic records. Delivering paper printouts of the requested records cannot be used to satisfy a request for computer records. Most states, however, have not been as prescriptive. In these states, public managers will need to make policy choices, particularly about whether or not certain records will be available on a public network such as the Internet. While elected policy makers are ultimately responsible for this choice, in practice, a nonelected public manager typically decides whether to include certain record sets as part of the Web offerings of the government.

POLICIES FOR STAFF USE OF PUBLIC AND PRIVATE NETWORKS

Ensuring effective and appropriate use of networked services (such as Web access, e-mail or File Transfer Protocol [FTP]) involves two major policy considerations—determining breadth of access and defining appropriate use.

Breadth of Access

Public managers will typically make and implement the policies that determine the degree to which the government will supply its employees with Internet and/or intranet access. Some governments have limited access to Internet services to certain managers who can justify the need. Others have taken a more universal approach to employee access, while still others are developing a variety of mechanisms (intranets, filtering, etc.) that shape, limit and customize the access to networks, files, databases and content based on an analysis of employee work needs. One of the latter governments might give all employees access to government materials that are "pushed" (automatically transmitted) over an intranet to their desktop. At the next level, internal e-mail access might be provided to all employees, while only a smaller group of employees is given external or Internet e-mail rights. Similarly, some employees might be given access to a set group of Internet Web sites (e.g., by means of a filter or a proxy server), while others would be given full access to the Internet. Finally, some employees could be given access to special services such as file transfers between the Internet and intranet or access to certain specialized application service providers (e.g., for getting use of the most recent graphics software). Unfortunately, little is known about the impact of each of these types of policies or access configurations on employee productivity. Moreover, researching this question would be difficult, since productivity is a function of so many factors, many of which would be more important than Internet access.

In this regard, access policies, because of their high visibility, are likely to form a major part of the technology culture of the organization. More wired or technology-oriented organizations will obviously provide broader access. Whether this broader access is justified may depend on how public managers in these organizations capitalize on the expanded access by "informating" more of the work of the organization (e.g., through expert systems and knowledge ware applications development and practices that make use of the enhanced communications technologies). Organizations that do not develop and implement plans to capitalize on the more developed technology culture that broader access helps create may be disappointed in the results of a broad-access policy. More generally, public administrators will need to manage the trade-off between the longer-term developmental benefits of providing broader access (than is justified by current work tasks) and the more immediate and potentially negative impacts on productivity that expanded access for employees with few information needs might have.

Appropriate Use

The use of networks can be categorized as involving active, passive and reactive activities. Passive use is typically the best understood and best addressed type of usage. Passive use involves workers receiving or searching for information, while active (and reactive) use involves employees creating new information for transfer (e.g., e-mail) or storage (e.g., Web page creation or news group posting) on the network. Most governments have policies in place related to employees surfing the Web for content or uses that have been designated as inappropriate (e.g., gambling, shopping or viewing pornography).

While inappropriate passive use is generally well understood, public managers probably need to be more concerned about developing policies related to the active production of information by employees. Here, policies may be called for in two areas. First, managers should establish policies that address content published by employees on the government's Web site. Limiting publication to content that has been reviewed and found appropriate should suffice to address possible concerns related to this type of active use. Second, policies may be needed to govern employees' use of e-mail (or second-tier, unofficial Web sites). Because most e-mail is seen initially by only a few people, some managers and staff may think, mistakenly, that e-mail is private and confidential. The predominant legal position in most states' case law is that e-mail sent through a local government's e-mail system is owned by that government and that the government has the right to audit or inspect e-mail messages sent over its system. Case law is less clear with respect to whether e-mail constitutes a record that is subject to open records legislation. However, even if privacy laws did protect e-mail sent by employees, the ease of copying or forwarding e-mail makes any controversial e-mail message sent by an employee potentially public. Unlike Web publishing—where password protection technology can prevent inappropriate publication—any such technological remedy for e-mail would essentially undermine the benefit of having e-mail in the first place. However, public managers can take steps to inform employees about the public nature of their e-mail and the potential liability for inappropriate use. Public managers can also take steps to clarify to the recipients of e-mail that, unless otherwise stated, the views of the person sending the e-mail do not necessarily represent those of the government itself. For a message to go out without this declaration, an employee might need the approval of a supervisor.

RELIABILITY OF BUSINESS OPERATIONS AND COMMUNICATIONS

Public managers will typically be charged with the development of policies related to the security and reliability of government servers and networks, as well as with the reliability of government personnel and procedures. While the security and reliability of government servers and networks will continue to be a moving target and one where professional IT consultation will be needed, the security and reliability of business operations will typically fall on the shoulders of the general public manager. Policies in this area address issues such as the following:

- The storage and/or deletion of electronic communication.
- The need to have paper copies or backup files of communications.
- The need for backup responders to communications when the particular staff member is not able to check e-mail or respond.
- The security measures that staff should take regarding passwords.
- Authorized impersonation or representation of another person when using e-mail or when amending or forwarding messages that have been received (such as when an administrative assistant is authorized to reply in the name of the manager).
- Levels and types of Internet use; such policies might be needed to prevent network congestion.
- Etiquette expected of employees when using the Web.

TELECOMMUTING

Telecommuting represents one of the chief ways in which wired organizations can potentially become more efficient than nonwired ones. Accurate data on telecommuting are difficult to obtain because of the variety of styles and levels of telecommuting. Conservative estimates by the U.S. Department of Transportation suggest, however, that 2 million U.S. workers telecommuted in 1992. By 2003 this number is expected to increase to between 7.5 and 15 million, or between 5 and 10 percent of the workforce (U.S. Department of Transportation 1992). According to a more recent survey conducted by the Association for Computing Machinery, the practice of telecommuting appears to be falling behind the stated desires of surveyed firms. That is, although some 62 percent of companies surveyed reported that they encouraged telecommuting, a mere 7 percent of the employees of these firms actually appear to be telecommuting. This finding has been characterized as the "telecommuting paradox" (Khaifa & Davidson 2000). The telecommuting paradox suggests that even though telecommuting benefits may be shared by employees and their sponsoring organization, a number of workers will not see themselves as suitable for telecommuting. Hence, if public managers are to gain the benefits of telecommuting, they will need to understand and implement the key drivers of telecommuting. Although there are likely to be a number of drivers, including support for home offices, supervisors' support, technical support and financial incentives, one of the principle social drivers of telecommuting, according to Khaifa and Davidson's study, is peer influence. Their findings suggest that it is critical that the organizational culture not simply accept telecommuting, but actively and enthusiastically promote it. In this regard, peer influence appears to outweigh even the influence of superiors. The importance of peer influence extends to the desire of telecommuting workers to feel that they still have social connections to the organization.

Public managers, rather than elected policy makers, will typically be charged with developing policies for telecommuting. Managers should be aware that telecommuting represents a dramatic shift in the long-dominant factory system model of production. (See Table 9.2.)

While the general trends in technology and human capital development favor a return to the cottage system via telecommuting, this is not always the case. Hence, public managers will need to develop clear criteria for choosing the work and employees suitable for telecommuting. Also, executive-level managers must ensure that the styles and skills of existing managers and general management practices will lead to successful, performance-enhancing telecommuting. The following lists offer a number of ideas and practices that public managers should consider when developing plans to promote or employ telecommuting (Thomas 1999; Fairweather 1999). The ideas in these lists for the most part represent commonsense approaches to telecommuting practices, since the management literature on this practice is not especially well developed.

Table 9.2
Comparative Advantages of Factory System Versus Cottage System

Factory System increased equipment costs and rent, but . . .	Cottage System is returning due to:
Reduced labor unpredictability. Reduced supply/production glitches. Increased labor productivity through both more effective supply of capital and systemization of work. Reduced monitoring and enforcement cost. Eliminated negotiation/decision making cost. Allowed for nonprofessional service-oriented work (e.g., banking) to be systematized.	Decline in remote monitoring, training and coordination costs. Use of computer assisted monitoring makes it possible to track nonprofessional service/manufacturing work. Computers/Internet make effective remote coordination feasible. Increased role of flexible specialization processes and customized products. Small batch/more craft-like production. Increased number of highly trained professionals who self-direct and incorporate a strong work ethic. Very sophisticated knowledge work can be done with low capital costs (e.g., $600 computer).

Types of Work

In general, the kinds of work that are most amenable to remote provision include:

- knowledge production
- processing that involves little on-site equipment or maintenance
- processing that does not require any exchange of physical objects
- processing where the inputs/outputs/controls are electronic
- work that produces an easily evaluated product
- work that does not depend on following a "one best way" procedure to produce effectively
- work that does not depend much on informal peer-to-peer knowledge transfer

Examples of the kinds of work amenable to remote provision include:

- Software production (issues that could make remote provision inappropriate: inability to evaluate the work; inability to evaluate informal learning)

- Sales (issues that could make remote provision inappropriate: learning best practices from other salespersons)
- Education/Research
- Customized design
- Order processing/Typing

Types of People

When trying to identify people who are likely to be successful at working remotely, managers should look for:

- People with established friendships/networks
- People with established loyalties to the firm/government
- People who have received sufficient training
- People who want to work remotely and who thrive on independence
- People who are adept with technology
- People who have the psychological ability to establish mental workspaces at home/remote sites
- People who have a trust relationship with their supervisor

Management Principles

While the literature on managing remote work is still at the stage of providing only anecdotal information, some key themes for successful management of telecommuting employees appear to be fairness, clarity and respect for privacy.

Fairness

- All workers get the same deal.
- Fair process for deciding which work qualifies for remote location.
- Fair process for deciding which work will be done at which remote site or sites.
- Fairness in terms of splitting the benefits/costs of remote work.
- Fair access by unions/government inspectors to remote sites for health/safety inspections.

Clarity

- Remote work guidelines are put in writing.
- Rules for who pays for what are clear, comprehensive and understood up front.
- Rules for on-site inspections/supervision of work are clear.
- Rules for supervision of work hours, processes and procedures are established.
- Level of support for remote work is made clear, and responsibilities for work when this support is not available are identified.

Respect for Privacy

- Remote site workers are not subject to extraordinary levels of computer-based performance monitoring.
- The need for remote site workers to conduct some personal business during office hours is understood.
- Remote site workers' private calls and e-mail are not examined without probable cause of wrongdoing.
- Monitoring of work is conducted only by people who understand the nature of the work and not by people from a special security unit.
- Notification is given to workers of home visits/video visits that involve viewing of private space.

Levels of Remoteness

Workers and managers have some choice as to the level/degree of remoteness. Choices might include:

- Telecommuting: workers with fixed offices who occasionally work from home.
- Tethered in office: Staff with some mobility who are expected to report to a fixed location. Staff move around buildings/campus.
- Hoteling: No fixed office space, but book a hotel room/productivity center cubicle as required.
- Home: home or customer office site.
- Fully mobile: office in vehicle.

Trial Periods

- Management negotiates a trial period with employee for remote work.

Support

- Managers create opportunities for informal contacts between remote and nonremote workers.
- Managers assess the psychological suitability of workers for remote work assignments.
- Provision of or support for designated workspace at home.
- Policies regarding the ability to control the means of communication. Can the worker choose to turn off the mobile phone/beeper/pager? If so, how often?

Training

- In effective use of e-mail/chat.
- In communication protocols. (How quickly does one need to read/respond to e-mail?)

Table 9.3
Relationship Continuum from Low to High

Relationship Level	Management Time-Burden for Managing Remote Work
Support: low degree of substitution; low degree of impact; outsourced work is not core and is usually of short duration, with alternatives easy to find. Example: food services	Low
Reliance: a higher extent of substitution and length of relationship, but still low strategic impact. Example: data warehousing	Low to Moderate
Alignment: low extent of substitution, but high strategic impact. Worker/contractor has unique expertise. Example: planning software design	Moderate to High
Alliance: High substitution, high strategic impact. Example: contracts for planning, design, building, and development and implementation	High

- In separating the emotions of intimate/family issues so that they do not spill over into workspace.
- In using a company/government knowledge base to solve one's own problems.

Training for Managers

- In becoming more like contract managers than line supervisors.
- In developing interdependent relationships. Example: choosing a contractor/remote worker who does not have too many other jobs will help maintain some degree of interdependence.
- In allocating time and resources to remote workers who need it the most. Studies of contract management suggest that work that is higher on the relationship continuum is more likely to need more consistent attention from managers. The relationship continuum is based on factors such as the degree to which the remote or outsourced work substitutes for work that would otherwise be done in-house, the degree to which the remote or outsourced work is part of the core capability or function of the organization, the time-length of the smallest units of remote/outsourced work that one can contract for, and the degree to which alternatives to the remote/outsourced work can be identified and used. (See Table 9.3.)

Managers will need to intuitively recognize that work has become a major center for friendship as other centers for this type of social relationship have declined (e.g., small towns, extended families). As such, for some employees, working in isolation may lead to a lower level of sociability and a higher level of perceived anonymity. These conditions can in turn lead to the potential for a relaxation of ethical or agency-oriented behavior. Clear, fair, supportive and comprehensive policies for telecommuting can help prevent this situation. A good beginning guide to issues related to telecommuting is the '98 *Telecommuting Guide*, published by Smart Valley, Inc. (available on the Web at http://www.svi.org/telecom_guide/).

PRIVACY

Privacy protection has become a major policy issue both regarding government policy to regulate privacy in relations between businesses and consumers and with respect to relations between governments and citizens and clients. In the latter area, federal and state statutes already define privacy rights in a number of areas such as education, health and mental health (Soler 1993). More recently, Congress and then-President Clinton proposed new legislation to help define consumer privacy regarding electronic transactions in health, banking and other commercial arenas. Similarly, the Office of Management and Budget has ordered that federal agencies have and post privacy policies. Given strong public opinion in support of privacy protection, public managers at all levels of government would be wise to develop privacy policies for their networked information, particularly for information that is solicited from citizens. While privacy concerns are most salient with regard to citizens, governments should also be concerned with the privacy of employees.

Components of a Privacy Policy

Generally, privacy policies have four main components:

- Notice: Citizens/employees are given clear and conspicuous notice of the government's information practices regarding what is collected; how it is collected (e.g., directly or through nonobvious means such as cookies); how it is used; how choice, access and security are guaranteed; and whether information is disclosed and under what circumstances.
- Choice: Citizens/employees are given choices as to how their personal identifying information is used beyond the primary use for which the information has been provided (e.g., to complete a transaction).
- Access: Citizens/employees are given access to the personal information collected about them, including opportunities to delete or correct errors in the information.
- Security: Citizens/employees are made aware of the adequacy of the steps used to protect the security of the information that the government has collected.

In addition to these primary components, privacy advocates point out that variations on these components can be used in numerous ways to either strengthen or undermine privacy protection. For example, having to take a specific action indicating that one is explicitly choosing to allow an organization to use one's private information (called the opt-in requirement) is substantially different than consenting to the use of one's private information unless one takes a specific action to indicate otherwise (called the opt-out requirement). Most computer usability experts agree that having to opt-in in order to relinquish one's private information probably provides stronger privacy protection than having to opt-out in order to receive the protection. This is particularly the case when the privacy notice is not especially visible. In such a situation, a user may have quickly made the move (e.g., clicking on the next Web page in a sequence) that indicated they were willing to relinquish privacy before they were really aware of the meaning of their choice. The opt-in requirement makes the choice a much more conscious one for all users. The opt-out choice assumes that people are already pretty aware of a possible privacy compromise and are already pretty good managers of their own privacy. Because of the increasing concerns about privacy, public managers will need to study their constituents' attitudes on this issue before designing the degree of privacy protection congruent with prevailing community attitudes.

Variations in State Law

While all public managers should be concerned with the development of adequate privacy policies, managers at the state and local levels also need to be aware that states vary substantially in their definitions of what is considered private and what is considered an open record. In Washington State, for example, any effort to develop databases of information that would allow for customization of government services would run up against the current requirement that all data not explicitly excluded from scrutiny by citizens must be open to citizens. As such, a public manager's ability to create strong privacy protection could be restricted. Variations in state law suggest that managers should be extremely careful in copying the information use and dissemination practices of other governments. For instance, if a manager in Arizona or Illinois were to authorize the dissemination of information regarding sex offender registration with local police to the general public, as is practiced in Washington State, that manager would be violating state laws.

Vulnerability to Privacy Assaults

As more governments develop Web-to-database systems and as governments increase their ability to share information, privacy protection will become even more salient as a policy issue. This concern will grow—not because of possible government decisions to release information not currently released, but because the wholesale linking of data from disparate sources can create the potential for the creation of new information. For example, currently the U.S. Census Bureau will not release sample raw data that have been stripped of identifying information—even to university researchers—if the size of the group is small enough to allow credible inferences as to someone's identity. Information that by itself is not particularly sensitive (such as the type of car a person owns) can become sensitive when combined with other information gathered from both public and private sources. It then becomes possible, for example, to develop individual profiles of people and to use those profiles to target marketing efforts or to infer political persuasion more effectively. Moreover, findings from research currently being funded by the National Science Foundation at the National Institute of the Statistical Sciences (Karr 2000) suggest that as an analyst is able to apply data from multiple data sources to the puzzle of individual identity, it becomes possible to solve the puzzle in cases where, all else being equal, it should be impossible to solve. This research suggests that as more data are matched across more data sources, governments at all levels will need to develop more sophisticated guidelines for allowing citizens and commercial firms to access sets of data that could eventually lead to a loss of privacy.

Although some personal data may always be accessible by physical means (that is, by visiting government offices), the costs of travel and the time required to go through paper documents one by one limit information gathering. Also, it is difficult to remain anonymous while gathering information systematically under the eye of government staff. When information is available over the Internet, such informal checks on data gathering no longer exist.

Balancing Privacy and Openness: Using Technology and Other Means to Reduce Harm

Finding the appropriate balance between protecting privacy and protecting openness will always be a policy issue. Moreover, no matter what balance policy makers attempt to strike, there persists a large element of administrative discretion and willingness to address the balance using alternative technologies and procedures. For example, federal law prohibits staff at a human services department in a southern state to see actual income information that is gathered and formatted into a database by Department of Labor employees. However, the Department of Labor can allow the human services staff access to query the database around particular parameters (e.g., Did Mrs. Jones make more than $700 last month?). Similarly, it may be possible for public managers to choose to employ digital technologies to help protect privacy in innovative ways. A comparison of the security characteristics of digital versus paper record-keeping can illustrate this point. Assume that a person's records are kept on paper and that this paper, for efficiency purposes, must be stored in an area with general employee access.

In this case, the only way to ensure privacy is to train employees to respect privacy and to hope that any breaches of this privacy are detectable. With digital records, however, one can both create elaborate password protection and use digital tracing of the individuals who access the data to ensure that staff are not able to invade a citizen's privacy.

Also, it is possible to replicate in part the difficulty of amassing large quantities of data from paper sources while still allowing electronic access. For example, the data retrieval engine can be designed so that the entire contents of the database cannot be downloaded at one time. Rather, one can only get a limited number of records during a particular period of time or on any particular query.

In addition to using technology to improve privacy, public managers may have other means within their discretion to—if not create a higher level of privacy—at least reduce the harm that an invasion of privacy could create.[3] Imagine the following scenario: A private firm purchases a database of arrest records of citizens and then puts these records up on the Web for public consumption. The public manager in this case was under no obligation to publish the same data on the Internet, but is able to use her discretion in deciding what data should be available on the government's Web site. In this case, the public manager may want to reduce the potential harm of the publication of the arrest data by also publishing the disposition of the cases (e.g., charges dropped) and data related to case circumstances or the citizen having successfully paid his or her debt to society.

SURVEILLANCE AND MONITORING

Wired governments will have a host of powerful information tools to help them in designing and delivering services more effectively. However, many of these tools can also be used to create or enhance surveillance of employees and citizens. Internet networks can be combined with electronic sensors that provide audio and video data, thereby radically enhancing the potential for widespread surveillance. The city of Los Angeles, for example, has installed cameras at hundreds of intersections and routes to be used to better manage traffic conditions. In developing the system, the transportation department chose to install filters in the high-resolution cameras to prevent the individual identification of vehicles or people (though numerous identity-marking attributes can still be seen) and chose not to videotape the traffic scene except for purposes of calibrating the system. These decisions were purposeful in that the department did not want to spend time providing information to law enforcement or to get involved in the controversies that would surely follow such a decision. This departmental-level administrative decision essentially let city of Los Angeles policy makers avoid having surveillance become a high-level policy issue. If this situation is in any way typical, public managers across the nation will likely be faced with similar policy-making decisions. While such decisions may in fact be more appropriate for elected officials, elected policy makers may prefer to have public managers address the issue. In such cases, public managers will need to clarify in their own minds what they believe to be the appropriate policies related to surveillance and monitoring. In this regard, they will need to consider:

- The specific uses of surveillance technologies (e.g., public safety) that might be considered appropriate
- The situations in which surveillance technologies can be used for individual or group identification (e.g., situations where harm of a particular level is threatened)
- The approval process for implementing surveillance technologies
- Appropriate notice requirements regarding the acquisition, implementation and use of those technologies

In addition to physical surveillance, governments may choose to monitor citizens' access to government data or employees' access to Internet sites. As suggested above, such monitoring can either be an invasion of privacy (e.g., were the government to monitor citizens' reading habits through review of public library records) or a protection of privacy (e.g., when tracking the unlawful entry by an employee into a database containing private information). As we move into the digital age, it is likely that more policies of both types will be needed. For example, in Minnesota the proposed Internet policy states that except when clearly authorized by state statute or federal law to do so, government agencies should not monitor citizen access to and usage of public government data. In addition to protecting or invading privacy, government monitoring of people's access to its Web site can provide valuable information about the site's quality and usability. As this level of monitoring does not need to involve the identification of individual users, public managers should ensure through administrative policy that IT staff do not in fact attempt such identification unless it is part of a larger effort that involves strong privacy protection (e.g., notice, choice, access and security).

Finally, it should be recognized that routine surveillance and monitoring of employees is probably incongruent with knowledge management approaches to running government operations. Knowledge management depends on trust and the willingness of employees to share their knowledge broadly. Surveillance and monitoring tend to undermine these behaviors.

PERSONAL USE OF GOVERNMENT-OWNED TECHNOLOGY

One of the areas where public policy has not yet solidified involves government employees' use of government-owned equipment and networks. Perhaps because many governments lack a technology policy development process, the vacuum is often filled by policies that are unnecessarily restrictive (e.g., policies that create a blanket prohibition on all personal use of information technology). Where a more concerted technology policy development effort is being tried, more flexible policies regarding personal use of government technology are being considered. For example, at the federal level the CIO (Chief Information Officers) Council's Interoperability Committee (1999) has proposed the following general policy on employee use of office equipment:

Federal employees are permitted limited use of government office equipment for personal needs if the use does not interfere with official business and involves minimal additional expense to the Government. This limited personal use of government office equipment should take place during the employee's personal time, not during official duty time. This privilege to use Government office equipment for non-government purposes may be revoked or limited at any time by appropriate Federal agency or department officials. . . . Employees are authorized limited personal use of government office equipment. This personal use must not result in loss of employee productivity or interference with official duties. Moreover, such use should incur only minimal additional expense to the Government in areas such as:

- Communications infrastructure costs (e.g., telephone charges, telecommunications traffic, etc.)
- Use of consumables in limited amounts (e.g., paper, ink, toner, etc.)
- General wear and tear on equipment
- Data storage on storage devices
- Transmission impacts with moderate message sizes such as e-mails with small attachments.

The draft policy goes on to note the usual list of prohibited uses. What is important about this policy draft is that it recognizes that computer and network equipment are very similar to the telephone. For both types of equipment, light use (e.g., no long distance calls, no storing gigabytes of information) will not substantially impact the government's bottom line. However, such light use can help transform a tool (e.g., e-mail) that would have only business impacts into a tool that can produce major social and civic benefits. At the same time, excessive or heavy use could have adverse financial and resource impacts.

PERSONALIZATION OF SERVICES AND INFORMATION

Data mining and information filtering technologies currently in use in the private sector could allow governments to create and use profiles of citizens who use governmental services. These profiles could be developed based on strong privacy protections (e.g., citizens would have to opt-in before a profile would be created or used). Profiles that could track interests (patterns of Web surfing, age, occupation, family situation, etc.) might be used benignly to help guide citizens more quickly and more effectively to the services or information they seek. Similarly, such profiles could be used to ensure better emergency response (e.g., Mr. Jones will need assistance to get out of bed in an emergency), more coordinated service delivery, and more individualized treatments, notices, and the like.

Intelligent agents ("bots") use profile data to estimate or predict a user's preferences, attitudes, characteristics or desires in order to customize responses. This ability to tailor a local government's message to individuals could radically change the way local governments communicate and interact with citizens. Many of the potential uses of intelligent response would unquestionably be desirable. However, public managers will need to develop policies to distinguish these benign uses of customization technologies from those that may have a more questionable impact. For example, at what point does personalizing a message to specific audiences become telling different citizens a different story or steering some citizens toward or away from a service or participation opportunity? Unfortunately, in many instances there is likely to be a trade-off between the immediate citizen-satisfaction benefits of personalization and the more diffuse and distant costs of this personalization effort to democratic governance.

Public managers would be wise to develop a level of consensus among policy makers and citizens on what is acceptable and unacceptable regarding the use of intelligent agents and similar technologies. In the absence of such a consensus, managers will need to develop their own policies in this area before experimenting with these cutting-edge technologies.

INNOVATION POLICIES

While wired governments generate innovation through internal knowledge creation and management practices, they can also help promote innovative technologies through their purchasing and standard setting activities. There are numerous examples of how government purchasing and supported research have increased the competitiveness of U.S. high-technology firms. The successes of the aircraft industry and the Internet in America represent the most dramatic examples. In these cases, government was able to advance a technology through high levels of resource support. However, governments can also do so through more prosaic and less resource-intensive practices or policies. Examples include the following:

- Giving discounts to firms, vendors and contractors who conduct business with the government electronically via the Internet and associated technologies.
- Requiring use of certain technologies when communicating with the government. Currently, the city of Singapore requires that businesses in its jurisdiction doing business with the government do so through online connections (Caldow 1999). In addition to the added efficiency for government, Singapore policy makers see this requirement as part of a larger economic development effort. By encouraging

Singapore companies to become wired, it is believed that these businesses will be better positioned to compete in emerging global electronic markets.

- Eliminating alternative technologies or practices. In Georgia, the state no longer prints the state employees' telephone book. State employees are expected to look up numbers online.

- Creating the organizational conditions that tend to enhance the chances for innovation (i.e., more complex divisions of labor, more organic organizational structures, and high-risk strategies) (Hage 1999).

SHARING OF THE GOVERNMENT'S BRAND

Popular government Web sites and popular governments have a "brand value" with which commercial groups may want to be associated. One easy way to achieve such an association is through a link to one's organization on the government's Web site. Executive-level public managers are likely to have a great deal of discretion regarding which groups will be allowed to be associated with the government through a Web link. They will want to refuse requests from some groups, as links from a local government site can potentially imply a sponsorship relationship. Public managers will need to craft fair and defensible policies to address such situations. In at least one instance, a city that established a policy of permitting only links to sites that promoted tourism, economic welfare and industry was sued by a local alternative newspaper for its refusal to establish a link to this newspaper's site. The federal district court found that this particular restriction was reasonable, and it upheld the city's policy. However, public managers who attempt to pick and choose sites to link to without a reasonable policy may run into more serious court challenges.

NOTES

1. For further reading, see Stephana I. Colbert and Oren R. Griffins, "The impact of 'Fair Use' in the higher education community: A necessary exception?," *Albany Law Review* 62, no. 437 (1998). Readers may also visit the U.S. Copyright Office Web site at http://lcweb.loc.gov/copyright/. A good source for further reading on linking issues is at http://www.computerbar.org/seminars/97jakab.htm.

2. For a good discussion of this issue, see "After Microsoft: The open-source society," *American Prospect* 11, no. 10 (March 27–April 10, 2000).

3. The following sources provide a useful sample of policies related to access and privacy: Final Report of the Information Policy Task Force to the Minnesota Legislature as Adopted for Submission to the Legislature by the Task Force at Its Last Meeting on January 19, 1999, found at http://www.state.mn.us/ebranch/admin/ipo/pipa/tfreport.html; Federal Trade Commission (May 2000), *Privacy Online: Fair Information Practices in the Electronic Marketplace. A Report to Congress*, Washington, DC: U.S. Department of Health and Human Services, Press Office. (October 29, 1999), HHS Proposes First-Ever National Standards to Protect Patients' Personal Medical

Records, *HHS News*; Center for Democracy and Technology. Government Agencies Ordered to Post Privacy Policies. Visited June 6, 2000, at http://www.cdt.org/previousheads/dataprivacy.shtml, posted June 3, 1999.

REFERENCES

Caldow, J. (1999). Surfing through a portal. *E-Commerce, a Supplement to Government Technology* (August): 22–26.

CIO Council Interoperability Committee. (1999). *Draft Recommended Executive Branch Model Policy/Guidance on "Limited Personal Use" of Government Office Equipment Including Information Technology.* Washington, DC: CIO Council, March 4.

Fairweather, N. B. (1999). Surveillance in employment: The case of teleworking. *Journal of Business Ethics* 22(1): 39–49.

Hage, J. T. (1999). Organizational innovation and organizational change. *Annual Review of Sociology* 25: 597–622.

Karr, A. (2000). Demonstration of National Institute of Statistical Sciences technology. Paper presented at a National Science Foundation Digital Government Meeting, Los Angeles, California, May 16.

Keegan, D. (2000). Survey: Americans e-mailing public officials. Found at http://www.fcw.com/civic/articles/2000/0501/web-survey-05-05-00.asp.

Khaifa, M., and R. Davidson. (2000). Exploring the telecommuting paradox. *Association for Computing Machinery, Communications of the ACM* 42(3): 29–32.

O'Looney, J. (2000a). *Local Governments On-Line.* Washington, DC: International City/County Management Association.

O'Looney, J. (2000b). Access: Making your community internet-ready. *IQ Service Report* 32(5): 1–20.

Rocheleau, B. (1999). The political dimensions of information systems in public administration. In *Information Technology and Computer Applications in Public Administration: Issues and Trends*, ed. David Garson. Hershey, PA: Idea Group.

Soler, M. (1993). *Glass Walls: Confidentiality Provision and Interagency Collaboration.* San Francisco: Youth Law Center.

Thomas, R. (1999). The world is your office. *Management Today*, July: 78–84.

U.S. Department of Transportation. (1992). *Transportation Implications of Telecommuting.* Washington, DC: U.S. Department of Transportation.

PART IV
THE NETWORK IS THE GOVERNMENT

10
Wires across Government Boundaries

THE DEMANDS OF NETWORKING IN THE PUBLIC SECTOR

Most of the important functions of government (education, economic development, welfare, rehabilitation and corrections) are no longer the sole
domain of a single bureau. Rather, many of these functions are carried out
through elaborate alliances involving different levels of government and
government agencies; profit, nonprofit, consumer and interest groups; and,
in some cases, unions, churches and foundations. At the beginning of the
twentieth century Max Weber identified the bureau as the dominant organization form, with its clear lines of hierarchy, task responsibility and efficient one-size-fits-all processes. However, by the end of the century Clegg
(1990) and others had identified a shift toward a networking form of organization. This organizational form rose to prominence as the stakeholders
in an issue or activity became more diverse and more specialized in their
choice of client groups and associated skills. This specialization of knowledge and focus meant that numerous agents would possess some piece of
the puzzle and be able to make some contribution to a policy, program,
treatment or project. Policy networks, program alliances, project partnerships and service delivery partnerships have certainly gained a dominant
place in the discussion of organizational forms and managerial concerns in
recent years. Nevertheless, there is little evidence that this new way of doing things has actually changed the degree of autonomy that organizations
possess with respect to core structural issues (funding, hiring, job design,
etc.). Rather, the salience of these topics has more to do with the realization
that managing well will mean giving considerable attention to the environment in which the governmental action will take place. That is, it is chiefly

the desire for better performance that will drive governments into more elaborate networks.

As Agranoff and McGuire (1999) and O'Looney (1996) have outlined, managing in a networked or collaborative environment demands new managerial skills, including skills in forming and maintaining networks, managing the legal, political and cost dimensions of networks, and knowing how to find and tap technical and nontechnical resources that exist in other organizations. Agranoff and McGuire advise that "public managers need to know who has the resources: money, technology, information, expertise, time and other necessary commodities" (p. 28). Furthermore, a manager in a networked environment must inspire purposeful interaction, team building and trust among the parties to the network if it is to be more than just a setting for talk. When these positive qualities break down, the manager will need good negotiation and conflict resolution skills. In contrast, as the alliance strengthens, the public manager will bring to bear more specialized skills of joint financing, joint production and multiparty contract development.

One of the key tasks for public managers in recent years has been to choose the opportunities for partnerships and for disengaging from partnerships. This task has been complicated by federal grant requirements and state executive actions that have resulted in the establishment of more and more diverse collaboration among parties in an issue area. Unfortunately, collaboration has costs as well as benefits. Coordination and communication costs will diminish the operational efficiencies that are the supposed goal of collaborative activity. In some cases the cost of maintaining the network can overwhelm the actual efficiency benefits. In the private sector, these excess costs will eventually be weeded out through competition among firms. Eisenhardt and Galunic (2000) advise business managers to assume that connections among business partners are temporary. They suggest that collaborations should be based on performance criteria rather than on any particular desire for collaboration or any top-down strategy. Hence, collaboration should only happen when business-unit managers from different companies believe that a partnership makes sense for their respective firms. The executive manager's role is to set the context and then let collaboration as well as competition drive the process.

In the public sector, there is no similar competition-based mechanism for limiting participation in networks. As such, public sector networks can become black holes that suck up the time and energy of public sector managers and staff. Because of the difficulty in developing strong performance indicators in certain public sector areas (e.g., human services), there is also a natural tendency for such public organizations to participate in collaborative exercises without any sincere effort to actually integrate services. That is, the natural tendency to maintain organizational autonomy will dominate unless public managers take a leadership position to foster more integrated services (Kagan 1993).

While public-public partnerships are difficult enough, public-private partnerships—the kind most widely touted as needed to bring new technology into government—present even greater challenges. Public managers involved in public-private partnerships often find that these partnerships have higher administrative costs than public-public partnerships. The added administrative costs are due in part to public managers having to educate private sector partners on issues such as the different ethical practices and codes that apply to public sector (but not private sector) actions in areas such as personnel management and contracting for services (O'Looney 1992).

While interorganizational and inter-sector collaboration is often accompanied by inescapable administrative costs, well-crafted partnerships can provide substantial benefits over the long term. In the human services area, for example, partnerships that enable human services workers to identify and effectively care for high-risk children and families whose problems would otherwise go untreated until they became severe could lead to substantially lower welfare and correction services expenditures. Technology can play a role in the development of the kind of cross-agency/cross-government collaboration that is needed. Moreover, there is some evidence that development of integrative information technology of this sort can also expand the partnership circle. That is, as information technology is used to lower transaction costs (e.g., for identification, intake, and billing of clients or services) across organizations, evidence from the private sector suggests that the potential for outsourcing to multiple suppliers is likely to increase (Malone et al. 1987). That is, as information technology lowers transaction costs, partnerships involving interorganizational contracting become easier to create and maintain.

Increased use of information technology is also associated with the creation of new organizational forms such as networks, virtual corporations, and value-added partnerships (Hitt & Brynjolfsson 1997). The importance of these new forms is evidenced in the development of a new publication, the *Journal of Organizational Virtualness*, dedicated entirely to the study of virtual organizations. Eva Fuehrer, a leading contributor to this area of study, defines a virtual organization as "a temporary network of independent institutions, enterprises or specialized individuals that through the use of information and communication technologies, spontaneously unite to utilize an apparent competitive advantage" (Sieber & Griese 1998, p. 11). Virtualness also appears to relate to the ability of an organization to obtain and coordinate critical competencies by involving external and internal constituencies to deliver superior value (Sieber & Griese 1998, p. 13). Additionally, what makes virtualness a unique form of interorganizational coordination is the extent to which the members of a virtual organization are separated by geographical, temporal and communal barriers (Sieber & Griese 1998, p. 14).

Evidence of the development of similar new forms of organization in the public sector based on new IT infrastructure and capabilities is still somewhat sketchy. In part, the greater difficulty in developing IT-grounded partnerships, alliances and knowledge networks in the public sector is due to the fact that public organizations have boundaries that are set in law. Even in cases where legal restrictions on collaboration are not overwhelming, the complexity and ambiguity of legal requirements tend to dictate against easy collaboration. One of the key knowledge areas where this can be clearly seen is in the sharing of client data among public human service agencies. The invocation of confidentiality as a legal basis for refusing to share information about service clients is perennially cited as a barrier to effective service integration. In fact, few federal or state laws actually prohibit information sharing among public human service agencies (Soler 1993). However, because so many laws and legal counselors need to be coordinated in any information or data sharing effort, an alliance of public human service providers rarely overcomes this barrier, even though the law does not explicitly bar sharing.

HOW DO KNOWLEDGE NETWORKS CHANGE INTERORGANIZATIONAL RELATIONSHIPS?

Often technical and social changes will mirror and shape each other. In this regard, the emergence of network organizations for the implementation of government strategy can be seen as having taken place in conjunction with the emergence of telecommunication networks. The successful development of organizational networks obviously entails significant changes in the quality, scope, direction and flow of information. As the Center for Technology in Government notes:

The most intractable problems (e.g., welfare reform, environmental protection and public safety) and the most far-reaching initiatives (e.g., electronic commerce and integrated portals to customer-oriented services) require extensive information sharing across organizational boundaries. Information sharing among agencies within government and between government agencies and private and nonprofit organizations has clearly become a crucial ingredient in these and other innovative problem solving and service delivery initiatives. (1999, pp. 1–2)

Table 10.1 outlines some of the key differences between traditional and potential forms of wired organizations. Wired organizations would allow, for example, a regional governmental partnership to take on joint responsibility for water system administration or geographic information system management and upkeep. Staff tasks related to these responsibilities might rotate

Table 10.1
Comparison of Traditional Versus Wired Governments' Interaction with Other Governments

Traditional	Wired Organization Makes Possible or Demands
Clear boundaries among governments and government agencies.	Boundaries between and among governments and government agencies become porous.
Partnerships are established for limited communications purposes.	Partnerships are established for expanded communications, coordination, and joint production purposes.
Staff are paid by, supervised by, work in and are accountable to a single organization.	Staff may be paid by, supervised by, work in and be accountable to a number of different organizations, including a virtual organization.
Focus of responsibility/accountability is on individual agencies.	Agencies identify joint responsibilities. Elaborate partnerships among governments become possible.

among different governments or governmental departments. Personnel time spent on these tasks might be reimbursed to the individual governments/departments from a pooled fund set up for this purpose. Similarly, in a community social services area, cross-agency partnerships might assume joint responsibility for the results of services that are provided by individual agencies according to an interagency strategic plan. For this approach to work administratively, integration of the individual agency data systems is needed (Joint Legislative Audit and Review Commission 1998).

The development of broadband, digital technologies combined with advances in knowledge management is likely to support and stimulate further change in the relationships among organizations that are currently networked through ordinary communication channels (e.g., meetings, telephone, newsletters, etc.). The increased ability to shape, store, analyze, integrate, and flexibly represent and transmit information (i.e., the capabilities inherent in digitized information) will provide public managers, their staffs, their constituents and their partners with an ability to know more than they currently know. It is too soon to say what the actual impacts of these new technologies will be on the willingness and ability of governments to lead or participate in alliances. As Dawes et al. (1997) have pointed out, many of the smaller governments, agencies and nonprofit service providers still do not have adequate access to or skill in the use of these technologies.

Moreover, as information technologies move in the direction of knowledge management and away from more linear and relatively easy to implement data processing, the abilities and willingness of front-line workers to actually use technologies for improved decision making become much more important. Within the context of a single organization, the existence of a hierarchical command structure can foster a willingness on the part of workers to at least go through the motions of adopting and using a new information system. Within an interorganizational alliance, there typically is no such command structure. Rather, the successful adoption of a new system is dependent on the willingness of all the partners to use their individual command and reward structures to further the adoption process. The difficulty of successful cross-agency implementation dramatically increases in cases where the usefulness of the system is dependent on every single agency adopting it at the same pace and to the same degree. Because the benefits and costs of adopting a new cross-agency system are rarely distributed equally, the needed levels of motivation to ensure the desired pace and depth of adoption across the board are not likely to be achieved. Instead, organizations that face high costs or low benefits will probably be less forthcoming in their efforts to develop and implement the network. My personal experience with a local effort to implement a common intake process for social services confirms this observation. In this effort, the key barriers were not technological; rather, they involved the changes in the administrative practices of one of the major agencies involved in the effort (i.e., welfare reform) and the inability of smaller agencies to spare additional personnel when a key participant from their agency was not able to attend meetings due to illness or scheduling conflicts (O'Looney 1998).

Although it is too early to predict the actual impacts of new technologies (such as video conferencing, instant messaging, and online news and discussion groups) on the willingness and ability of governments to lead or participate in alliances, some educated guesses can be made based on experience with similar enhancements in communication and coordination technologies.

First, if all else remains equal, increased access to bandwidth and knowledge management systems should enable organizations to participate more actively in a larger number of networks. This prognosis is based on a couple of assumptions, the first being that managers and staff should be able to save time by moving from physical meetings to online ones. Travel time can obviously be saved and redirected toward participation. In addition, online communication allows time to be used more effectively. This is particularly the case whenever online meetings become to a certain degree asynchronous. With asynchronous participation, managers and staff can use small units of time between communications in one arena to participate in additional networks. Moreover, managers and staff typically possess large amounts of time that is unusable because it comes in segments too small to use in traditional collaborative-oriented communications. For example, if a particular collaborative task requires calling ten people on the phone, there may not be enough time to do this. However, with a group e-mail list or listserv, a manager could contact everyone within a minute or two.

Second, and more importantly, if the power of knowledge management systems is extended beyond organizational boundaries, it becomes possible to use these systems to quickly and more effectively perform some of the alliance network maintenance functions that currently can be quite costly. For example, knowledge management systems should be able to assist public managers to identify who has the resources (money, technology, information, expertise and time) needed on any particular collaborative project. Equally important, these systems can be used to help create a record of contributions by collaborative partners. This record might form the basis of workload sharing in projects that demand substantial, but unequal, contributions by the individual parties to the collaborative. Without such an ability to track charges or contributions across agencies, a number of collaborative projects would not be possible. One such project, for example, is the Common Access intake form, which is designed to allow a social services client to apply for six different federal benefit programs using one form. When the data demands of this form were examined, I discovered that over 70 percent of the data fields would be used by only one agency (the Georgia Division of Family and Children Services). As such, other agencies might be reluctant to contribute staff time to the Common Access effort without some added contribution from the agency receiving a disproportionate share of the benefits from the collaborative effort. Information technology can be used to help allocate the exact level of the additional benefits and costs among the collaborative participants and to automate an exchange of resources that would reestablish a balance between workload and benefit. Alternatively, creating a sense of equality among collaborating partners need not be based on a direct monetary or resource exchange. As the example of the Xerox service representative knowledge base described in Chapter 4 indicates, it might be enough for agency contributions that are above the norm to be recognized as such and for those contributions to be celebrated by the members of the collaborative.

Portals and New Roles for Mediating Public Institutions

Although the development of knowledge networks and information exchanges typically occurs through project-specific efforts of agencies, departments and whole governments, another model for development of these networks and exchanges is emerging. Two trends in the private sector may be harbingers of similar types of information exchange and networking in the public sector. These trends—the development of portals and the syndication of information—are interlinked. The key concept of a portal is the idea of there being no wrong door for a person who enters the portal. While the concept of the portal is simple and logical, the early development of government Web sites, which tended to grow out of department-specific efforts, worked against this logic. This developmental path resulted in there often being a Web site for every department, each with a separate Web address. With anywhere from ten to one hundred different agencies or departments in a single government, the potential for confusing citizens was substantial. Even when governments created a single Web site, many of these sites simply offered a place from which a citizen could then jump to the individual departmental Web sites. The problem with this solution is that it still requires that citizens know that in their city the department that deals with mosquitoes is called Community Services rather than Public Health or Environmental Control. Also, it might require citizens who want the government to spray their neighborhood for mosquitoes to go to two or three departmental Web sites to complete the request and payment for services. In contrast, a portal Web site is one designed to enable a naïve citizen to obtain all the information and conduct all the transactions necessary within a specific domain. A portal Web site is designed from the beginning to interconnect information and processes from any number of departments, agencies and governmental jurisdictions. Unfortunately, citizens do not tend to separate the domains and jurisdictions of government in the way that is customary for public administrators, and not all citizens understand these domains in the same way or have the same needs. For example, a citizen who wants to open a new business may need information and may need to transact business with a number of agencies within each of the three levels of local, state and federal government. Another citizen with a similar desire to open a new business may only need information from a single local government department. Oftentimes citizens will not know ahead of time what level (or complexity) of service they will need. Transactions as seemingly simple as obtaining a building permit can quickly involve state and federal agencies when the land in question is in a flood plain, is environmentally sensitive or is near a major road or airport. For a portal Web site to be effective, someone has to make all the links and interactions among the various levels of government visible and easy to navigate.

Organizationally speaking, a portal site could be the product of intergovernmental collaboration or it could be the product of a single government (or mediating institution) making the connections among independent government providers of information or transaction opportunities. In the latter case, the single government or mediating institution would act as a syndicating agent—one that ties together information from a variety of sources so as to facilitate a business process. Syndication has been recognized as a strong emerging business model for the private sector Internet (Werbach 2000). Syndication tends to be an effective business model for information goods when the information in question is part of a larger whole and there are a number of possible distribution points for the information. With respect to government information, information from the federal government is potentially of interest to all other governments (state and local), while state government information will be of interest to all the localities in the state. Moreover, whenever a government holds information such as economic or health data that can be customized for individual localities or regions, this information is potentially amenable to syndication.

Whether syndication will become a widespread and effective model for the public sector Internet is still an open question. Opportunities for syndication tend to be most prevalent in fields where there is substantial standardization of information and transaction procedures. (See discussion of EDI and XML later in this chapter.) Hence, some of the best uses of syndicated data in the private sector relate to standardized corporate finance data. In this field, for example, proprietary Web sites such as Merrill Lynch On-Line will purchase information from a syndicating agency that has in turn put together packages of charts, earnings reports, advisors' opinions and economic forecasts that have been customized for use within the Web site. Unfortunately, much public sector work and information have not been effectively standardized. For example, individual local governments will typically have their own systems and information requirements for such things as issuing building permits, business licenses, swimming pool or well permits, renting public property and so on. Without standard data elements, it becomes difficult for any agency to set up a syndication service that could, for example, allow one to use a single common information gathering interface to apply and pay for building permits across jurisdictions. It should be recognized that in some areas (e.g., the use of geographical information system data) the development of standards is making possible a certain level of syndication. For the most part, however, the public sector, particularly in local home rule states, is not prepared to take advantage of the possibilities for highly effective portals.

MANAGING INFORMATION IN INTERORGANIZATIONAL SPACE

Public sector alliances, and ultimately the various constituents of the participating governments, should benefit from better digital networks and related systems. However, for this to occur, these systems must be used effectively to aggregate and compare data from various parts of an organization or across organizations so as to lead to improved understanding of complex and interdependent problems and issues (Goodhue et al. 1992). Data integration can support service delivery streamlining, increased levels of communication, and summarization of ideas with less distortion of meaning (Huber 1982). Organizations or alliances that lack ways of integrating disparate information will often experience increased tensions due to the existence of informational ambiguity across units or agencies. Data repositories can integrate disparate sources of data in ways that can help resolve tensions about the intersection of programs and services, business drivers, data, technology, and the policy environment (Center for Technology in Government 2000).

Data integration has probably gone the furthest in the area of law enforcement. A number of state governments (e.g., Pennsylvania, Indiana and Wisconsin) have begun to develop integrated systems for law enforcement data. While law enforcement officers who are connected to the federal government's TIME (Transaction Information for Management of Enforcement) system can retrieve basic arrest and criminal history information, the lack of more integrated systems creates numerous problems, including the following:

- Inability of officials in one county to check for a suspect's activities in other counties or states.
- Inability of public defenders to locate their clients housed in corrections facilities because of reliance on paper files.
- Lack of access to court documents (such as restraining orders or bail conditions).
- Officers having to enter the same information again and again, thereby wasting time.
- Lack of standards and systems for managing photographs, leading to a waste of officers' time (Justice Professionals Still Lack Information 1999).

Although law enforcement officers can eventually get the data they need, under traditional procedures data sharing is sometimes delayed or does not occur due to administrative barriers. For example, changes in law enforcement personnel or the loss of data sharing agreements negotiated in prior years can impede the flow of information. A major advantage of an integrated data system is that once data sharing problems are resolved, the sharing itself becomes automated, and as a consequence potential sharing problems do not recur.

One of the main ways in which data integration improves our understanding of problems is by facilitating the development of a common language for communications in a problem or issue space. The problem with searching for photographs across law enforcement jurisdictions represents a classic case of the lack of a common language. For example, one jurisdiction might categorize photographs by crime type, while another categorizes them by evidence type. Even when systems agree on the basic indexing scheme (e.g., crime type), it may be difficult to retrieve the data one wants because the jurisdictions may have different category names or define crime types differently.

As this example suggests, while data integration projects can help identify the need for a common language, the creation and updating of such a language is typically beyond the scope of information technology technicians. Rather, public managers responsible for program areas must work collaboratively across programs and jurisdictions to create this language. Their goal in this regard should be to integrate data systems so as to allow the people who will be using them to more quickly and accurately extract meaningful information. ("Data warehousing" is the term under which most data integration efforts are currently described.)

Unfortunately, most managers of data warehouse projects do not spend the needed resources on developing this common language and understanding. According to participants in a seminar project on data warehousing sponsored by the Center for Technology in Government, "A vast majority, between 50 and 80 percent, of data warehouse projects fail because participants don't fully understand the value of integrated data and aren't sure how to use the combined information" (2000, p. 2). The Center for Technology in Government suggests that a number of steps can be used to help ensure that the data warehouse system is one that fulfills its promise. These steps include:

- defining a service objective that meets real business needs;
- developing a business case that shows how the project will work and what benefits it will provide;
- establishing partnerships with all key stakeholders;
- encouraging open communication among all participants;
- building and testing a data warehouse prototype of relevant data;
- resolving problems; and
- being persistent.

Prototyping is a particularly valuable part of this process as it allows developers and users to work together to refine the system so that it becomes ever more useful to the users. Furthermore, prototyping establishes a small user group who will assume some ownership of the system and therefore champion it within the organization or alliance.

Experts in system integration also suggest that data warehouses should be phased in through an evolutionary approach rather than a revolutionary one and that real data should be used from the beginning. In the evolutionary approach users obtain value from the data generated from the first phase. Succeeding phases build on and refine information that has already proven valuable. In this way, user acceptance is more likely to be achieved. Employing real data, rather than dummy data, helps users obtain value from their very first use of the system.

Development of integrated data systems is often less about technology than about understanding the structure, limitations, gaps, quality, size and historical changes in the data and data definitions. The Center for Technology in Government (2000) estimates that 80 percent of the effort in data warehouse projects goes into the management of the data. Additionally, policy issues will often stand in the way of data sharing, particularly in cross-agency projects. Here, issues of data ownership, data authenticity and appropriate use, the rules for changing or adding data, the authority basis for new practices in data entry or change, and the privacy and security of the data are often major issues. Such policy issues can doom a system more effectively than technical difficulties, such as agreeing on an appropriate architecture or data keys for data matching across disparate databases.

Barriers

Data integration can have a positive impact on costs by reducing redundant design efforts (Goodhue et al. 1992). However, because multiple subunits or divisions are involved, data integration can also increase costs by increasing the size and complexity of the design problem or increasing the difficulty in obtaining agreement from all concerned parties. Key barriers to cost effectiveness summarized by Goodhue et al. (1992) include:

- The need for compromises in system development in order to meet local information needs
- Bureaucratic delays
- The reduction in local flexibility, which also impacts development speed
- Higher up-front costs for the design and implementation of multiparty information systems

Organization-wide data integration can also result in a loss of local autonomy in the design and use of data. Even in cases where such loss is minimal and outweighed by potential benefits, local entities will often resist the implementation out of fear that the loss of control may have more severe consequences later on. In some cases an integrated system can involve not just a loss of local control, but also a decrease in effectiveness. This can occur when field units face tasks of different complexities or challenges (Sheth & Larson 1990). For example, a resource management system that has to be designed to serve the needs of the largest municipal government in a state is likely to be overly complex for the smaller municipal governments. The larger government is likely to need more modules (to address the larger number of governmental departments and functions) and more complex applications (to allow executive managers to keep tabs on the more complex operations). Essentially, the "one size fits all" approach to system development forces personnel in the smaller governments to spend time learning a system that is more complex than is needed. Not only are training costs increased, but systems that are overly complex also tend to take more staff time to enter or retrieve data or to complete transactions.

Additional barriers to effective data integration include issues such as timing and information overload. Although data integration efforts can reduce data entry redundancy, it is sometimes the case that one entity needs a certain piece of information before others in the shared system. If this agency is dependent on another agency—one that cannot meet the timeliness criterion—for the collection or reporting of the particular piece of information, the redundancy reduction advantage of an integrated system may not outweigh the loss of timeliness.

Information overload may be the most critical barrier to using integrated information systems effectively. Information overload results whenever agencies in the aggregate collect more data than they truly need. The excess data and the excess systems that hold the data will often make research that much more expensive, as people not only have to learn multiple systems but also have to continually make judgments about the appropriateness of using Data Set or System A rather than Data Set or System B. Overload typically occurs when agencies fail to work with others to come to agreement on a single "official" version of data and related systems that can be used by all stakeholders. Obviously, whenever information overload occurs, it should be taken as a sign of administrative failure rather than technology failure. A primary task of any system integration effort is to identify and eliminate unnecessary information overlaps before building a new system. Left unresolved, information overload can lead to a system that is integrated only at a surface level. A system of this type will appear overly complicated to users, who often will reject the system before it is fully implemented.

Principles and Practices

System or technology compatibility (often referred to as *interoperability*) is often thought to be the primary barrier to effective intergovernmental efforts to deliver services. Obviously, the lack of interoperable systems acts to keep service delivery within a traditional mode. For nontechnical public managers, however, interoperability is more a result than a cause. This is because interoperability tends to occur only when public managers and other public decision makers choose to force an interoperable design. Such designs have to be forced because the alternative, non-interoperable systems, is both less expensive and less demanding in terms of mental and emotional energy. Perhaps for this reason, the Kennedy School of Government's report in barriers to intergovernmental partnerships, *Standing in the Way of Tomorrow* (Mechling 1998), does not emphasize technology compatibility. This topic did not make the list of top barriers. Rather, the authors of this report identified four less technical barriers as being most important: (1) funding constraints; (2) cultural conflicts and lack of trust between jurisdictions; (3) resistance to collaboration (skepticism); and (4) lack of political empowerment.

While *Standing in the Way of Tomorrow* lays out the difficulties of building integrated systems, another publication, the Center for Technology in Government's *Tying a Sensible Knot* (Dawes et al. 1997), begins to identify the principles and practices that can help government managers avoid or minimize the barriers to effective system integration. Listed below are the broad recommendations found in that document along with commentary that draws on sources in the literature as well as my own experiences in collaborative efforts. (See also O'Looney 1996.)

1. Expand existing efforts to build statewide information infrastructures that encompass technology, data and human resources. This effort might include development of a statewide secure intranet like New York's, or state-sponsored digital certificates like those being developed by a number of states. The key to such an infrastructure is that it becomes attractive to smaller governments that might otherwise be tempted to either go it alone or not connect at all. One of the incentives for local governments to participate in the building of such an infrastructure would be the state's provision of technical assistance and training to local staff, and the potential to improve recruitment and retention of technical staff. It should also be recognized, however, that, as with all state-local efforts to collaborate, needed local involvement may not be forthcoming unless local governments are also given a role in decision making about standards and the governance of the system.

2. Establish formal linkages and communications mechanisms that encourage awareness of other models and experiences. Attempting to build a system collaboratively can sometimes result in one or another group attempting to get the entire collaborative to adopt a version of their existing system. While it may be the case that their system would meet the needs of the entire collaborative, acceptance may still not be forthcoming because partnership participants have not experienced the full range of possibilities and therefore are reluctant to simply capitulate to the wishes of a stronger partner. In these cases, peer reviews and periodic peer consulting from outside the collaborative group is suggested.

3. Establish and support a project management "academy" for both state and local managers. Using information technology to help deliver complex, multiagency service programs involves IT managers, general public managers and program staff developing a new commitment and sense of responsibility to goals that are over and above the goals of their own home agency. At one level building this new commitment will require increased exchanges of information among governments and between public agencies with a range of missions. More specifically, however, it will involve public managers being willing and able to develop binding interagency agreements and contracts that could potentially result in a shrinking of their own agencies' empires. This degree of commitment is unlikely to occur without training and experiences that will convince public managers that the whole is truly greater than the sum of the parts. Hence, the idea of an academy would be to instill both new management skills and new attitudes.

Information as a Common Pool Resource

In addition to these general recommendations, public managers may need to go a step further if they are to successfully complete system integration projects. Specifically, the literature on the management of common pool resources is relevant to system integration efforts. A common pool resource, such as a fishery or water basin or open pasture land, is one that is potentially renewable as long as it is managed in a way that does not deplete the stock from which the resource units are drawn. Common pool resources are often difficult to privatize for two reasons. First, the physical properties of the stock (e.g., fish that swim from place to place) make it difficult to maintain steady ownership of the resource. Second, even when an agreement on use rights to the stock can be made, unscrupulous owners of a common resource will have opportunities to cheat without getting caught (e.g., by drawing more than their share of water, fish or other common resources).

Some data sources seem to act like common pool resources. Take, for example, citizens or service clients as a typical data source. One can survey or question these citizens or clients only so often without exhausting their patience or time. As the number of agencies attempting to tap a data source (e.g., a public assistance client) increases, the quality of the data will deteriorate, as the client gets tired of giving the same information several times. This client is likely to shortcut the process or may even drop out of the system. More progressive businesses have addressed this issue through the use of data depositories that can be accessed across functional units. They collect information and documents only once and then store the results. Staff in the various function units can go to the depository and get the needed information. Insurance companies such as USAA that combine several types of insurance with savings, checking, and other types of accounts can access each other's data as needed to serve a customer.

Essentially, companies like USAA set up a collective action scheme in which stakeholders share data while a central data office tracks changes in the data. Unfortunately, few public agencies have developed similar systems that work across agencies or that lessen the demands on citizens or clients. Even in cases where the law provides for and one would expect data sharing (e.g., between federal and state tax collection agencies), the burden is still put on citizens to make copies of tax returns and related documents. As more demands for information are placed on citizens, governments need to take more seriously the potential for data deterioration due to exhausting citizens' patience and time.

Unlike a physical common pool resource, which literally can be exhausted from overuse, a data common pool resource is unlikely to experience catastrophic depletion. Rather, it is more likely for data sets or agency budgets to deteriorate as data fields are not completed or government workers spend more time attempting to fill in blanks in the data. More seriously yet, citizens may cease to participate in government programs due to an unwillingness to negotiate the paperwork. This reluctance to provide data could work to both the citizens' and to society's detriment. For example, imagine a case where Mrs. Jones fails to provide current income data to her caseworker. As a result, her food stamps are cut off and she is unable to take care of her children. This in turn is deemed to be child neglect, which leads to the state's placing her children in foster care, a very expensive decision. It may very well have been the case that Mrs. Jones had already given the school system this information (e.g., for the reduced price lunch program), but forgot to give the social services department the same information and does not now have easy access to the verification documents she gave the school system. For want of a way for Mrs. Jones to authorize a sharing of information between two government agencies, the state expends several hundred dollars a week unnecessarily and causes tremendous emotional harm to a family.

While this hypothetical scenario suggests that a lack of systems for information sharing can result in new and serious harms, the more likely result of such systems inadequacy is less dramatic, but nevertheless equally undesirable. That is, the primary result of there not being adequate systems of this type is more likely to be a situation where Mrs. Jones, due to exhaustion with paperwork, fails to seek out help with problems that are not currently experienced as severe. As such she will fail to fill out all the duplicative forms needed to receive the support and prevention-oriented services that will lead to long-term independence and strength. The overall result of inadequate systems is that participation on the part of people like Mrs. Jones in the programs that will help cure underlying causes of distress will typically fall below desired levels. Adequate systems would be ones that not only allowed data sharing, but also automated the links between programs in ways that would ensure that Mrs. Jones received all the services she and her family needed when they needed them. Such links obviously involve procedural steps (e.g., the school nurse automatically signs up Mrs. Jones in a public health nutrition program run by a different agency) as well as information system connections (Gardner 1992).

If we accept that data in the public sector represent a form of common pool resource, certain implications follow. In particular, common pool resources appear to be best managed through mechanisms for collective action. The alternative mechanisms—centralized state control or privatization—each have their own problems with respect to the management of common pool resources. One difficulty with having the state regulate common pool resources, Ostrom (1990) suggests, is that agents of a centralized state often have very incomplete information about specific strategies, which would induce the users of a common pool resource to do so wisely. In the scenario of a client needing multiple public assistance programs, the "bringing in the state" solution would look very much like the federal government attempting to tell local welfare program managers how best to treat their clients. Given the incredible diversity of local resources, cultures and histories, one can easily see how such a strategy would fail.

With respect to the privatization option, Ostrom argues that many existing common pool resources cannot be divided in a manner that would allow for effective or efficient use. This is obviously the case with many nonstationary resources such as air, fisheries or underground water, but whether it is the case with respect to data resources is more difficult to say. (It should be noted that the equivalent of the "privatization option" in this case of deciding how public sector agencies are allowed to access data sources essentially involves a distribution of limited data collection rights to individual public agencies.) One could potentially imagine, for example, a system under which people had to give certain data only once to a designated data collection agency (e.g., an agency responsible for name and address, another agency responsible for social history, and so forth). Were the rights to collect certain data to be distributed in this manner, it would also be necessary to enforce those rights. An enforcement mechanism is suggested in the federal Paperwork Reduction Act. For example, were an agency's rights to impose data provision duties on citizens limited to a very short time period, agencies would of necessity have to learn to minimize their requests and support their data needs through data sharing. While this privatization solution to the common data resource problem is theoretically feasible, it is not likely to be adopted. For this quasi-privatization to work, legislators would need to have a much more detailed understanding of the data needs and data sharing possibilities of numerous government agencies. Even were this level of understanding to exist, there would be little political support for such a tying of administrators' hands.

Given the weaknesses of the alternatives, Ostrom has suggested that mechanisms for self-organized collective action can often provide the most appropriate way to handle common pool resource problems. Collective action institutions for common pool resources do not just arise because there are common pool resources. Rather, certain design principles need to be followed. Seven such principles are outlined below.

1. *Clearly defined boundaries.* With respect to integration of data systems, reasonable boundaries are needed in light of the desired tasks or goals. For example, although it might be desirable for all social service organizations in a particular area to agree to be part of a common data system, in reality the inclusion of many smaller organizations would likely complicate the boundaries of the resource pool. These small organizations often do not have the skill sets or resources to engage in boundary setting activities such as standard setting or data dictionary creation. Furthermore, it will be difficult in a number of governmental areas to determine the optimum trade-off between the feasibility benefits of clearly defined boundaries and the substantive benefits of having integrated data systems that have an extensive scope. Practically speaking, this might involve questions such as when and where it is worth including juvenile justice data with child welfare data.

2. *Congruence between appropriation and provision rules and local conditions. Appropriation rules restricting time, place, technology and/or quantity of resource units are related to*

local conditions and to provision rules requiring labor, material and/or money. This design principle suggests that as government agencies develop data integration collaboratives they will also need to identify the appropriate levels and types of contributions that will be demanded from the partners. It might be the case, for example, that one agency is rich in technical expertise while another agency might be more appropriately staffed and equipped to gather information that is common to participants in the new system. Still other agencies may be willing to restrict their desire to gather data immediately (i.e., demand less than their accustomed share of citizens' time) in return for not having to contribute specific human or monetary resources.

3. *Collective choice arrangements. Most individuals affected by the operational rules can participate in modifying the operational rules.* This design principle is generally accepted within the IT development community, but is stated in terms of principles of end-user involvement or development. Typically, end-user involvement activities connote a high degree of involvement by the actual users of a system in its overall functionality and look and feel (as opposed to the traditional primacy of IT specialists in systems development). In an intergovernmental context, these principles would simply be extended to the different sets of end-users in the different agencies. In such cases, for example, one might ordain that:

   • a group of representative users from the different agencies jointly manage the whole project.

   • a user group from the participating agencies undertake the analysis of the current business processes across the different organizations.

   • a cross-function, cross-agency user group choose among various design options or get to veto options.

   • a cross-function, cross-agency user group write the system's user guide documentation.

4. *Monitoring. Monitors, who actively audit the condition of the common resource and the appropriators' (or users) behaviors, are accountable to the appropriators or are themselves the appropriators.* This design principle suggests that effective oversight of data integration projects will involve identifying monitorable goals related to more effective and efficient data collection and manipulation. One measure of a successful data integration effort might be that citizens, government clients and staff spend less time as a group entering and searching for data than was previously the case. While measuring time in this manner is a straightforward task, it may not be an entirely satisfactory measure. We can imagine a case, for example, where Agency A receives a particularly large benefit from the data integration effort. This benefit might come in the form of Agency A clients not needing to spend thirty minutes filling out paperwork. Such a result would meet the definition of success that we postulated. However, if we further assume that Agency A does nothing else to change its routine, we can see how this measure might be inadequate. For example, if the result of the time saved through an integrated data system was simply that Agency A clients spent more time simply waiting in line (rather than filling out forms as they waited), little would have been gained in the process.

What an interagency monitoring group possibly brings to such a situation is an ability to look at the whole and to recommend adjustments across the entire system to capture desired system-wide benefits. In this hypothetical case, for example, Agency A may have been unable to take advantage of this benefit due to an inability to hire new caseworkers. Such caseworkers would have made it possible to decrease the time Agency A clients spent simply waiting to more economical levels. With interagency, system-level monitoring of common resources, it might be possible for the monitoring group to identify a system-level solution that would not be possible at the level of individual agencies. For example, imagine that the same data integration project had resulted in Agency B's staff becoming much more efficient without any efficiency impacts on Agency B clients (i.e., just the opposite of the impact on Agency A). As a result of this increased staff efficiency, Agency B's staff now processes more clients in less time. Assuming no new demands on their time, Agency B now has slack resources in the form of additional time in staff work schedules. An interagency monitoring group would be able to measure these slack resources and, theoretically, could recommend moving staff or resources to Agency A, where they are needed.

An interagency monitoring team can contribute a sense of responsibility to the whole system development effort. Moreover, the agencies involved in the collaborative effort will need to identify measures that the group as a whole can understand in the same way.

5. *Graduated sanctions. Appropriators[1] who violate operational rules are likely to be assessed graduated sanctions (depending on the seriousness and context of the offense) by other appropriators, by officials accountable to these appropriators, or by both.* This design principle is probably the most difficult for intergovernmental collaborative efforts to implement. Beyond excluding an agency from a partnership entirely—a step that could easily be self-destructive—governmental collaborations have few tools with which to develop graduated sanctions. This is in stark contrast to private sector collaboratives. Whereas private sector collaboratives can require a pooling of funds, or dues, and can easily exchange resources in support of innovative or extraordinary efforts on the part of particular partners, the public sector is typically restricted in these practices. Without pooled resources that can be lost for a failure to follow the collective action rules, governments tend to retain too much sovereignty and protection against sanctions. In this regard, they are often restricted to existing appropriation or cross-agency/cross-government subsidies that have been approved by the appropriate legislative oversight committees.

6. *Conflict resolution mechanisms. Appropriators and their officials have rapid access to low-cost local arenas to resolve conflicts among appropriators or between appropriators and officials.* Here the weakness of many governmental collaborative efforts is related to slow conflict resolution. In many cases a conflict will smolder so long that it is overshadowed by the emergence of a new crisis or hot issue. For example, in a multiyear effort to develop a common intake system for Georgia's social service systems, the question of how existing laws and regulations would impact the project was referred to an informal group of agency lawyers who failed to come to any quick agreement and who never reported the results of their study. As such, the conflict between those who thought that the project was impossible (e.g., because of confidentiality restrictions) and those who did not believe this was the

case was essentially tabled until the energy behind the project was redirected to other issues.

7. *Minimal recognition of rights to organize. The rights of appropriators to devise their own institutions are not challenged by external governmental authorities.* This design principle has particular application to efforts of state and local governments to build integrated systems when the federal government has the power to override the project. In such cases, the impact of the federal government's actions on the state or local government's system integration efforts is often unconscious. For example, states working on a common intake system for social services (e.g., one that would involve a number of state agencies and local field offices and programs) at the time welfare reform was passed soon learned that their efforts would be derailed by the need for the major social service agency (i.e., the one responsible for the Temporary Assistance to Needy Families program) to stop everything to revamp its IT systems to conform to the new law. Unfortunately, a recognition of the right to organize a collaborative IT project at the state or local level without federal interference is likely to exist in only a few areas of governmental activity.

Fostering Structural Interdependence

In addition to following these design guidelines, public managers who are considering long-term data integration projects should also look for opportunities to create stronger intergovernmental partnerships overall. In particular, managers should identify possible resource configurations and transactions that would tend to create positive interdependence among the parties to a partnership. With respect to collaboratively built, integrated IT systems, a structure in which Agency A depends on Agency B for hardware and networking expertise, while Agency B depends on Agency C for end-user training, and Agency C depends on Agency A for software development is one that will lead to much stronger and longer-lasting partnerships than arrangements where each agency supplies its own needs in all of these areas. Explicitly designing organizational interdependence runs counter to the natural desire of executive managers to achieve and maintain organizational autonomy. In addition, designing for interdependence also runs counter to traditional public administration training and experience. (See Sabatier 1986 on the impact of multiple veto points on implementation success.) Public managers for the most part learn from experience to avoid dependence on others. Unfortunately, lessons learned from such experiences may be the wrong ones for meeting the challenges of a wired government. It is typically not that public managers take away the wrong lesson from their experiences. Rather, it is that managers may confuse one-directional dependence, which will often hamper organizational effectiveness, with multidirectional interdependence. Whereas the former leaves a public manager with no bargaining chips with which to obtain needed resources, the latter provides all the players with the potential to engage in win-win exchanges (Tjosvold 1986). Dependence is frequently worse than independence, but interdependence is often better than independence, particularly when independence leaves one with only the resources provided to the agency. The manager of a wired government will want to combine efforts to foster interdependence with the development of collective action institutions for building and managing integrated information systems.

Fostering Trust within Knowledge Networks

In addition to creating structural support for information and system integration, public managers will need to attend to the softer side of collaboration. That is, they will need to help create the psychological conditions that favor self-evolving order across organizations (e.g., trust, common goals, the expectation of a long-term relationship, etc.). (See Tjosvold 1986; Gray 1985; U.S. Department of Health and Human Services, Office of Inspector General 1990; Kagan 1993; Ellickson 1991.)

While the development of trust is generally considered a necessary foundation for collaborative efforts to integrate services, public managers should recognize that there are different ways to develop and support trust. One is to create an environment where the costs of not trusting are greater than the benefits of trusting. Even though this "calculative" form of trust building can effectively create trust conditions in some circumstances, it may be the least effective form of trust building in a knowledge-oriented environment or organization (Doney & Cannon 1997; Jarvenpaa & Shaw 1998) because for it to work, people need to be able to visualize instances of trust breaking. In a knowledge-oriented environment, trust breaking might involve failing to share knowledge or information. However, such a failure would most likely go undetected, and so could not be included in the trust calculus. Alternative bases for trust, such as regular, in-depth exchanges of social information and explicit activities designed to help parties learn about each other, appear to be a sounder basis for trust in a knowledge-based environment (Lewicki & Bunker 1996).

Example Efforts

The Office of Justice Programs (OJP) is developing a nationwide network of criminal justice information systems. The network will give state and local stakeholders with responsibilities for law enforcement, courts, prosecution, corrections, probation, parole and public defense immediate access to all information necessary to respond to and resolve the consequences of criminal activity. OJP plans to create an intergovernmental architecture for facilitating the interoperability of locally autonomous criminal justice systems. The effort involves a combination of technical assistance grants and training and the coordination of state and local efforts to build a national integrated criminal justice information architecture that would be based on existing state standards. "Standards" would mean technology and data standards at the information "sharing" layer. The goal would be for vendors to then develop products that meet the standards.[2]

The Iowa Intergovernmental Information Technology and Telecommunications (IITT) Task Force was developed by the Iowa Department of Management in order to create an intergovernmental technology plan. It is comprised of stakeholders working on technology issues at the federal, state and local levels. The task force is charged with creating a plan to provide an electronic government network that will enhance services to businesses and citizens and streamline government services across federal-state-local lines.

The task force has developed plans in five issue areas: general government; electronic commerce; human services; geographic information systems (GIS); and criminal justice and public safety.[3]

Oregon Pathways is a state-local collaboration designed to improve the efficiency and accessibility of human services. Currently, the collaboration has created a user-oriented tool for agencies to share basic information about their services. The standards creation effort to date appears to have resulted in a set of common service definitions and an agreement to use Internet-based technologies. Agencies are able to use a password to register and update their service delivery offerings. Proposed efforts for the future include the more difficult tasks of creating a multiagency eligibility screener, common electronic applications for social services, and other tools to support the coordination of services and case management.[4]

The charge to the Minnesota Intergovernmental Information Systems Advisory Council (IIAC) illustrates the full range of tasks that need to be undertaken by a group designed to create wired organizations across the range of state and local government activity. Specifically, the council is asked to do the following:

Assist state and local agencies in developing and updating intergovernmental information systems; facilitate participation of users during the development of major revisions of intergovernmental information systems; review intergovernmental information and computer systems involving intergovernmental funding; encourage cooperative efforts among state and local governments in developing intergovernmental information systems; present local government concerns to state government and state government concerns to local government with respect to intergovernmental information systems; develop and recommend standards and policies for intergovernmental information systems to the office of technology; foster the efficient use of available federal, state, local, and private resources for the development of intergovernmental systems; keep government agencies abreast of the state of the art in information systems; prepare guidelines for intergovernmental systems; assist the commissioner of administration in the development of cooperative contracts for the purchase of information system equipment and software; and assist the legislature by providing advice on intergovernmental information systems issues.[5]

A sample IIAC project is the Local Government Financial Reporting Project (FINREP). Its goal is to reengineer the local government financial reporting system. When completed, the project should reduce the number of reporting forms, make financial reporting to the state more accurate, make comparisons among local governments easier, and speed the turnaround time for reports back to local governments by making them available online.

In San Diego, the New Beginnings project, which provides comprehensive service delivery including medical care and housing, required cooperation among city and county governments, a school district, a housing commission, a health center, nonprofit agencies and state agencies. Implementation of the integrated case management information system overcame barriers of intra- and inter-institutional communication in order to deliver effective services to families (Marzke et al. 1994).

KEY TECHNOLOGIES OF INTERORGANIZATIONAL NETWORKS

While most of the same knowledge management technologies identified in Chapter 4 can be applied to interorganizational environments, two important technologies have nevertheless been specifically developed to enhance the ability of organizations to share information and to automate business transactions: electronic data interchange (EDI) and extensible markup language (XML) for the Web. Although these terms have different connotations, if one accepts a broad and inclusive definition of EDI, then it is possible to identify XML as a particular instance of EDI. However, if one adopts a more narrow definition of EDI, a distinction can be made between the terms.

Development of Electronic Data Interchange

Electronic data interchange (EDI) refers to the direct exchange of standardized information from computer to computer for the purposes of furthering or completing a business transaction. The exchange may involve documents, applications, data fields, invoices, work or purchase orders, electronic funds, or any piece of information that is organized in such a way as to be prepared for processing by the recipient (e.g., data designed to provide for error-checking) (Laudon & Laudon 1996). EDI is used by governments for a variety of interjurisdictional and interorganizational transactions, such as export documentation, the transmission of crime data and criminal records, purchasing, and the processing of health insurance claims and personnel benefits (Anderson 1998). The advantages of EDI include lower error rates, higher processing speeds, lower inventory costs, increased productivity, and better business relationships (Scala & MacGrath 1993). However, setting up and maintaining an EDI system involves substantial capital costs, and therefore may be justified only in cases where there is a high volume of transactions. Moreover, EDI is only feasible when one's trading or exchange partners also use EDI (Anderson 1998).

EDI and other technologies for interorganizational networks essentially make it possible to extend process reengineering and knowledge management activities beyond the boundaries of the organization. That is, even though a government may have streamlined its in-house work processes, the benefits may yet be trivial if many of the bottlenecks in the processes being redesigned exist outside of the organization itself. In these cases, unless public managers incorporate suppliers, collaborating organizations, and even customers into the process streamlining effort, the potential benefits may never be captured.

Although use of EDI has been somewhat limited in scope because of the high entry costs, the development of business-to-business e-commerce Web sites may prompt expanded use of EDI or EDI-like technologies. As such, public manages should be aware of impacts that may be less visible, but still important to the success of work-transformation projects. One obvious impact is a decrease in flexibility. It takes time, effort, collaboration and resources to develop an EDI system. However, over time it is typically the case that the system will need to be changed. In these instances, additional resources must be spent at both (or all) ends of the system. In addition, because of the setup costs of EDI, it is often the case that certain suppliers, partners or customers may not be able to participate, thereby reducing the flexibility to work with these groups. As the selection of suppliers or partners is restricted due to entrance costs, there is a potential for the government to miss out on partnership opportunities. Also, because EDI will typically involve agreements about system maintenance and operational reliability, there is a potential for an organization to become dependent on suppliers or partners maintaining their end of the system. A second factor is that even though EDI is based on standards, there are many instances where different but related EDI networks will use different standards or codes for identifying the same product or data. In such cases, it may become difficult, for example, to control the supply of warehoused goods using electronic bar codes (Anderson 1998). A third complicating factor with respect to implementing an EDI system is the need to adjust other organizational practices. For example, if one sets up a purchasing system that employs EDI standards that are used nationally, it makes sense to open up competition for supplying the government with goods or services to a national market even though the traditional practices have limited the competition to local or regional suppliers. The original factors that led the government to limit competition (e.g., the need for speedy delivery and the time spent on notifying vendors and comparing prices) often become moot with the implementation of an EDI system. For instance, once an EDI system is in place much of the time spent in bid notification, bid response, price comparison and sale negotiations can be eliminated through automated processes. With a substantial amount of the processing time being cut, it then becomes possible for distant suppliers to ship goods within the desired time frame.

Despite the complexity of the decisions that lead to successful EDI, it is generally recognized that in many areas, particularly in the public sector, the potential benefits of EDI have only begun to be tapped. As such, a case can be made that governments should take a proactive stance toward developing EDI systems in both the public and private sector. For example, recognizing the benefits of EDI, the Singapore government developed and implemented TradeNet, a nationwide EDI system that allowed government agencies to process and exchange export and import trade documents with private shipping companies. The effort required a number of government agencies involved in trade regulation to develop much closer, more collaborative relationships. The benefits of the TradeNet system were evident in the high rate of adoption of the system by private trading companies: by the end of the second year of operation, 90 percent of all trade documents were transferred through the system (Tan 1998). The system also led to a reduction in trips per transaction by clerks from at least two to zero, an elimination of interpersonal interactions related to document submission, the full automation of document checking and approval, a reduction in fees charged, a reduction in turnaround time from two days to fifteen minutes, the automated routing of documents for customs processing, and a reduction in staff from 134 to 88 (Neo, King & Applegate 1993).

Even though EDI can provide government suppliers, partners and customers/citizens with substantial benefits, the impetus to promote EDI in the public sector may be weak for a couple of reasons. First, as monopolies, public sector organizations do not generally experience the same type of pressure to introduce new ways of doing business, at least in the short term. Second, because of public organizations' monopoly status they are often subject to political pressures that inhibit radical change. That is, because governments could use their monopoly position to order their partners, suppliers and citizens to use an EDI system, they are under political obligations not to do so—at least not to do so rapidly or in a way that would leave out whole groups of stakeholders who do not wish to invest in new technologies such as EDI. Instead, governments will often be obligated in their reform efforts to maintain dual systems—a traditional (e.g., paper document) system along with the new EDI system. Obviously, more democratic societies will feel this obligation more strongly than less democratic ones.

Anderson (1998) suggests that governments should take a number of direct and indirect steps to promote the use of EDI, including:

• Teaching public managers about the most innovative practices of their peers
• Building knowledge about EDI

- Participating in EDI councils and standard setting bodies
- Direct subsidy of EDI projects
- Setting goals for EDI deployment
- Participation in EDI projects
- Coordination of e-commerce activities among governments

XML and Internet-Based EDI

With the development of the Internet there has been a movement, particularly in the United States, to implement EDI across the Web rather than through private networks. This movement was for many years stymied by fears about the security of Internet transactions and by the lack of a standard language and translation software for identifying particular pieces of data within documents. With the development of increased Internet security (e.g., the use of the secure socket layer, or SSL, and browsers that allow for encryption and decryption of data), this barrier to using the Internet as a network for EDI is receding. Web users now can sequentially query Web sites or download needed documents in order to further a business need—and to do so securely when needed. While this step essentially set Web-based EDI on an equal footing with more private EDI systems, the development and use of extensible markup language (XML) promises to make Internet-based EDI a more powerful technology than traditional EDI.

XML is essentially a set of codes or tags that describe the text in a document such as a Web page. Just as the HTML tags in the sequence of Bold when interpreted by a Web browser render the word "Bold" in bold letters, so too do XML tags help to render text in ways that make it more meaningful or useful to a user. Unlike HTML, which is comprised of a limited and preset group of tags, XML allows Web page producers to build their own system of meaning and to share it with others. For example, one might create an XML tag set that looks like this:

<payer="John Doe" category="utility" type="residential water consumer" bank="American Savings" amountdue="$125">

This XML phrase might reside on a government water utility Web page that John Doe could bookmark and access from his browser. More important, John Doe could use a personal accounting system that would automatically visit this Web site, gather the needed bill information and automatically prepare a check or authorize electronic payment on a certain date.

XML is intended as the universal format for structured documents and data on the Web. The "structured data" that XML is designed to help convey over networks could be things like the data in spreadsheets, address books, financial statements or transactions, or even technical drawings. Generally programs that produce such data can store it in a text format. In this format, it is possible—given the right set of rules, guidelines and conventions—to look at the data without having to have a copy of the program that produced it. XML essentially supplies the set of rules, guidelines and conventions for designing text formats for such data. XML tells you how to mark up text so that you can design effective ways of describing information, usually for storage, transmission or processing by a program. The XML markup is based on a combination of predefined tags, which represent categories of information (like data fields) and definitions of how these tags relate to each other in a treelike hierarchy (e.g., which information is a subset or a sibling of other information). While tree hierarchies cannot represent all information, they can represent most types of data and their structures. When fully implemented, XML tags perform the same functions as EDI codes used to identify specific pieces of data within documents or data files. Like EDI, XML allows for such things as media-independent publishing, workflow management in collaborative environments, and the processing of documents by intelligent clients—but does so in a Web environment based on text (or Web page) documents.

Media/Vendor Independent Publishing and Data Exchange

If one only needed to exchange a copy of a document and if all of one's business partners, suppliers and customer/citizens agreed to use the same set and version of the needed application software (e.g., WordPerfect, Acrobat, Excel, ArcView, etc.), XML would probably not be necessary. One would simply download the files needed and open them with one's own copy of the software that originally produced the file. However, it is rarely the case that all stakeholders have the same software, and it would be difficult to enforce such an agreement among a diverse group of stakeholders. Moreover, it is often important to be able to integrate data directly from one application to another.

Workflow Management in Collaborative Environments

Because XML helps support automated exchange of data among diverse applications, it can help organizations to better manage workflows across organizational or unit boundaries. This is possible because XML enables the assembly into a single digital document the multiple data fragments (e.g., word processor files, database queries, graphics, video clips, or even real-time data from sensing instruments) that might be needed to complete a work process. Because XML is Web-based, different agents within a work process can use the data in an XML document for their own purposes.

Processing by Intelligent Systems

Because the Web is now the primary context in which software developers are creating intelligent agents (for gathering and analyzing information and automating decisions), XML is being integrated with these intelligent systems at a fairly rapid pace. As such, instead of individual government employees having to arrange for a number of sequential queries to acquire information from diverse sources, the use of XML in an Internet-based intelligent system can support numerous exchanges of information taking place simultaneously and automatically with governmental suppliers, partners and customers (or at least those who are on the Web and formatting their text documents or Web pages using the same XML-based format). When governments purchase goods from vendors or provide services to citizens, a tremendous amount of information is typically exchanged. Vendors, for example, will supply prices, codes for the type of good, quantities available, warranties provided, expected payment terms, delivery dates and the like. Citizens and consumers of government services will supply a similarly complex array of information that will vary with the service being requested. With XML all of these data can be shared electronically. Moreover, once the government, vendors and citizens set their preferences for arriving at agreements with each other, terms can be agreed upon and deals closed without further human activity or intervention (Explaining XML 2000).

Because XML is a set of rules for defining a markup language, it allows the creation of any number of enumerations of domain or transaction-specific languages. Specialized XML languages are being built for everything from air travel to banking to health information. In the public sector, XML languages are being developed first in areas where there is substantial overlap among the levels of local, state and federal governments (e.g., criminal justice, land and environmental issues, and health care). To draft a new XML language, the language authors must achieve agreement on which tags will be allowed and how tagged elements are going to nest within one another. For example, a health record XML might have a high order "person ID" tag that contains elements (with their own tags) for address, phone number and the like. An XML language's vocabulary and structure are codified in a document type definition, which is then referred to by all documents of that particular type. Once document types are defined, programmers will be able to use the various types of information in a document to create customized versions of the document for different audiences or abilities. Using XML style sheets (or Web pages that tell other pages how to display information), programmers will even be able to help people with disabilities by rendering XML into Braille or audible speech. The key benefits of XML are simplicity and extensibility.

Simplicity. Because it is text-based, programmers do not need sophisticated tools to debug a problem or to create documents that can be read across computer platforms. XML provides the ground rules that eliminate layers of programming details so that people with similar interests can concentrate on the key task in any data exchange/transaction effort—agreeing on how to represent the information that they will routinely exchange, rather than spending time agreeing on which programming tools will be used. As a result, the cost of implementing an EDI-type system can be considerably reduced, allowing a larger number of moderate-volume transactions to take advantage of EDI-type systems and related benefits. Similarly, as XML becomes a widely used standard, the authoring tools for XML document creation will become more sophisticated and less costly, reducing development costs even further.

Hence, even though XML was developed primarily to meet the requirements of large-scale Web content providers for industry-specific markup, it is likely to make the exchange and customized use of data more widespread than would have been the case were traditional EDI protocols followed. What XML does not eliminate is the costs to stakeholders of developing standard ways of categorizing or tagging data elements.

Extensibility. The extensibility quality of XML means that Web publishers can extend the capability of basic HTML tags by adding their own tags. These tags can be used to create a much more extensive set of metadata, or data about the data, in the Web page or document. In this way, the efficiency of searching should be greatly improved. Data managers in an area of interest (e.g., public finance) can even create their own descriptive tag sets and document types. Use of these tags can then in turn make it possible for data from a Web page to be automatically extracted from the page and entered directly into an existing database or system. Essentially, XML provides Web-based publishers of documents with the capabilities of sophisticated document coding without the rigors imposed by traditional EDI coding and document design and validation. In addition to facilitating data exchange, XML will also aid the development of powerful Web-based interfaces with data. For example, XML will enable users to click on a hyperlink and then choose among several linking options; alternatively, XML will allow documents to place data within different contexts. As these capabilities are developed, XML applications will merge the strengths of databases, expert systems and "what-if" modeling applications such as pivot tables. This extended capability, moreover, will take place within the context of being able to draw data from any XML formatted source on the Web.

How Might Governments Use EDI/XML?

The following briefly describes how EDI/XML technologies might be used in different functional areas of public sector activity.

Health Information Networks

Currently, it may be possible for a doctor to search a database that contains your health records and access your drug reaction history on her Web browser. However, if she wanted to then include these data in a specialized expert system for identifying potential drug interaction problems, she would not be able to do so. Were the doctor able to access a patient's drug reaction history within an appropriately formatted XML document, the data contained in the document could then be directly pulled into a database or expert system for further processing (Bosak & Bray 1999).

Surplus Property Auctions

System users could view and submit bids on various pieces of government property for sale. With minimal round-trips to the server, users could watch as the application revealed new bids and bidders.

Integrated Justice Systems

Judges could view in one integrated document criminal histories, psychiatric reports, arrest reports, related civil/criminal justice filings and outcomes, corrections and probation reports, child support history, and so on.

Integrated Economic Data

Government Web sites often become stale because their authors do not update data that changes often. The sites may provide links to various outside data sources (e.g., Census Bureau, Bureau of Labor Statistics, etc.), but the person interested in data about the community (e.g., as part of a new business location siting effort) must maneuver through several links and search queries at each site to receive the most recent data. With an XML enabled site, these data could be integrated into Web pages that pull data from the most recently updated sources.

Modeling of Water System Threats

Recently, I was involved in an effort to develop a drinking water monitoring system for the state of Georgia. The short-term purpose of this system was to identify communities whose drinking water was being threatened by drought. The system that was built supported water system operators, public managers and ordinary citizens reporting problems with drinking water sources such as well pumps that are sucking air. The longer-term goals of the system include an ability to model, map out and predict threats to drinking water sources. To accomplish this latter goal, it will be necessary to gather data on such things as stream flow and rainfall rates in areas near the water sources that are experiencing problems—at the proximate time that the problem is reported. Fortunately, there are agencies (e.g., United

States Geologic Survey, University of Georgia School of Agriculture, etc.) that gather and store such information and publish it on the Web. Unfortunately, these data are not published in an XML format that would allow them to be automatically linked with and included in a water source problem report. As these agencies adopt an XML standard the data sharing needed to produce the kind of predictive models public policy makers have requested will become possible.

The Implications of XML for Public Managers

The good news about XML-based data exchange is that it is relatively simple and much more flexible and powerful than traditional EDI. The challenge of XML for public managers will be to reshape their human resource development strategies related to interorganizational information exchange. Currently, moderate to large governments tend to possess a mixture of two types of IT specialists. The first type are trained in data processing and familiar with mainframe and client/server database technologies, but relatively inexperienced with Web-based technologies. A subset of these staff may be capable of developing traditional EDI systems. The second type of IT specialists are self-trained or minimally trained Web masters. With the development of XML, both of these groups will likely need retraining. The data processing group will need to learn how to use XML structures to exchange data between existing database systems and the Web, specifically, learning how to pull information from the Web into existing systems. Tomorrow's Web designers will face the challenge of learning much more about structuring data (e.g., building multilayered, interdependent systems of DTDs [Document Type Definitions], data trees, hyperlink structures, metadata and style sheets) (Bosak & Bray 1999). This means that the typical training of Web masters, which has emphasized graphics and relatively simple document design factors, will be insufficient to enable governments to take advantage of the much more robust infrastructure afforded by XML.

FUNDING INTERGOVERNMENTAL IT PROJECTS

The Intergovernmental Advisory Board (IAB), chartered as an advisory board under the Federation of Government Information Processing Councils (FGIPC) in May 1997, has identified seven broad approaches for funding IT initiatives. The following list enumerates these approaches along with some sample project descriptions drawn from a number of sources, including IAB's publication *Innovative Funding Approaches for Information Technology Initiatives* (Intergovernmental Advisory Board 1998). This publication provides full descriptions of numerous examples of innovative funding of intergovernmental IT projects.

Partnerships:

- New York, Maine and Missouri are investigating the possibility of a joint testing program for information technology accessibility to establish state access standards and modify purchasing methods to include independent verification of access performance (Intergovernmental Advisory Board 1999).

- The state of Georgia induced private industry to build proof-of-concept digital signature applications and technologies on a pro bono basis. Private firms probably participated because of their desire to be first down the learning curve.

- American Management Systems (AMS), the systems integration firm that developed a billing and financial system for the state of Massachusetts, gave Massachusetts a royalty of $150,000 from the subsequent sale of the system to other clients.

- The Department of the Treasury's Financial Management Service, the Department of Energy, the Environmental Protection Agency and the Bureau of the Census have partnered in the effort to define public key infrastructure (PKI). Each agency contributes funds to pay for the project.

Fees:

- The Information Network of Kansas (INK) charges fees for premium information services. The premium fee services are related to legal, banking and other industry-specific business information and applications. The private firm that operates the fee service for the state receives a regulated return but remits most of the network's revenues to the state of Kansas.

- The state of Massachusetts uses a contingent fees agreement to develop and implement information technology projects within the state. If the system does not work as specified, the state does not have to pay the fee.

- A number of states (e.g., Georgia and West Virginia) use phone line surcharges to support crisis line technology services such as Emergency 911.

- The state of Texas is outsourcing its statewide procurement system on a fee basis. The state will pay nothing for development of the system. The system vendor will receive its return on the basis of a small fee for each transaction (e.g., each online purchase order transmitted). Connecticut's online procurement system is similarly funded—product sellers pay a fee to the system managers, with the state having provided only limited assistance to the system creators for their startup costs (Walsh & Dizard 2000).

Taxes and Bonds:

- In 1996 Nebraska designated two cents from the state's existing cigarette tax for the newly created Information Technology Infrastructure Fund (ITIF).

- The city of Philadelphia has created and funded a productivity bank from a bond issue for funding productivity improvement projects. The bank can lend money for project-specific investments to achieve cost savings and/or revenue gains and service improvements. IT projects are eligible, but loans must be repaid in future budget years when the productivity improvement is expected to occur.

Sale of Public Assets:

- The city of Pittsburgh dedicates the proceeds from the sale of old computer, telephone, cabling and communications equipment to the purchase of new equipment. This program gives managers an incentive to get top dollar for used equipment.

- A number of governments have developed ways to use public rights of way to either generate funding for technology or to trade access for a share in the technology infrastructure being laid in the right of way (O'Looney 2000).

Grants:

- One of the largest grant programs for innovative intergovernmental IT projects is sponsored by the Department of Commerce's Telecommunications and Information Infrastructure Assistance Program (TIIAP). This program provides matching grants to government and nonprofit organizations involved in projects designed to improve the public's access to education, health care, public safety and other community-based services. The response to the TIIAP grant program has been more than ample, indicating a high level of recognition of important opportunities to improve service delivery through intergovernmental partnerships.

Seized Assets:

- Funds from the Justice Assets Forfeiture Fund are shared with state and local law enforcement agencies that participated in investigations that led to a forfeiture. A portion of the funds allocated to state and local governments is being used to fund law enforcement technology development efforts.

Combination Funding:

- Maryland has developed a technology investment fund to provide resources for technology projects that will lead to improved efficiencies, service expansion and increases in educational opportunities. The fund represents a combination of revenues from technology leases and sales, documented savings from better technology contract management, and general fund appropriations.

NOTES

1. Appropriators is Ostrom's term for persons or organizations that appropriate common pool resources for their own use.

2. For more information, see *Report of the Intergovernmental Information Sharing Conference of States*, July 30–31, 1998, found at http://www.ojp.usdoj.gov/integratedjustice/julyrep2.htm.

3. For more information, see http://www.state.ia.us/government/iitt/.

4. For more information, see http://www.anydoor.org/.

5. Minnesota Statutes, 1999, Section 16B.42, Intergovernmental Information Systems Advisory Council. Found at http://www.revisor.leg.state.mn.us/stats/16B/42.html.

REFERENCES

Agranoff, R., and M. McGuire. (1999). Managing in network settings. *Policy Studies Review* 16(1): 18–41.

Anderson, K. V. (1998). *EDI and Data Networking in the Public Sector*. Boston: Kluwer Academic Publishers.

Bakos, Yannis. (1997). Organizational partnerships and the virtual corporation. Chapter 4 in *Information Technology and Industrial Competitiveness: How Information Technology Shapes Competition*. New York: Kluwer Academic Publishers.

Bosak, J., and T. Bray. (1999). XML and the second generation Web. *Scientific American* 280(5): 89–94.

Center for Technology in Government. (1999). *Knowledge Networking in the Public Sector*. Albany, NY: SUNY.

———. (2000). *Putting Information Together: Building Integrated Data Repositories Summary Report*. Albany, NY: SUNY, February 9.

Clegg, S. R. (1990). *Modern Organizations: Organization Studies in the Postmodern World*. London: Sage.

Dawes, S. S. (1996). *Making Smart IT Choices: A Handbook*. Albany, NY: Center for Technology in Government.

Dawes, S. S., T. A., Pardo, D. E. Green, C. R. McInerney, D. R. Connelly, and A. DiCaterino. (1997). *Tying a Sensible Knot: A Practical Guide to State-Local Information Systems*. Albany, NY: Center for Technology in Government.

Doney, P. M., and J. P. Cannon. (1997). An examination of the nature of trust in buyer-seller relationships. *Journal of Marketing* 61(2): 35–51.

Eisenhardt, K. M., and D. C. Galunic. (2000). Coevolving: At last, a way to make synergies work. *Harvard Business Review* 78(2): 33–45.

Ellickson, R. C. (1991). *Order Without Law: How Neighbors Settle Disputes*. Cambridge, MA: Harvard University Press.

Explaining XML. (2000). *Harvard Business Review* 78(4): 18.

Gardner, S. L. (1992). Key issues in developing school-linked, integrated services. *The Future of Children* 2(1): 85–94.

Goodhue, D. L., M. D. Wybo, and L. J. Kirsch. (1992). The impact of data integration on the costs and benefits of information systems. *MIS Quarterly* 16(3): 293–311.

Gray, B. (1985). Conditions facilitating interorganizational collaboration. *Human Relations* 38(10): 911–36.

Hammer, M., and J. Champy. (1993). *Reengineering the Corporation*. New York: Harper Business.

Hitt, L. M., and E. Brynjolfsson. (1997). Information technology and internal firm organization: An exploratory analysis. *Journal of Management Information Systems* 14(2): 81–102.

Huber, G. (1982). Organizational information systems: Determinants of their performance and behavior. *Management Science* 28(2): 138–55.

Intergovernmental Advisory Board. (1998). *Innovative Funding Approaches for Information Technology Initiatives: Federal, State and Local Government Experiences*. Washington, DC: Federation of Government Information Processing Councils, January.

———. (1999). *New Responsibilities for Managers Providing Information Technology Services: Federal-State Issues Alert*. Washington, DC: Federation of Government Information Processing Councils.

Jarvenpaa, S. L., and T. R. Shaw. (1998). Global virtual teams: Integrating models of trust. *Organizational Virtualness: Proceedings of the VoNet—Workshop*, ed. Pascal Sieber and Joachim Griese. Institute of Information Systems, Department of Information Management, University of Bern, April 27–28.

Joint Legislative Audit and Review Commission (JLARC). (1998). Review of the Comprehensive Services Act. Senate Document No. 26. Richmond, VA.

Justice professionals still lack information to make good decisions. (1999). *BJIS Update* 2(4): 1–4.

Kagan, S. L. (1993). *Integrating Human Services: Understanding the Past to Shape the Future*. New Haven: Yale University Press.

Kraus, A., and J. B. Pillsbury. (1993). *Streamlining Intake and Eligibility Systems: A Review of the Practice and the Possible*. Washington, DC: Center for Assessment and Policy Development.

Laudon, K. C., and J. P. Laudon. (1996). *Management Information Systems: Organizations and Technology*, 4th ed. Upper Saddle River, NJ: Prentice-Hall.

Lewicki, R. J., and B. B. Bunker. (1996). Developing and maintaining trust in work relationships. In *Trust in Organizations: Frontiers of Theory and Research*, ed. R. M. Kramer and T. R. Tyler. Thousand Oaks, CA: Sage Publications, 114–39.

Malone, T. W., J. Yates, and R. I. Benjamin. (1987). Electronic markets and electronic hierarchies. *Communications of the ACM* 30(6): 487–97.

Marzke, C., D. Both, and J. Focht. (1994). *Information Systems to Support Comprehensive Service Delivery: Emerging Approaches, Issues, and Opportunities*. Des Moines, IA: National Center for Service Integration.

Mechling, J. (1998). *Standing in the Way of Tomorrow: The Federal Views of Barriers to Intergovernmental IT Initiatives*. Cambridge: Harvard University, John F. Kennedy School of Government.

Neo, B. S., J. L. King, and L. Applegate. (1993). *Singapore TradeNet: Beyond TradeNet to the Intelligent Island (Case-9-196-105)*. Boston: Harvard Business School.

O'Looney, J. (1992). Public-private partnerships in economic development: Negotiating the trade-off between flexibility and accountability. *Economic Development Review* 10(4): 14–22.

———. (1996). *Redesigning the Work of Human Services*. Westport, CT: Greenwood Press.

———. (1998). Identifying opportunities for effective cross-agency electronic services delivery: Spanning the gap between consumers' needs and the real prospects for system integration and success. Background paper for Designing the Digital Government of the 21st Century: A Multidisciplinary Workshop. Albany, NY: Center for Technology in Government. http://www.ctg.albany.edu/research/workshop/background.html.

———. (2000). *Local Governments On-Line*. Washington, DC: International City/County Management Association.

Ostrom, E. (1990). *Governing the Commons: The Evolution of Institutions for Collective Action*. Cambridge: Cambridge University Press.

Sabatier, P. (1986). Top-down and bottom-up approaches to implementation research: A critical analysis and suggested synthesis. *Journal of Public Policy* 6: 21–48.

Scala, S., and R. MacGrath, Jr. (1993). Advantages and disadvantages of electronic data interchange, *Information and Management* 25(2): 85–91.

Sheth, A., and J. L. Larson. (1990). Federated databases: Architecture and Integration. *ACM Computing Surveys* 22(3): 183–236.

Sieber, P., and J. Griese, eds. (1998). *Organizational Virtualness: Proceedings of the VoNet—Workshop*. Institute of Information Systems, Department of Information Management, University of Bern, April 27–28.

Soler, M. (1993). *Glass Walls Confidentiality: Provision and Interagency Collaboration.* San Francisco: Youth Law Center.

Tan, M. (1998). Government and private sector perspectives of EDI: The case of TradeNet. In *EDI and Data Networking in the Public Sector*, ed. Kim Viborg Anderson. Boston: Kluwer Academic.

Tjosvold, D. (1986). The dynamics of interdependence in organizations. *Human Relations* 39(6): 517–40.

U.S. Department of Health and Human Services, Office of Inspector General. (1990). *Service Integration: A Twenty-Year Retrospective.* OEI-01-91-00580. Washington, DC: U.S. Government Printing Office.

Walsh, T., and W. F. Dizard. (2000). Online buying's a boom or bust proposition. *Government Computer News: State and Local* 6(7): 1.

Werbach, K. (2000). Syndication: The emerging model for business in the Internet age. *Harvard Business Review* 78(3): 85–93.

11

Wired Governments in the Context of Wired Communities and Economies

A key difference between the wired organization and traditional organizations is the permeability of the boundary between the government and businesses, civic groups and individual citizens. A wired organization is one that enables, through multiple channels for communication and exchange, a quantitative and qualitative change in the interaction among these entities. Depending on how the wiring gets done, a wired government can achieve greater control over its external environment or give external actors greater control of the government. Most likely, a wired government will enable both.

Historically, changes in technology, economic engines and political relations are intertwined. Knowledge transmitting technologies and languages, in particular, have been strongly associated with particular forms of governance and political culture. For example, the primacy of complex languages and scripts (e.g., Chinese ideograms) and difficult communications media (e.g., clay) has tended to support monopolistic forms of government and civic culture (e.g., autocracies or theocracies). With the development of less exclusive technologies (e.g., papyrus and paper) and alphabet-based scripts, literacy became widespread and larger groups were able to share in political decision making and civic life (Ong 1982). The development of the printing press and written forms of vernacular languages further facilitated a movement toward democracy. The emergence of broadcast technologies has had a more ambiguous impact on democracy. On the one hand, these technologies allow for more widespread transmission of information, but on the other hand, the ability to broadcast, being an expensive technology, has become concentrated in the hands of a few individuals or corporations.

A similar set of impacts on political culture can be traced to changes in forms of economic production. Slave and feudal economies helped create a caste system in which only certain persons were allowed to exercise the rights of citizenship. The opportunity for "free land" in the New World helped to create a new model of free labor and broader-based citizenship. With the emergence of industrialization, work became more productive and more social. The first factor led to opportunities to eliminate child labor and create the mechanisms for mass education, while the second provided the impetus for workers to organize labor unions and to participate in mass political parties (Tapscott 1999). In the twenty-first century, wealth will flow from knowledge and from the capacity to identify and exploit niche markets throughout a global economy. This capacity, Tapscott (1999) suggests, will change the distribution of power and lead to an "Age of Networked Intelligence," at least for the two-thirds of the workforce that will be knowledge workers.

While there is general agreement about the increased importance of knowledge, particularly knowledge that can be exploited on a global scale, the specific political impacts of this development are still unclear. Theoretically, a knowledge-based economy would appear to provide the basis for a greater distribution of power among the citizenry. This is the case because, unlike land or capital, which are limited and cannot be distributed without a diminishment in the share of the resource, knowledge can be reproduced and widely distributed without any diminishment. At the same time, however, not all knowledge is of equal value, and as long as a large segment of the population does not participate in the knowledge economy, the potential exists for greater inequality. Robert Reich (1993), the former secretary of labor, has suggested this very impact—that is, that the knowledge economy is, in part, responsible for an increase in income inequality in the United States. Assuming Reich is correct, a major challenge for America in the next few decades will be to prepare the great majority of its citizens for the knowledge economy.

One of the factors to watch in this regard is the development of broadband networks and multispectrum transmission technologies. Theoretically, these technologies will allow all citizens, at a low entry cost, to become broadcasters of information-rich media, including full-motion video. If these technologies develop as expected, they should support more citizens entering the knowledge workforce as well as greater democratization. As these networks and technologies spread, knowledge and power can also be spread more widely. While it is unlikely that this technology trend will, by itself, effectively undermine the dominance of television advertising, the fact that the new media are interactive and provide the user with greater control suggests some cause for optimism. That is, the new media are at least congruent with democratic aspirations.

As was outlined in Chapter 5, although the new media channels facilitate proliferation of knowledge and the exchange of ideas, they simultaneously create new problems for public administrators—specifically, how to manage the increased communications load coming from citizens. In this regard, governments will need to explore the potential for new technologies and new practices to help facilitate constructive communications between citizens and governments. With regard to new technologies, research will be needed to help understand how, for example, governments can effectively use intelligent agents to manage communications and service interactions with citizens—and how citizens will react to the use of such technologies to mediate their exchanges with their governments. In addition, with the help of information technologies and networks, governments should be able to offer more personalized services as well. Notably, the model of personalization does not fit well with a traditional bureaucratic administration of government in which all citizens in a jurisdiction are treated the same. In the traditional model of government, the only personalization option for citizens was to move to a different jurisdiction.

The expected changes in technology and economic organization suggest that the historic bases—economic and technological—for the current arrangement of governmental jurisdictions may no longer be viable. One example of the outdated nature of governmental jurisdictions can be seen in Georgia. Here, the rationale for the size of county governments goes back to the pre-automobile era. The appropriate size for a county was determined by the distance a person could ride on a mule in a day's time. This arrangement resulted in Georgia having 159 counties, many of which are too small to provide services with any degree of efficiency or economy of scale.

Now the existence of easily accessible global networks for commerce and communications makes the arrangement of small-scale jurisdictions much less supportable. Looking toward the future, however, public managers may find that new technologies and economic realities will do more than lead to the emergence of a particularly efficient jurisdictional size—the traditionally dominant impact of these forces. Rather, it is likely that these new technologies and economic realities will support new configurations of authority, influence and responsibility. Some futurists (e.g., Toffler & Toffler 1995) suggest that the changes we are now seeing in our technologies and economies indicate a need to reallocate decisions among levels of government and civil society. Some decisions, such as those related to environmental problems, may need to be moved up to a more regional and global level, while other decisions and responsibilities may be more effectively made in areas that are removed from the center.

Although public managers will not make the major decisions about changes in jurisdictional form, authority or size, their day-by-day shaping of communication channels and service delivery environments will likely play a role in whatever devolution or reconfiguration of authority occurs. In particular, public managers will make important choices about adopting technologies that establish or give precedence to particular architectures for communications and exchange. Lawrence Lessig (1999) has highlighted a number of ways in which the embedded code or architecture of computer mediated communications can impact governance and the distribution of power among participants in a technical system or network. Lessig suggests, for example, that when governments sponsor online public forums, the characteristics of the forums shape the nature of the power that the participants will be able to access and use. In this regard, Lessig tells the story of how two online service providers were impacted differently by their subscribers due to the difference in the way the providers shaped the online services. One service provider allowed unlimited membership in any of its chat spaces, while the other, America Online, placed a twenty-three-person limit on its chat or discussion spaces. In the former case, Lessig notes, when the service provider attempted to censor speech that was negative about the service, the affected subscribers were able to quickly communicate with other members and to organize a "rebellion" that led to the service provider backing down on its practices. A similar rebellion, Lessig argues, was impossible among America Online users because of the embedded barriers to communication across the different discussion spaces.

Lessig's work suggests that as organizations become more wired, the technical rules governing the wiring system will likely play a more important role in the distribution of power and influence among the system stakeholders. Moreover, it is often the case that the new distribution of power and influence will occur in ways that current stakeholders will not immediately be aware of. With respect to citizens' influence on government, one can imagine any number of possible configurations of network interfaces by citizens who interact with and participate in governmental decision making. Taking a cue from Toffler and Toffler (1995), one can conceive of an interface specifically designed to support the development of neighborhood-level decision making, perhaps leading to a devolution of authority to virtual neighborhood councils. Such online, possibly asynchronous councils might help overcome one of the major historical barriers to a more direct town-hall-meeting style of democracy—the inability of citizens to attend meetings. As public managers begin to build wired connections to citizens, they will also be making architectural choices about such things as whether citizens will be allowed and technologically facilitated in efforts to organize fellow citizens around particular issues. Choice of technologies will also play a major role in determining whether individual citizens will be able to personalize the electronic interface they will have with their government (and with their fellow citizens). Such personalization could result in an entirely different cultural pattern of citizens and public officials listening, talking and writing to each other. As a result of such changes in technologies, citizens may choose to tune in or tune out particular voices or information flows.

Some cyber theorists feel that as long as the creators of the technology allow people to make choices and exercise control—such as who you talk informally with at work or what you can buy in the supermarket—technology will allow us to achieve a more pervasive and substantive democracy (e.g., Tapscott 1999). In fact, the nature of digital technology is such that citizens will have a wider range of choices to make than is implied by the market metaphor. Should the technology emphasize individual or group choices? How will group-level choices be structured—by interest area, by geography, by knowledge, and so on? For good or for ill, public managers who have responsibility for creating new system interfaces for citizen-to-government interaction will be the ones to answer many of these questions.

In the area of citizen-government interaction, there is substantial concern that some citizens have greater access to information and communication technologies than others. This is the prime focus of those who speak or write about the "digital divide." While the digital divide should be of great concern to public policy makers, it is an issue that is more likely to be tackled by elected policy makers than by public managers per se. However, public managers are more likely to have a substantial impact on the second order question, which is, Once connected, what are the information needs, patterns of retrieval, points of connectivity to content and participation, and social and logistical barriers to accessing information? Proponents of a "community informatics" approach to issues of digital democracy, in fact, argue that this second order question is really the primary one in that the value of information technologies to citizens is "heavily contingent upon the type and quality of 'content' to which they provide access" (Hague & Loader 1999, p. 11). Table 11.1 outlines four changes in the area of citizen participation and connectivity to government that are related to these second order digital divide issues. Public managers choosing to implement certain technologies, points of connectivity, and procedures for citizen participation will likely play a deciding role in whether these changes, in fact, occur. According to the community informatics perspective, public managers who arm themselves with knowledge about citizen information needs may then be "empowered to apply pressure on the relevant information providers (across public, private, and voluntary sectors) if the required information is not forthcoming" (p. 11).

According to many of those who have studied actual public sector electronic services initiatives, the promise of these initiatives to enhance strong (or highly participatory) democracy has not been fulfilled. Hague and Loader's (1999) summary of public sector practices to date suggests that:

- there has been a greater willingness to use information technologies to put out information to citizens rather than to receive information from them.
- there has been a greater focus on citizens as customers or service recipients than on citizens as active co-participators in governance.
- when citizens' views are requested, governments have tended to use technologies or procedures that aggregate citizens' views on predetermined issues rather than promoting deliberation among citizens or input into actual agenda setting.

Table 11.1
Citizen Participation and Connectivity to Government

	Traditional	Wired Organization Makes Possible or Demands
Information filtering and aggregation	Communications filtered through representatives and media choices.	Direct communications between citizens and public managers and technical staff. Information filtered through artificial intelligence and through citizen-to-citizen dialog.
Citizen influence	Influence is strongest during elections for representatives and through professional polling.	Citizens can track and influence decision making at every step in the process from agenda setting to final vote.
Citizen organization	Organization is limited by resources for communication linkages such as mailings, television and radio, and travel to meetings.	Citizens are also enabled to communicate with each other and to form affinity groups that would be impractical without electronic network linkages.
Public managers' communications with citizens	Official communications involve a standard, one-message-fits-all approach.	Official communications are personalized based on individual profiles of citizens' interests and needs.

Hague and Loader's conclusions about public practices related to online citizen participation suggest a broad critique of electronic public administration. The remedy, Coleman (1999) suggests, would involve not electronic plebiscites but a series of channels in which citizens would be able to engage in deliberations via online linkages to governmental committees and advisory bodies.

However, even this more moderate level of digital democracy would likely cause concern among public management theorists who see public managers as making key decisions regarding "when the public is to be involved and how the public should be invited and engaged" (Thomas 1995, p. 11). While Thomas is supportive of increased levels of public participation in public decisions, he nevertheless favors public executive managers deciding how influence will be shared with the public, which publics will be involved, and what will be the procedural rules and environments for the participation.

Thomas outlines an analytical process (e.g., What are the quality requirements? Is there sufficient information to make a high-quality decision? Is there likely to be conflict?, etc.) that will lead a manager to choose one type of public participation rather than another (e.g., an advisory group, a public hearing, citizen surveys, etc.).

If one accepts Thomas' contingency approach to public participation, the community informatics critique of current digital democracy practices would need to be tested in a more sophisticated way. That is, one would need to identify situations where a more open and thorough approach to public participation was called for but was not implemented by public managers.

INTERACTION WITH THE NGO SECTOR

Nongovernmental organizations (NGOs) have traditionally formed the primary intermediaries between citizens and their governments. As governments become more wired and as they open channels for individual citizen-to-government interaction, this may change. However, even if a government is fully wired and open to online citizen participation, the average citizen will usually not have the time to participate to the degree that the network might make possible. Convenience is of little use when citizens do not have the leisure time to participate effectively. As a result, it is likely that most citizens will still rely on associations and mediating institutions (churches, political parties, civic groups, etc.) to shape government policy and practice to their liking.

What new networks allow that would not be feasible in their absence is the rapid development of temporary associations and coordination among persons and existing associations that have an immediate need to influence government. For example, neighborhood groups that would find it difficult to plan joint meetings and collaborative lobbying efforts can easily use listserv and Web technologies to keep members informed and to coordinate activities such as yard sign distribution, online petitions, and emergency called meetings (Baym 1995). Similarly, nonprofit organizations have been able to use networks to more effectively coordinate policy development at the national level. For example, the Electronic Policy Network (http://www.epn.org) coordinates the efforts of dozens of progressive policy and research institutions via a Web interface. Citizens are able to use the site to discover common policy directions in a topic area or quickly identify the policy priorities of particular research or policy organizations in the network. Here the network enables groups with like interests and views to work together. While networks theoretically can also help one group understand the very different points of view of other groups, examples of such cross-interest group uses are much more difficult to find.

With respect to the more immediate relationships between individual

Table 11.2
Role of NGOs in Traditional Versus Wired Organizations

	Traditional	Wired Organization Makes Possible or Demands
Exchange of Information	NGOs provide annual or occasional reports.	NGOs and government share data and collaborate on joint tasks such as client case management.
Financial Relationships	NGO grantees make once-a-year grant/contract requests.	NGOs bill the government for services rendered as they are rendered.
Overall Role of NGOs, Associations and Research Organizations	Governments make occasional use of associations and research organizations to overcome severe problems or crises.	Continual coordination with and use of associations/research organizations to help design, create and refine knowledge management applications.

NGOs and a government that depends on NGOs to deliver services, one can postulate a set of changes that is similar to the changes expected in the relationship between citizens and their governments. In addition, however, a wired relationship of this kind provides a number of new possibilities for governments and NGOs (see Table 11.2).

INTERACTION WITH THE PRIVATE SECTOR

Government interaction with the private sector can take a number of forms. At one end of the spectrum is the well-known practice of outsourcing of government services. Such outsourcing has become a larger and larger part of government activity, particularly at the federal level. At the other end of the spectrum is what might be called in-sourcing or government enterprise work. In-sourcing allows businesses to come to government to get their needs met. By far the largest instances of in-sourcing occur at public universities that contract with private firms to conduct research. However, governments have sometimes been able to charge fees for services that they are well positioned to provide and that are of particular interest to the private sector. Examples of this type of service include the sale of business, land, personal, demographic or economic data collected in the course of government operations. Between in-sourcing and outsourcing are a variety of public-private relationship forms, including:

- Research and development alliances (e.g., the Garden City Information Technology Cooperative, which involves local governments and private sector IT firms in efforts to promote increased use of technology throughout the community).

- Partnerships that involve the exchange of informal goods, services or opportunities for consulting and marketing (e.g., the partnership program sponsored by the Center for Government Technology at SUNY Albany, which includes IT firms as co-sponsors of research and development of government IT applications).

- Business partnerships in which government and private businesses share in a tangible asset such as a fiber optic network (e.g., the city of LaGrange, Georgia's partnership with its local cable operator; O'Looney 2000a).

As these examples of government interaction with the private sector suggest, the attempt to develop wired governments is often itself an area for growth in intersector activity. In particular, as the private sector gains more experience in advanced IT applications and management techniques while governments simultaneously lose in-house technical expertise, the private sector is being asked to take on more and more IT functions (Ferris 1998). While the trend toward private sector provision of IT has its pitfalls (see discussion of Brown and Brudney's [1998] study later in this chapter), the development of wired, networked governments will tend to promote more private sector provisioning—and for more than the obvious reason of an increase in demand. As governments become more wired and connected to large-scale networks such as the Internet, the common functions of government IT also become more amenable to economies of scale that large private sector IT firms can provide. This is the case because with extensive connection to the Internet, private IT firms are able to offer a package of services (e.g., application service provision, or ASP; seat management;[1] network maintenance; and help desk services) without having to dedicate resources exclusively to one government for these services. That is, the same personnel who service Government A can also service Governments B and C, thereby using human resources more efficiently.

In addition to enabling greater private sector participation in creating and maintaining IT functions, outsourcing, in-sourcing and partnerships with wired governments should become more cost-effective, particularly with respect to promoting greater competitiveness within the vendor community and increasing the effectiveness of contract monitoring. For example, with the development of online procurement systems, it should be easier for geographically distant firms to get appropriate notice and to participate in contract negotiations to a degree similar to that afforded to local firms. Also, network linkages to contractors should enable more frequent communications and data exchanges between governments and contractors—factors that tend to promote greater satisfaction with outsourced services (O'Looney 1996).

Table 11.3 summarizes some of the potential changes in the contractual

Table 11.3
Role of Private Sector in Traditional Versus Wired Organizations

	Traditional	Wired Organization Makes Possible or Demands
Interaction with private sector	Outsourcing, in-sourcing and partnerships are limited by: • Inability to effectively monitor contract obligations in real time • Lack of a sufficient number of competitive contractors • Inability to compare prices or quality of work	Partnership opportunities are expanded as: • Data sharing and early warning capabilities enhance trust • Geographically distant competitors enter the competition • Real costs and prices become transparent • Control of inventory and supply improves • Transaction and paperwork costs are reduced

and partnership relationship that might be expected as governments and their private sector partners become more connected via networks and computer mediated communications.

WILL WIRED GOVERNMENTS HAVE BOUNDARIES?

While a wired world can suggest that geographic or jurisdictional boundaries and physical space will no longer be important, the evidence for such an impact is still ambiguous at best. Malone and Laubacher (1998) propose that the twenty-first century may not be dominated by large organizations to the extent that has been the case in the twentieth century. In place of large organizations and their relatively stable teams of managers and employees, they suggest that businesses (and by extension, governments) may be made up in large measure of independent contractors or e-lancers. In this view, small organizations will be able to take advantage of large networks to make external transactions cheaper and more efficient than they are today. As a result, one would expect to see an organizational environment rich in external relations with contractors and temporary workers. These independent workers would be connected through computer networks, and their work would be time limited and fluid. Malone and Laubacher (1997) also suggest, however, that the small company/large network scenario may not come to pass. This model is being challenged by the alternative of the all-encompassing virtual company model. The city of Singapore illustrates many of the features of this later model. The all-encompassing virtual company model has advantages whenever there is a need for authority or strong organizational alliances to bring together the resources for service improvement. There is some evidence for the e-lance hypothesis in the increase in the number of freelance workers in the business world, and in the long-term increase in the amount of government work that is conducted through contracts. However, there is also some evidence that the increase in outsourcing of public sector work may be due as much to political needs as to a desire for organizational innovation (O'Looney 2000c).

The particular nature of work conducted by government, especially knowledge work at the state and local levels, suggests that there may be limits to the idea of an ad hoc, virtual or outsourced government. That is, while it may be easy to outsource sanitation services without unduly undermining civic values, it may be more difficult to outsource the information services of government, as this calls into question the neutrality and objectivity of the information on which public decisions are made. Brown and Brudney's (1998) study of the use of geographic information systems in local government provides one of the few examples of an attempt to measure the added value of outsourced information technology. This study suggests that there is probably a limit to the cost-effectiveness of outsourcing core information systems functions. These researchers found that moderate levels of contracting for the implementation of geographic information systems (GIS) yielded clear benefits for organizations. With higher levels of outsourcing, however, not only did the positive effects not appear but, as governments moved more toward exclusively providing services through contractors, the delivery time and cost factors increased to unacceptable levels. In addition, contract-only projects tended to produce fewer benefits in terms of operational productivity and performance, organizational decision making, and improved customer service. The estimated break-even point for outsourcing of GIS projects in this study was 25 percent. That is, projects in which more than 25 percent of the total budget was spent on outsourced services tended to produce diminishing returns.

While it is hard to generalize from this one study, the findings do indicate that outsourced IT service providers may have as many disadvantages as advantages with respect to carrying out IT projects. The key disadvantage is probably related to private sector consultants not having the time to identify and understand end-user needs to the degree that in-house IT staff have. Obviously, improvements in network connections between private and public sector organizations and improvement in remote sensing and communications may help future contractors to do a better job in this area. However, in the short term public managers should probably maintain a substantial in-house role in development of IT applications and services.

More generally, the predictions about replacing physical organizations with virtual ones have generally been overblown. For example, predictions that online learning would replace classroom learning have for the most part been unfounded. Rather, the research seems to suggest that online learning complements classroom learning (Hutton 1999). In a similar manner, most predictions about e-commerce replacing the old economy are overblown. It is much more likely that combinations of e-commerce and brick-and-mortar commerce will provide the model for success for the coming few decades at least.

Finally, although networks could potentially favor weak, broad and distant ties rather than strong, deep and community-based connections among people, the research so far in this area suggests that a network link (such as that provided by the Internet) will support a variety of social ties. That is, it can facilitate both strong and weak, instrumental and emotional, and social and affiliate relationships. As Hampton and Wellman (1999) have observed, relationships are best sustained through a combination of online and offline interactions, and are rarely maintained through computer-mediated communication alone. They also observe that much of the online activity seen in the highly wired communities they have studied occurs among people who live and work near each other, rather than among people who are more distant. That is, networks help to bring neighbors and co-workers together to socialize, to arrange in-person gatherings, to provide mutual aid, to exchange gossip and information, and the like. In fact, one of the emerging potentials of wired organizations is the increased awareness of political or organizational change and an increased ability to organize protest activity and mobilize resistance to undesired change. In this sense, while networks can be a liberating force through the potential for increased awareness of ideas and activities outside of the organization, they can also act as a conservative force to maintain desired status quo relations and routines. While networks may generally act to enhance community and local cooperation, the shape or architecture of the communication channels and the nature of the available content can either facilitate or frustrate this effect. (For an argument that cyberspace may be helping to dissolve local communities, see Slouka 1995.)

WIRED ORGANIZATIONS EXIST WITHIN A WIRED INNOVATIVE COMMUNITY

Like all governments, wired governments will depend on the existence of supportive elements in the larger community. It is no wonder that the best governmental Web sites (e.g., Boston, San Francisco, San Diego, Austin) are sponsored by cities where there is a strong high-tech base of industry and workers' skills. Research on industrial innovation, for example, indicates that such innovation is built on institutional arrangements that facilitate exchanges of different types of knowledge among a wide spectrum of occupational, government and business groups. In short, innovations occur as a result of a complicated network with intricate feedback connections, rather than through orderly pipelines of separate investments in basic research and process innovation. This research also suggests that the most effective innovation efforts require both abstract and practical knowledge. This fortuitous mixture, for example, can be seen in the close relationships between a key center for abstract thought—Stanford University—and the computer industries in Silicon Valley. A key value of links between the research community and practitioners is that the people in the research community (i.e., people trained to think scientifically and who are skilled in using investigative tools) will have interesting and fruitful conversations with people in the field who are experiencing problems that could benefit from new approaches.

Local governments that choose to become wired organizations will do their part to help stimulate an innovative community environment. However, additional steps can also be taken to help build a wired community. Many of these steps, such as creating a community broadband network, wiring buildings for high-tech industrial development, and creating public-private partnerships for network creation, are outlined in a recent *IQ Service Report* entitled Access: Making your community Internet-ready (O'Looney 2000a). In addition, however, a case study of San Francisco's Multimedia Gulch suggests that the general principles found in the business literature for successful business "incubation" (e.g., reduce overhead resource requirements for start-ups and provide an array of business support services targeted at the needs of companies in the emerging stages of development) apply equally well to specialized information technology businesses. That is, local governments should not make a lack of expertise in IT a barrier to recruiting and developing IT firms in the community.

While necessity may be the greatest prompt to innovation, competition also has a major impact on the degree of innovation that occurs. For the most part governments do not engage in direct competition with each other because each is sovereign within its own jurisdiction. However, this does not mean that governments cannot compete indirectly for recognition as leaders in innovation or in becoming wired organizations. At the state level such competition is promoted by the efforts of *Government Technology* and *Governing* magazines to rate the level of digital sophistication in a variety of areas. Similarly, Public Technology Inc. and the Kennedy School of Government provide innovation awards that frequently go to local and state governments that have successfully introduced new technologies and techniques into service delivery.

ORGANIZING FOR THE WIRED GOVERNMENT AND COMMUNITY

If wired governments exist within wired communities, then governments will likely need to take a substantially different approach to developing the capacities of a wired government. Specifically, governments will need to create a greater degree of partnership and collaboration with interested community groups as well as with providers of new technologies.

Existing Community Alliances

Generally, the most active partnerships among governments, communities and the providers of technology have been built around the need to bring high-end telecom (or broadband) services to a community that might otherwise receive these services only after they have already been implemented and exceeded in the more urban and affluent communities. While these alliances serve a very useful purpose and often involve a broad educational mission in addition to the pooled purchasing of bandwidth, for the most part they do not engage citizens and providers of technology in the business or operations of government. Rather, these groups tend to exist as fairly fluid networks that coalesce around issues of interest to the dominant players or sponsors. These interests tend to be economic in nature. Unfortunately, other interests, such as those of grass-roots community groups or groups that may have an interest in privacy, citizen participation, government service delivery, or the future shape of democratic institutions, are less represented and often invisible to key policy makers (Cawood & Simpson 2000). However, a few governments have made efforts to provide for a more expansive participation by citizens in IT strategic planning. One effort in Orange County, Florida, which began in 1994, was called the Well-Connected Community. For this effort, a number of task forces were organized. A citizen volunteer chaired each task force, and the meeting agendas, times and places were collaboratively set by the task force members. Areas of work included:

- Design of a network architecture model
- Cataloging and prioritizing information resources and topics
- Identifying the most desired information services to be provided

The local government helped facilitate steering committee meetings, and supported the creation of a local online bulletin board. The leadership of the organization included representatives from both city and county government, the Orlando Public Library, the University of Central Florida, and the Economic Development Commission of Mid-Florida (Babington 1995). The Well-Connected Community model is one that other communities can duplicate to move forward with wiring both governments and the surrounding community. The key to such development lies in balancing the content and transaction needs of the citizens and local businesses with the production capabilities of the government and its partners in economic development. By involving citizens and business leaders in their Web application and network development strategies, governments are more likely to fulfill real needs. The positive feedback from successfully meeting such needs is likely to help support further development of the government's Internet presence and capabilities.

The Rationale for Improved Government-Constituent Alliances

Three areas to consider in improving alliances between governments and constituents are trust, syndication and sharing, and asset-based approaches to government effectiveness.

Trust

While serious efforts to create community involvement in the development of wired government are difficult to sustain, public managers should support such involvement for a couple of reasons. First, online communities have come to expect that they will be involved in the development of public sector Internet services. A number of online communities have developed their own organizational networks focused on increasing public participation in government. Democracy On-line, for example, is one of a number of organizations that promote online civic participation and democracy efforts around the world (http://www.e-democracy.org/do/). The Web site for this organization provides a substantial amount of educational and technical assistance resources for online communities that share these goals. Steven Clift, the director of Democracy On-line, is a tireless advocate for improving the public sector facilitation of democratic processes. Clift's vigilance in this regard can be seen in a short excerpt from his Web-published book, *E-Democracy E-Book—Democracy Is Online 2.0*:

The clogged e-mail in-boxes of elected officials without the tools to sort, filter, and respond to incoming e-mail is leading to a situation where e-mail is the least effective way for an average citizen to influence their government. On the other hand, e-mail is an extremely effective tool for an insider who knows staff e-mail addresses or other addresses used by the elected official. This disparity must be addressed head on.[2]

Clift notes that a number of governments around the world are taking steps to use the new online technologies as channels for greater citizen participation. Specifically, he notes that:

• The Scottish Parliament has officially recognized and agreed to accept online petitions.
• The Netherlands government is working on policies that would establish guidelines for public managers to follow in replying to citizens' comments and questions in a timely and thorough manner.
• The European Commission's Fifth Framework (http://www.cordis.lu/fp5/) initiative provides funding for online democracy projects.

Second, implementing some of the new forms of network-mediated communications will necessitate that public managers gain the trust of the community regarding the government's use of technology. If a public manager
attempts to introduce technologies that are not in congruence with community values, the chances of success are few. This is particularly the case
with respect to

- developing new virtual meeting spaces
- creating customized services or implementing personalization technologies
- implementing online constituent-government exchanges that could involve variable
  pricing of goods or services

In these areas, core issues and concerns about democracy, privacy, equal
treatment and fair pricing are at stake. Public managers who move forward
with technologies that impact these values without prior consultation with
the community do so at their peril.

Syndication and Sharing

One of the key design guidelines for new knowledge-based organizations
is the idea of syndication. Syndication involves the sale of the same good to
numerous customers. These customers then individualize and integrate the
syndicated material (Werbach 2000). Governments should be interested in
syndication both as producers of syndicatable materials and as consumers of
these goods. For example, currently if a citizen visits a local government
Web site and wants to learn more about the demographics of the community, the Web site often will have a link to the homepage of the U.S. Census
Bureau's Web site. Through a long series of clicks, the citizen eventually is
able to obtain the information sought. Such a situation is ripe for syndication. In this instance, the Census Bureau might become a producer of a
customized Web page for each community in the United States. Such a page
would become part of the local government's Web offerings and provide
one-click-away access to all the different types of census data relevant to that
community. Identifying opportunities for syndication is most likely to occur
when governments connect and consult with providers of information outside of the government. Hundred of opportunities for syndication exist
within and among communities. These might include newspaper alliances
providing automated clipping services for the local government's Web site.
Similarly, local governments could syndicate a compendium of news from
groups of governments. Local information and referral services could package information for local government Web site offerings on community
services, while local governments could build an interface with the I&R (information and referral) provider that would allow automated entry of social

service provider information on grant applications being made by these providers to the local or state government. The potential for information sharing and syndication is endless.

Asset-Based Approaches to Government Effectiveness

Another reason why public managers should work with communities of constituents (i.e., citizens, suppliers and partners) in developing new technologies for effective government is based on the idea that community members are active agents for change rather than passive consumers of services. In this view, community members, appropriately mobilized, can contribute to governmental effectiveness by bringing assets to the table that would otherwise lie dormant. Asset-based community development generally involves two phases: the identification or mapping of community assets, and the mobilization of these resources so as to multiply their effectiveness (Kretzmann & McKnight 1993; O'Looney 1998). Asset-based development is closely akin to the idea of using social capital or the norms and networks of civil society to provide mutual support among people. The key to this approach is encouraging people to use their skills (or assets) in ways that will naturally lead them to call on others to join in their effort or enterprise. This joint action toward a common goal will often lead to the formation and strengthening of associations that in turn make valuable contributions to the community. An asset-based approach is one that is built on a view of learning as being most effectively engaged in as an activity of constructing. Simply put, people learn more quickly and thoroughly if they go about constructing or creating things that they have a strong interest in and that demand new knowledge and skill—as opposed to being passive consumers of knowledge that is disembodied from activities. A refinement of this idea—called social constructionism—revolves around the notion that learning can be enhanced by people sharing in a constructive activity in a social setting (Turner & Pinkett 2000).

What would this encouragement mean in terms of technological offerings? Obviously, the new communications technologies can play a role in community building, and communities can play an advisory role in the development of government technologies. Important in this regard is a need to recognize that not all technologies are equal when it comes to encouraging learning, asset-oriented development, and the creation and maintenance of networks that support learning in a social context.

Currently, we can distinguish between technologies that are grossly antithetical to these goals and those that are probably supportive. For example, in the former category one should probably include "push" and other one-way delivery technologies; technologies that do not allow users to modify key elements; and technologies that encourage unproductive conflict, social divisiveness, or antisocial or irresponsible behaviors such as flaming, hacking or the production of destructive code. On the other hand, desirable technologies allow people to construct their own versions of an application or to explore the underlying assumptions of the technology (such as game or simulation software). Further, these technologies facilitate free and easy inquiry and the cross-referencing of ideas and information, or empower people by helping to put knowledge or information within a local context. Examples of such technologies provided by Turner and Pinkett (2000) include "personalized web portals for residents, an online community newsletter, a community asset-mapping database, and customizable templates for residents, associations, and institutions to create their own web pages" (p. 164). Elsewhere, I have similarly proposed using GIS and database technologies to promote the exchange of skills and services among community residents based on location as well as intersecting needs (O'Looney 1996).

While it may be easy to identify technologies that are obviously disempowering or that run counter to the development of a knowledge-oriented community or organization, identifying technologies that are likely to support these desirable developments in an unadulterated way will sometimes be more difficult, for a couple of reasons. First, technologies rarely have a single impact. Rather, they are likely to enhance some values or capabilities while undermining others. As suggested earlier, personalization represents one of these technologies. Although the ability to personalize a technology or communications channel can enhance the user's sense of personal empowerment, it can potentially narrow the perspective and the range of information that reaches the user. In the extreme, the risks of extensive personalization are similar to the risks run by a teacher who allows a child of five to personalize his learning plan for the school year. Because the child has not yet been exposed to mathematics, it is unlikely that he would choose to study this subject. Similarly, adults who lack exposure to alternative points of view will tend to become more convinced of their own opinions and less tolerant of others. This is not to say that personalization is undesirable in many instances, only that personalization and the establishment of broad social networks may in some circumstances run counter to each other. Similar ambiguities can be identified in other technologies that would make the list of desirable asset-and-learning-enhancing technologies. For example, while in the abstract a community database of job or service exchange opportunities represents an ideal asset-enhancing technology, there may be occasions or circumstances in which the economic cost of exchanging locally (rather than in the global or more organized marketplace) outweighs the community building benefits of the technology. Admittedly, in comparison to most choices regarding the introduction of technologies, the ambiguities I am describing represent subtleties rather than major concerns. However, all technologies can have major long-term consequences as they tend to shape the path of further development. As such, we need to be as careful in how we design and choose environments for implementing what seem like "good" technologies as we are in choosing not to design and implement the more obviously bad technologies.

CONCLUSIONS

The development of cyberspace creates new possibilities for and challenges to governments and governance at all levels. In the pre-wired world, governments had the primary social role of weighing and integrating diverse values and interests. As James Madison pointed out in *Federalist 10*, one of the advantages of large republics is that the level of diversity is so substantial as to prevent the formation of any faction (built around any particular interest) from long sustaining the power of the majority. At lower levels of government that comprise less expansive jurisdictions, however, the diversity of interests has often not been broad enough to prevent the formation of sustaining majority factions that are able to undermine the interests and rights of citizens who find themselves in a minority. At the national level, the new communication channels allow small interest groups to be better organized and to more effectively collaborate with other groups across distances that once stymied such organization and collaboration. At the state and local level, the creation of cyberspace has made it more feasible for a greater diversity of interests, knowledge and skills to be applied in areas previously dominated by provincialism. At the same time, the development of cyberspace may be further undermining already weakened local ties and economies in favor of what some believe are more shallow relationships between people from distant communities. Government at all levels will play a role in addressing these challenges, and public managers, whether they like it or not, will often find themselves in the middle of a large debate.

Progressive public managers of wired governments will:

- Be aware that governmental use of technology will be a major subject in this debate
- Engage the larger community in discussions about the path of technological development
- Research the likely impacts of technology before, during and after its implementation
- Provide channels for all the stakeholders (citizens, staff, program managers, end-users, etc.) to refine, reject or institutionalize the technology

Public managers who succeed in these tasks will truly be leaders for our time. This leadership in decision making about broad technological development paths cannot occur in a vacuum. Rather, it is built on knowledge and experience with technology itself. Public managers who will lead in the technology policy arena will likely have a vision of how they want to move their organization down the information technology learning curve. This book has outlined the developmental nature of this curve and has identified knowledge management as a "higher level" stage in the learning process. One implication of this model, however, is that public managers may need to walk before they can run. In this regard, the lesson of IT project management is not to adopt the most recent IT business fad, be it knowledge management, ERP or otherwise. Rather, public managers should map out IT projects within a larger strategic plan that outlines how the project will be congruent with the desired organizational vision, culture, budget, and relationship with the larger environment of partners, citizens and communities. Ultimately, as organizations develop and gain experience with the basic uses of IT, they will likely move in the direction of using these technologies for managing organizational knowledge. At the leading edge, knowledge management may even be used to manage the knowledge about how information technologies are best implemented and used within certain task and public value contexts. This is indeed a tall order. What makes this an even more demanding challenge is that public managers are likely to be "policy makers in practice" in this area of wired governments. Evidence for managers playing a stronger than ordinary role in policy development related to technology is found in the results of a recent national survey of public managers on the future of public sector Internet services (O'Looney 2000b). While an equal number of respondent group surveys were sent to chief elected and chief administrative officials, only a handful of elected officials chose to complete the survey. Moreover, the chief administrative official often passed on the survey to an information technology specialist.

With regard to the policy development void, public managers will need to take a sixfold approach. First, they will need to educate elected policy makers on the importance of becoming more versed in the challenges that information technology is likely to pose for government administration and governance. A starting point for enticing elected officials to take more interest in digital government issues may be the idea of Internet voting. Because Internet voting represents a specific wiring project whose implementation is likely to be decided by elected policy makers, it was not a primary focus of this book. However, the intricacies of the subject and its inherent interest to elected officials should offer the public manager an entry point for enhancing elected officials' willingness to grapple with the challenges of digital government.

Second, public managers will need to base their decisions about what technologies to implement and how to implement them on a shared vision of the future and shared values regarding the appropriate roles and responsibilities of citizens, staff, policy makers and public managers. In this regard a number of questions need to be answered, including the following:

Who can speak for the government online?
Who will have access to what information, under what circumstances?

When and where should citizens be able to participate online?

When, where and how often should public officials (elected and administrative) make themselves available online?

Who can publish what, and what approvals are needed, if any?

To what degree, if any, will the government personalize information and services for citizens and businesses?

When, if at all, can government employees use e-mail for personal correspondence?

How will electronic meetings and electronic rule making take place online, if at all?

Third, public managers will need to learn from their peers through exchanges of information on the effective and appropriate uses of technology in other organizations. In this regard, public managers should participate in the knowledge exchange activities sponsored by groups such as Public Technology, Inc. (PTI), the Center for Digital Government, the International City/County Management Association, the National Research Council, the National Science Foundation (Digital Government Initiative), and the CIO Council.

Fourth, because practical knowledge is still rather thin with respect to alternative technology policies, public managers should help to sponsor controlled experiments in which they agree to experiment with an alternative technology policy. In this regard, Keith Johnson's leadership in the effort to allow citizens to transmit their comments on a proposed Department of Agriculture rule is exemplary. Obviously, just as Johnson had to get clearance from the department's legal counsel, so too will many experiments need to receive some level of approval from policy makers. However, the explicit labeling of a practice as an experiment can help obtain the needed permissions.

Fifth, public managers will need to analyze how their experimental policies (or "policies in practice") actually impact the organization and the larger community. This will require that public managers have a strategic vision and priority goals for the government they administer. Answering the question of "technology for what purpose?" is essential before undertaking such an analysis. With a clear sense of purposes and goals, a public manager can then identify whether and how a specific technology or set of technologies will advance these goals. The key to understanding the digital revolution is this idea of infinite malleability. Digital technologies can be designed to maximize any of a variety of objectives. Without specific objectives in mind, the technologies produced are not likely to achieve their potential effectiveness and may even promote objectives that are at cross purposes with each other.

Finally, public managers must assess technologies within the context of the organizational and environmental reality. Even though a primary goal for the government may be enhanced citizen participation, the organization may not be able to support new channels for online citizen-to-government communications. Obviously, if the organizational culture is technophobic, if the jobs have been designed to require little in the way of higher-order skills, or if the culture of governance does not favor strong citizen participation, the public manager's choice of technologies to move the government toward becoming a wired one will be more limited. In this regard, administration of technology and technology policy in practice, like politics itself, becomes the art of the possible.

NOTES

1. Seat management involves the consolidation of all desktop hardware, software, help desk, PC maintenance, and local network services under a single umbrella contract.
2. Found at http://www.publicus.net/ebook/edemebook.html#egov.

REFERENCES

Babington, T. (1995). Becoming well-connected means putting citizens first. *Public Management* 77 (11): 8–11.
Baym, N. K. (1995). The emergence of community in computer-mediated communications. In *CyberSociety: computer-mediated communications and community*, ed. S. G. Jones. Thousand Oaks, CA: Sage.
Brown, M. M., and J. L. Brudney. (1998). A "smarter, better, faster, and cheaper" government: Contracting and geographic information systems. *Public Administration Review* 58(4): 335–45.
Cawood, J., and S. Simpson. (2000). Can public policy widen participation in cyberspace? *DIAC 2000: Shaping the Network Society*. Seattle. Annual Conference of Computer Professionals for Social Responsibility, May 20–23, Washington.
Coleman, S. (1999). Cutting out the middleman: From virtual representation to digital deliberation. In *Digital Democracy: Discourse and Decision Making in the Information Age*, ed. B. N. Hague and B. D. Loader. New York: Routledge.
The Digital State. (1998). Washington, DC: Progress and Freedom Foundation. (Government Technology conducted a follow-up to the study in 1999.)
Ferris, N. (1998). The big IT handoff. *Government Executive*, October.
Fountain, J. E. (N.d.). The virtual state? Toward a theory of federal bureaucracy in the twenty-first century. Draft paper. Kennedy School of Government, http://siyaset.bilkent.edu.tr/Harvard/fountain.htm. Visited January 22, 2001.
Hague, B. N., and B. D. Loader, eds. (1999). *Digital Democracy: Discourse and Decision Making in the Information Age*. New York: Routledge.
Hampton, K., and B. Wellman. (1999). Netville on-line and off-line: Observing and surveying a wired suburb. *American Behavioral Scientist* 43(3): 475–92.
Hutton, S. (1999). Course design strategies—Traditional versus on-line: What transfers? What doesn't? *Alberta Association for Continuing Education Journal* (26): 43–50.

Kretzmann, J. P., and J. L. McKnight. (1993). *Building Communities from the Inside Out: A Path Toward Finding and Mobilizing a Community's Assets*. Chicago: ACTA Publications.

Lessig, L. (1999). *Code and Other Laws of Cyberspace*. New York: Basic Books.

Malone, T. W., and R. J. Laubacher. (1997). *Two Scenarios for Twenty-first Century Organizations: Shifting Networks of Small Firms or All-Encompassing "Virtual Countries"?* MIT Scenario Working Group, Sloan School of Management, Massachusetts Institute of Technology. MIT Initiative on Inventing the Organizations of the 21st Century, Working Paper 21C WP #001.

———. (1998). The dawn of the e-lance economy. *Harvard Business Review* 77(4): 122–39.

Mowery, D. C., and N. Rosenberg. (1998). *Paths of Innovation: Technological Change in Twentieth-Century America*. Cambridge: Cambridge University Press.

O'Looney, J. (1996). *Redesigning the Work of Human Services*. Westport, CT: Greenwood Press.

———. (1998). Mapping communities: Place-based stories and participatory planning. *Journal of the Community Development Society* 29(2).

———. (2000a). Access: Making your community Internet-ready. *IQ Service Report* 32(5): 1–20.

———. (2000b). Future of public sector Internet services for citizen participation and service delivery. (Preliminary report found at http://www.cviog.uga.edu/govtech/egovhome.html).

———. (2000c). Selecting services for outsourcing. In *Local Government Innovation*, ed. Robin Johnson. Westport, CT: Greenwood Press.

Ong, W. (1982). *Orality and Literacy*. New York: Methuen.

PTI. (2000). *1999 Top 25 Technology Solutions*. Washington, DC: Public Technology, Inc.

Reich, R. B. (1993). *American Competitiveness and American Brains*. New York: Baruch College, City University of New York.

Slouka, M. (1995). *War of the Worlds: Cyberspace and the High-Tech Assault on Reality*. New York: Basic Books.

Tapscott, D. (1999). *The Digital Economy: Promise and Peril in the Age of Networked Intelligence*. Toronto: Alliance for Converging Technologies.

Thomas, J. C. (1995). *Public Participation in Public Decisions*. San Francisco: Jossey-Bass.

Toffler, A., and H. Toffler. (1995). *Creating a New Civilization: The Politics of the Third Wave*. Paducah, KY: Turner Publishing.

Turner, N. E., and R. D. Pinkett. (2000). An asset-based approach to community building and community technology. *DIAC 2000: Shaping the Network Society*. Seattle. Annual Conference of Computer Professionals for Social Responsibility. May 20–23, 161–69.

Valery, N. (1999). Survey: Innovation in industry: Networks, not pipelines. *Economist* 350(8107): S8–S14.

Werbach, K. (2000). Syndication: The emerging model for business in the Internet age. *Harvard Business Review* 78(3): 85–93.

Wolfe, M. R. (1999). The wired lot: Lifestyle innovation diffusion and industrial networking in the rise of San Francisco's Multimedia Gulch. *Urban Affairs Review* 34(5): 707–28.

Ziegler, J. Nicholas. (1997). *Governing Ideas: Strategies for Innovation in France and Germany*. Ithaca, NY: Cornell University Press.

APPENDIX A
The Technology of Digital Signatures

A digital signature that conveys a high level of confidence, trust and legal enforceability is one that will involve some level of authenticating both the person and the document. Authenticating that someone is who they say they are generally involves a non-automated process. That is, some person who has authority and can be trusted must certify the identity of the person who will be using a digital signature. Once this has occurred, there is a large role for technology to play. This role is threefold:

First, the certificate authority (CA) doing the authentication (or its agent) will issue a certificate. The certificate that the CA issues is a password-protected, encrypted data file that has itself been digitally signed by the certificate authority. The data file consists of a public and private key pair, which is simply a pair of numbers that has no inherent association with any identity. This dual-key (or asymmetric or public key encryption) technology involves the use of separate keys for encrypting and decrypting. People's public keys are used to encrypt the messages sent to them, and they use their private keys to decrypt these messages. The two keys are mathematically related, but the private key cannot be derived from the public key, so the public key can be freely distributed. The private key generally stays on the owner's computer.

When Ann wants to send a secure message to John, she encrypts the message with John's public key. When John receives the message, he decrypts it with his private key. To send an encrypted message, Ann needs to have access to John's public key, which she can get by going to a public key repository or possibly to John's Web site. If John is a merchant involved in e-commerce (or works for a government agency involved in e-government) John's public key will be built into the Web site and will be automatically recognized by a Web browser. As such, the purchaser/citizen will send encrypted information without ever personally seeing the public key used for encryption. Since decryption requires the private key that is associated with the public key, only the recipient will be able to read the message.

Second, technology is used to create the digital fingerprint of the document being sent as part of a digital transaction. The generation of a digital fingerprint or code that is unique to a document usually takes place along with the encryption of the message. However, these processes are conceptually and sometimes functionally distinct. For example, in government operations officials often need to know not only that a document has been signed, but that it has not been changed by anyone since the signature was affixed. At the same time, these government data are public records and as such should be readable by the public. Encryption obviously can work to prevent changes to a document (one cannot meaningfully change what one cannot read), but encryption is not necessary for ensuring that one is reading an unchanged document. If the document's digital fingerprint at the point of reception is the same as the fingerprint originally generated by the document's author/signer, then one can trust that the document—even though it was not encrypted—has not been changed.

Third, technology is used to provide security for the host servers and databases. This technology essentially involves computer security firewalls and the following of protocols for securing passwords and other data that need to have limited access.

Although state and local government policy will do little to affect the nature of the technology used to provide electronic documents and transactions with desirable attributes (e.g., person or document authentication), government leaders need to understand the nature of these technologies to be able to decide when and where to use which technologies. Currently, there is little understanding as to what degree government leaders and administrators understand these technologies, their relative costs, or how they might best be employed in particular transaction environments.

APPENDIX B

The Administrative Infrastructure for Governmental Electronic Transactions

Administrative policies as well as technical systems are needed to enable governments to conduct transactions electronically.[1] Had the states and the federal government chosen a more restrictive, "digital signature only" approach to producing, sending and storing electronic documents, public managers would not be faced with difficult choices as to the administrative policies and technical systems that are needed to conduct business in different circumstances. Under more open-ended electronic signature legislation, public administrators will have a great deal of leeway to conduct electronic transactions according to any number of protocols. For this very reason, these administrators will need to have a good understanding of the key features of electronic documents.

Governments, like businesses in general, need to be able to communicate in ways that provide for a sufficient level of confidence that they have reached an understanding with the people, corporations, and agencies with whom they are dealing. As the typology in Table B.1 indicates, governments are involved in internal communications among managers, staff and elected officials, and in external communications with other governments, major corporations, consulting firms and ordinary citizens.[2] While the concepts of security and authentication have a general meaning in the everyday business world, these concepts can be broken down into five separate characteristics:

- *Non-repudiation*: the ability to prove that someone received a message or communication.
- *Confidentiality*: the ability to prove that a message was not read by an unauthorized party.

Table B.1
Typology of Transaction Characteristics by Type of Communication

		Type of Communication		
		Internal	**External with Major Agencies/ Corporations/ Consultants**	**External with Citizens**
Type of Security/ Authentication Characteristics of a Transaction	Non-repudiation	Receipt of new policies or important memos	Notices of bids or replies to offers	Notice of a zoning change
	Confidentiality	Client case records; correspondence on personnel issues	Sealed bids	Anonymous complaint or suggestion; sending of a private record; correspondence on a land or personnel issue
	Non-tampering	Travel vouchers/purchase orders	Contract document drafts with changes	Survey responses
	Signed	Travel reimbursement	Signed final contracts	Requests for zoning change; voting on a minor issue
	Witnessed	(see below)	(see below)	(see below)
	Combination of features to achieve a high level of security/ authentication	Deed transactions; court orders; sealed case records	Final signed contracts with a new business partner for a highly valued service	Voting on a major issue

- *Non-tampering*: the ability to prove that a document is the same as it was when it was originally drafted by its author.
- *Acknowledged/Signed*: the ability to show that a document was acknowledged as the intended writing of a specific individual, group or corporation.
- *Witnessed*: further evidence that a person attested to the contents of a document they signed.

It should be noted that in particular cases only one or two of these characteristics of more secure/authenticated transactions are needed. For example, it is often the case that one simply needs to know that a person has actually received a message that one has sent. In the nonelectronic world, certified mail performs this function. Similarly, in the electronic world, a third party or an automated e-mail server operated by a third party can perform this function.

While not every transaction needs every one of the security/authentication features, often many of these features can be bundled as part of a single software or security/authentication package. Moreover, some of the more demanding features, such as an electronic document signature, tend to require the presence of other features such as non-tampering to be effective. The following section outlines in more detail the key elements and requirements of electronic transactions from a legal defensibility point of view.

THE BASIC ELEMENTS OF E-TRANSACTIONS

In many cases, the demands of e-government will be the same as the demands of e-commerce. In some cases, however, it is more difficult to implement e-government than to implement e-commerce. In particular, certain business transactions frequently take place with only a fairly low-level security check. Before laying out the specific demands of e-commerce and e-government, it may be useful to identify the elements of a general system of transactions—or what may be needed to ensure a particular level of confidence in the enforceability of a transaction. These elements are essentially three: person authentication, document authentication, and authentication of the goods, services and considerations being exchanged.

In nonelectronic transactions, the authentication of the *persons* in the transaction occurs through a variety of means, including signatures, seals, and marks; the use of witnesses and notary publics; handshakes; and documents indicating the presence of a party in the facility when the transaction is claimed to have taken place. Contrary to popular opinion, signatures are not needed to conclude valid contracts, but because they tend to dramatically increase the enforceability of a contract, they have become viewed as an essential component of certain types of transactions. As the American Bar Association guidelines on digital signatures suggest, "A signature should indicate who signed a document, message or record,[3] and should be difficult for another person to produce without authorization."[4]

In nonelectronic transactions, the authentication of the *documents* in the transaction occurs through the linkage between the signature (and other signs of person authentication) and the document, and through the use of page signatures and numbering that limit the ability of parties to add to or falsify the document without detection.[5]

The authentication of the *goods, services and considerations* being exchanged typically occurs through the use of receipts, bank deposit slips, cancelled checks, shipping and receiving records, and the like. While lawsuits often arise related to the quality of the goods or services received or to the failure to receive certain goods, services or considerations, disputes over whether the actual exchange of these has taken place are rare.

Authentication and Basic E-Commerce

The vast majority of electronic commerce transactions involve credit card purchases. The level of data authentication/security needed for the typical in-store credit card purchase is somewhat lower than the maximum possible. For example, in many credit card transactions, the identity of the bearer of the card is never questioned. A major reason for this failure to perform a signer or person authentication check is the $50 limit on liability that the major credit card corporations have established as part of the incentive for using a credit card. This limit essentially means that the card user and the merchant in the credit transaction will often find it more efficient to skip an authentication check (since the vast majority of users are authentic and the penalty for being wrong in a few cases is so small). Additionally, with in-store purchases, the criminal use of a credit card is further discouraged by the potential for the merchant to identify the user at some future legal proceeding. With respect to authenticating the goods, services and considerations, in-store purchases allow for the immediate transfer of goods to the purchaser while the merchant checks on whether the purchaser has sufficient funds to purchase the goods. Similarly, with respect to document authentication, in-store purchases generally produce duplicate copies of a receipt document. The merchant and the purchaser can both check these documents before completing the transaction. The validity of these documents is further advanced by the fact that a third copy is often produced and retained by the credit card company.

Internet-based use of a credit card to purchase goods and services retains some but not all of these features. Specifically, in the Web-purchase situation, the merchant is still able to authenticate the consideration (i.e., by checking the credit card number), and the purchaser can usually authenticate delivery of the goods through tracking and records kept by a shipping company. However, the Internet transaction differs from the in-store one in a couple of ways.

The most important of these differences is the lack of insurance for fraud committed by consumers against merchants. Whereas consumers who use credit cards are protected by a $50 liability limit, merchants are not protected against consumers who are attempting to commit fraud over the Internet. Fortunately, the things that most governments might offer in exchange for a payment tend to be things that would not tempt someone to make an improper use of a credit card (e.g., taxes, fees, licenses, etc.). Furthermore, in an Internet purchase situation the level of person authentication is obviously lower than that of on-site purchasing. This could potentially be a problem were someone interested, for example, in getting a professional license based on having someone else take a licensing test for them. The bottom line here is that governments will have to be careful to ensure that in cases where personal authentication is needed, it can be assured.

Person Authentication

Being assured at a distance that someone is who they say they are is not an either/or proposition. Rather, one can experience several different levels of assurance. The components at each of these levels involve essentially two types of assurance: (1) validation of the person and (2) security of the system. Each of these types of assurance can have different levels of confidence. For example, to validate that someone is who they say they are at a 99 percent confidence level from a scientific, high-security point of view, it might be necessary to have them provide (once in person and subsequently through a digital sensing device over the Web) fingerprints or even a DNA sample. This level of person authentication is probably unnecessary for most transactions with either a business or a government entity. Rather, person authentication in business and legal transactions will typically involve a somewhat lower level of confidence, such as one of the following (see Table B.2):

- an in-person authentication by a third party or government agency.
- a document-based (mail-in) authentication by a third party or government agency.
- an electronic document-based authentication by a third party or government agency.
- an in-person, mail-in or electronic mail-in authentication by a party to the transaction.
- a trust-type authentication based on past transactions.

An in-person authentication demands that the person who will be conducting a transaction actually visit the offices of an authentication agency. The authentication agency may be a government agency or it may be a trusted third party that is in the business of authenticating the identity of

Table B.2
Levels of Authentication

		Authentication Process		
	Trust	**Via E-Mail Documentation**	**Via Mailed Documentation**	**In-Person**
Authenticating Organization	Party to the Process	Lowest Level Authentication		
	Third Party or Govt. Agency			Highest Level Authentication

the person(s) who will be conducting transactions. The person may also be asked to provide other documentation of their identity on visiting the authentication agency office. In a slightly lower level of authentication, a person may simply be asked to present a set of documents through the mail. This is the level of authentication that the U.S. government demands for the issuance of a passport. Lower still in the hierarchy of person authentication would be a process by which a person e-mailed supporting documents to an authentication agency.

Finally, in many cases authentication is sufficient based on repeat experience. For example, if a company has accepted a number of small credit card purchases across the Internet from a person using a particular computer (one with a unique Internet identification number), the company may approve a larger purchase based on this experience with what has come to be a "known customer" even though this customer has never been seen in person or authenticated by any other means than the validation of the credit card number.

The authenticating organization can be an important element in the authentication of identity, as the courts have long given credence to the corroborating testimony of third parties or of government officials. As such, when a person's identity has been authenticated by one of these agencies, the level of trust between the parties to the transaction can typically be much higher. However, for many transactions, such as those between longtime business partners, this level of authentication may not be necessary.

Document Authentication

The levels of electronic document authentication can be conceived in terms of a typology similar to that for person authentication. That is, confidence in the authenticity of a document is a combination of who is doing the authentication and whether the authentication includes a process such

Table B.3
Levels of Document Authentication

		Authentication Process		
		Trust	Use of Hash Functions	Use of Hash Plus Timestamp
Authenticating Organization	Party to the Process	Lowest Level Authentication/ Security		NA
	Third Party or Govt. Agency			Highest Level Authentication/ Security

as the use of hash functions that can provide assurances that the document has not been altered from the time it was sealed. Hash functions are essentially mathematically generated fingerprints of a document that can be used to tell whether it has been changed by even a single bit. Timestamps are a means by which third parties in the business of providing assurances that documents are unaltered can hold a copy of the fingerprint of the document. This copy of the fingerprint can be traced to a particular moment in time, and can be validated by a chain of authentication agencies, thereby providing even greater assurance that the document is what it claims to be and allowing for assurance underwriting by multiple parties. Probably only a minority of e-commerce and e-government transactions would demand the timestamp level of authentication. (See Table B.3.)

DEVELOPING THE AUTHENTICATION INFRASTRUCTURE

As with any process for authentication, the product (e.g., a digital certificate that guarantees that someone is who they say they are) is only as good as the guarantor. As such, the highest level of trust in a system of authentication will be generated by enabling the agents involved in authentication activities (which might be the parties to the transaction or a professional authentication service) to themselves be certified by an even higher authority. At the highest level, such an authority could be a national, state or local government or a highly capitalized business that can back up its authentication with a bond. For example, although the authority that will issue digital certificates in Washington State is a private firm, the firm was chosen by the government. Similarly, Utah's digital signature legislation lays out the responsibility of the Utah Department of Commerce Division of Corporations and Corporate Code to act in the capacity of the certificate authority of last resort. This division is authorized to license and regulate private certification authorities within the state, thereby enabling these authorities to generate a high level of confidence.

Utah's act also outlines the responsibilities of the subscriber (i.e., the person who applies for and accepts a digital certificate from a certificate authority). Accepting a certificate imposes a responsibility on the subscriber to indemnify the issuing certification authority (CA) for any loss or damage caused by reliance on a certificate that was issued based on false representation or failure to disclose relevant information. Essentially, the subscriber "certifies to all who reasonably rely on the certificate that the subscriber rightfully holds the private key corresponding to the public key listed in the certificate, and that all representations made by the subscriber to the CA or otherwise incorporated into the certificate are true."[6] In accepting a certificate, a subscriber assumes a duty to retain control of the private key and to prevent its disclosure to any person not authorized to create the subscriber's digital signature.

Enabling legislation can also outline such elements of an electronic transaction as expiration and revocation, liability or the defined limits on liability for licensed certificate authorities and operators of public key repositories,[7] and the status of a digital signature as evidence in a court of law.[8]

Public Managers and Digital Signatures

Unfortunately, legislation by itself does not assure that digital signatures will be used appropriately and effectively. In some cases, the legislation will not even provide adequate guidance for public managers. For example, the Utah act has been criticized for failing to adequately specify a standard for what would be reasonable care on the part of subscribers (or users of a digital signature) with respect to their duty to safeguard their private keys. As a consequence, public managers whose agencies use digital signatures will need to develop appropriate policies and training regimes to ensure that government employees understand their responsibilities and their level of potential liability. Moreover, as legislatures or the courts clarify liability levels and allocations (e.g., among subscribers, recipients, payers, encryption and other software manufacturers, and certificate authorities) and standards of evidence for liability determination, public managers will need to adapt training and agency policies to the new realities.[9]

As states move away from enabling legislation that requires digital signatures, existing legal principles will tend to govern the complex relationships among certificate authorities, merchants and consumers. Currently, legal scholars distinguish between two types of structures for CA relationships: closed structures in which the consumer does not have a choice in terms of which certificate authority to use, and open structures in which the consumer can choose among competing authorities. Since the trend appears to be toward open structures, the Internet Law and Policy Forum[10] commissioned a study of the legal principles that would govern these open structure relationships in the absence of specific laws. The forum's findings suggest that:

- the relationship between CAs and consumers who purchase a digital certificate is likely to be governed by existing contract laws. That is, digital certificates would be treated as a service, not a good, and therefore the common law is likely to apply (instead of the Uniform Commercial Code or other rules covering "goods"). However, the forum suggests that the contracts formed between CAs and consumers are not likely to completely resolve the matters that could arise from the relationship. As such, some default rules will be needed. Some of these default rules may be found in proposed additions to the Uniform Commercial Code. In other cases, however, default rules may need to be developed by the states.

- the relationship between CAs and merchants who receive the digital certificate from consumers is likely to be governed by existing tort law, not contract law. In particular, the "negligent misrepresentation" tort is likely to provide the most applicable set of rules to govern the certificate authority's liability to merchants if the digital certificate is incorrect.

The forum's draft position is that a party's liability for losses arising from the CA structure should generally be connected to whether or not the party acted reasonably. The party acting unreasonably should bear the resultant loss if the other parties acted reasonably. However, if all parties act reasonably and a loss is nevertheless experienced, the forum believes that the loss should be borne by the merchant. Moreover, the forum supports legislation that would limit consumers' losses whenever they act unreasonably but not fraudulently. Losses not covered by the consumer would then be borne by the merchant, because merchants are generally in the best position to take action to avoid losses or to insure or spread a loss among all consumers. In many cases, governments would be in the position of a merchant.

Although the forum's policy recommendations go a long way toward outlining how states might proceed in developing support for an open digital certificate structure, the forum members recognize that further study is needed.

In cases where the government decides to issue its own digital certificates, public managers may find themselves having to design and implement special standards for employee hiring and management, record keeping, bonding, and insurance in the office(s) that administer the certificates. Public managers may also need to develop allocation of loss rules when more than one party in a government-to-government or citizen-to-government transaction acts unreasonably.

NOTES

1. Much of the discussion of the technical infrastructure for electronic signatures is based on the American Bar Association's *Digital Signature Guidelines*, produced by

the Information Security Committee Electronic Commerce and Information Technology Division, Section of Science and Technology, American Bar Association, 1995, 1996.

2. The types of communication could be broken down further. For example, within the government some staff are authorized to access information that others are not. Also, it might be the case that an outside consultant may have more access to information than a low-level internal staff member. The types of communicators outlined here are rough categories that tend to correspond to the ease with which governments are able to implement a set of higher-level transaction security/authentication features. For example, it is much easier for governments to implement security/authentication features in a local area network that serves internal staff than it is to provide the same level of security/authentication with citizen communicants. Major agencies and corporations tend to be in between these extremes. Such entities are becoming more equipped with the needed technology to enable secure/authenticated transactions and have the resources to purchase digital certificates from third party certification authorities that provide a type of insurance against fraudulent transactions.

3. In U.C.C. Art. 2B (May 3, 1996 Draft), "Record" is defined by 2B-102(30) as "information that is inscribed on a tangible medium or that is stored in an electronic or other medium and is retrievable in perceivable form." See also *Model Law on Electronic Commerce*, United Nations Commission on International Trade Law (UNCITRAL), 29th Sess., art. 7(1), at 3, U.N. Doc. A/CN.9/XXIX/CRP.1/Add.13 (1996) ("Where a law requires a signature of a person, that requirement is met in relation to a data message if: (a) a method is used to identify that person and to indicate that person's approval of the information contained in the data message"). Throughout these guidelines "message" means the digital representation of information (generally, computer-based information), "document" means information inscribed on a tangible medium (generally, paper-based information), and "record" can be used to refer to a message or to a document, consistent with the definition of "record" in U.C.C. 2B-102(30), above (American Bar Association *Guidelines*, p. 15, n. 13).

4. The ABA *Guidelines* (p. 15, n.12) state that: The U.S. Comptroller General's rationale for accepting digital signatures as sufficient for government contracts under 31 U.S.C. 1501 (a)(1): "The electronic symbol proposed for use by certifying officers . . . embodied all of the attributes of a valid, acceptable signature: it was unique to the certifying officer, capable of verification, and under his sole control such that one might presume from its use that the certifying officer, just as if he had written his name in his own hand, intended to be bound." *In re National Institute of Standards and Technology—Use of Electronic Data Interchange to Create Valid Obligations*, file B-245714 (Comptroller General 1991).

5. A paper signature identifies the signed matter less than perfectly. Ordinarily, the signature appears below what is signed, and the physical dimensions of the paper and the regular layout of the text are relied upon to indicate alteration. However, those mechanisms are not enough to prevent difficult factual questions from arising. See, e.g., *Citizen's National Bank of Downers Grove* v. *Morman*, 78 Ill. App. 3d 1037, 398 N.E.2d 49 (1979); *Newell* v. *Edwards*, 7 N.C. App. 650, 173 S.E.2d 504 (1970); *Zions First Nat'l Bank* v. *Rocky Mountain Irrigation, Inc.*, 795 P.2d 658, 660-63 (Utah 1990); *Lembo* v. *Federici*, 62 Wash. 2d 972, 385 P.2d 312 (1963).

6. C. Bradford Biddle, Comment: Misplaced priorities: The Utah Digital Signature Act and liability allocation in a public key infrastructure, 33 *San Diego Law Review* 1143 (1996): 8.

7. For example, the Utah act calls for certificate authorities to (1) not be liable for any loss caused by reliance on a false or forged digital signature of a subscriber, in cases when the certification authority complied with all material requirements of the enabling legislation; (2) not be liable in excess of the amount specified in the certificate as its recommended reliance limit; (3) be liable only for direct, compensatory damages in any action to recover a loss due to reliance on the certificate. (Direct compensatory damages do not include punitive or exemplary damages; damages for lost profits, savings, or opportunity; or damages for pain and suffering.) Also, the Utah act specifies the duties of operators of public key repositories but limits their liability for failure to record suspension or revocation of a certificate in cases where less than one business day has elapsed since notification of a problem.

8. Utah's act provides that a certificate issued by a licensed CA is an *acknowledgment* of a digital signature verified by reference to the public key listed in the certificate. As such, digitally signed documents are deemed to be "acknowledged" and self-authenticating and are therefore prima facie admissible evidence under rule 902(8) of the Utah Rules of Evidence (identical to rule 902(8) of the Federal Rules of Evidence). In adjudicating a dispute involving a digital signature, a court in Utah will presume that if a digital signature is verified by the public key listed in a valid certificate issued by a licensed certification authority, that digital signature *is* the digital signature of the subscriber listed in that certificate; and that the digital signature was affixed by the signer with the intention of signing the message.

9. Biddle, Comment: Misplaced priorities.

10. The Internet Law and Policy Forum was established by a consortium of companies from Europe, the Americas and Asia in order to provide a neutral venue in which commerce, government and the stakeholders in the Internet community may gather to develop solutions to the challenging law and policy questions of the Internet. Further information on the forum may be obtained on the Internet at www.ilpf.org.

APPENDIX C
Highly Rated State Government E-Commerce Web Applications

This is a list of sample Georgia Web sites that allow citizens to conduct business with a state agency. Georgia was ranked very high in a *Government Technology* sponsored study of state Internet capabilities. The Department of Administrative Services' (DOAS) Georgia Procurement Registry provides a single point at which potential state vendors and contractors can identify business and proposal award opportunities in all areas, including construction, transportation, professional consulting and general bids. http://www2. state.ga.us/departments/doas. DOAS also allows state agencies to order supplies online and to pay for them using a State of Georgia Purchasing Card as well as corporate Visa and MasterCards. http://gasupply.doas.state. ga.us/apps/gss/supply.nsf

At the Consolidated Registration Information for Businesses section of the Secretary of State's Web site one can download the basic forms and contact information needed to start a business. One can also order and pay for Corporation Status Certificates online, search the corporation and trademark databases, and reserve a corporate name or obtain an annual registration form to be filed for an existing entity. http://www.sos.state.ga.us/. In addition, physicians, nursing home administrators, physical therapists, low voltage contractors and architects can renew their licenses online.

At the Department of Human Resources Web site you can order program documents for long-term care, childcare licensing, and health care online. However, payment for these documents must still be sent through the mail. https://www.ganet.org/dhr/OrderChildCare.cgi

The Public Service Commission allows citizens and business owners to search its filing docket for up-to-date filings with the commission on all regulatory issues. http://www.PSC.State.Ga.US/cgi-bin/searchdocument.asp

The Georgia Department of Transportation provides summary information on planned construction and repair projects by area or district as well as real-time traffic maps to improve route planning. http://www.georgia-navigator.com/

The Insurance Commissioner's Office allows citizens to file a consumer complaint form online at http://www.InsComm.State.Ga.US/feedback.htm

Index

About the Author

JOHN A. O'LOONEY is a Public Service Associate at the Carl Vinson Institute of Government, University of Georgia. He has worked with local and state government officials as an advisor, consultant, and program evaluator, and is director of the Internet Education Project. Among his many publications are three earlier books with Quorum: *Economic Development and Environmental Control* (1995), *Redesigning the Work of Human Services* (1996), and *Outsourcing State and Local Government Services* (1998).